Business Blunders

A former journalist, Geoff Tibballs worked in television for 15 years with ATV and then Central before leaving in 1989 to concentrate on a full-time career as an author. Since then he has had over 50 books published on a wide range of subjects taking in everything from *Titanic* to Sooty. Other titles include *The Guinness Book of Innovations, The Guinness Book of Oddities* and *Great Sporting Eccentrics*. Married with two daughters, his biggest business blunder to date has been choosing the wrong lottery numbers each week.

Business Blunders

Geoff Tibballs

Robinson
LONDON

Robinson Publishing Ltd
7 Kensington Church Court
London W8 4SP

First published in the UK by Robinson Publishing Ltd 1999
Copyright © Geoff Tibballs 1999

The moral right of the author has been asserted.

A copy of the British Library Cataloguing in Publication data is
available from the British Library

ISBN 1-84119-011-X

Printed and bound in the UK

10 9 8 7 6 5 4 3 2

Contents

Contents

Introduction

Sir John Harvey-Jones

With the possible exception of Del Boy in *Only Fools and Horses* (whose business book I was also asked to introduce) I consider myself one of the most eminently qualified business people to write the introduction to *Business Blunders*. This book is essential reading for every business blunderer as well as for the apparent minority who have, so far at least, avoided joining a club of which I am lifetime president emeritus. In fact, the more I think about it the more convinced I become that it is almost impossible to be in business at all without adding, wittingly or unwittingly, to Geoff Tibballs's files.

The difficulty for we innocent practitioners is that the borderline between business blunder and business brilliance is the merest hair's breadth. After all, the highly professional and successful businessmen at Sony threatened mass hara-kiri at the concept, so wonderfully masterminded by Akio Morita, of a portable cassette-player – the Sony Walkman, as it became known. Unfortunately there are far more examples of disastrously 'brilliant' concepts which are backed remorselessly by their conceivers, despite continual rejection by an ungrateful public who fail to appreciate a potential boon and blessing which the manufacturers have striven at length, and regardless of cost, to produce. Everyone remembers the Ford Edsel, Clive Sinclair's C5 electric car or the DeLorean sports car, but these are only the tip of an enormous iceberg of products that are only differentiated by the excessive hype preceding their failure. It is of course true that the higher you try and fly the further you fall, as Icarus and Richard Branson's balloon exploits demonstrate, but at least death is swift, even if not particularly merciful. Far more damaging from a business point of view is the long-running campaign that continues until the company either runs out of money (usually) or of corporate determination.

I can recall more than one instance that falls into this category but the case of the polyester film packaging for carbonated soft drinks at ICI is etched particularly indelibly on my mind. A technical marvel of its time, its failure to achieve any impact on the public was always blamed on mysterious vested interests. The concept was, as so often, disarmingly simple and an obvious winner. We had discussed a means of coating polyester film that made it impervious to carbonated gases. Of course, being ICI, the idea of applying this to the production of the polyester *bottles*, which are now *de rigueur* in the drinks business, was rejected as being too unimaginative and failing to exploit the potential advantage of our invention. We believed firmly that the world really didn't like bottles. After all they'd been around for some thousands of years and were plainly due to go. We knew that if we produced a sort of condom which could be pressure-filled (just like condoms are) the public would fall over themselves to show their preference and good taste, if you see what I mean. Not only that, but the entire needs of a soft drinks factory could almost be supplied, in deflated condition, by post instead of freight trains full of empty bottles filled with nothing more than air. The advantages were legion, as we soon realized. Unlike bottles these containers couldn't be used to fight with: a slug with a flabby piece of film just didn't match up to the potential of the jagged end of

Britain's favourite duelling weapon (supplied free, to boot). It couldn't be refilled and hurled, making the use of umbrellas on football terraces redundant in one blow. Goodbye to bottle banks. Truly we had on our hands an invention that would have immense sociological advantage and transform life as we knew it. Of course we saw a few minor snags. The container wouldn't stand up unsupported so a cardboard sleeve was required. It was not easy to drink from without significant spillage down suit, dress or bosom. But we just knew that the vast bottle-swilling public would see it our way. Five years later we sadly and reluctantly decided that, due to entrenched interests and the conservatism of the consumer, the world was not ready to change. Have you noticed that in a case like this it is always the conservatism and stupidity of the customer that is really to blame – never the designers, marketing and businessmen who promoted the idea in the first place.

The second category of business blunder is so nearly universal that it is barely considered a blunder but virtually recognized as normal business practice. This is the project where completion time extends by a week every week and of course the costs increase in the same manner. Once the pattern is established it is only sheer exhaustion and the abandonment of much of the original idea that forces a conclusion. Of course, business life being what it is, the conclusion is only reached when the total costs (isn't compound interest a wonderful thing?) are such that the original project can never make money. In fact the problem invariably is that so much has been sunk into the project that none of the investors dare pull out and cut their losses. Accountancy is a wonderful concept. It takes accountants and bankers to realize that as long as you go on losing money you still have a 'bankable' asset. The brakes are only put on because at some stage the project runs out of cash.

Introduction

The Channel Tunnel and Eurostar trains spring to mind, but only as the most obvious recent examples of a long and distinguished line. The groundnut scheme, Concorde, the Eurofighter, the British Advanced Passenger Train all owe something to the ability of businessmen to encourage a bad business decision to live and live. I sometimes wonder why we never seem to learn, but then of course if we did we'd never have a London Underground extension or a Millennium Dome. Our lives would be the poorer, even though scores of investors would be richer.

It seems tragic that, when almost every project comes in over cost and over time, company annual reports don't give credit to the distinguished businessmen and women who don't break ranks and who *do* actually manage to achieve exactly what they said they would. It seems even more sad that they don't just double the cost estimate and time involved so that they would be in budget. The problem, of course, is that if they did, most of these life-enhancing projects would never actually happen. It is only through self-deception that we can be encouraged to throw our hard-earned savings away.

The next category of business blunder, which causes more pain and more business failures than any other, is that old chestnut – the belief that our problem is solely that we haven't lost *enough* money and the solution is quite simply to put more in. This is a favourite strategy because, by definition, *you* don't have the money, it is someone else's that you are about to spend. It constantly amazes me how anxious people are to spend money they haven't got and how unappealing it is to live within their means. Expenditure below receipts doesn't seem to be the recipe for happiness – or even for a good night's sleep. When sales are down and costs are up you would expect that people would concentrate on what they *do* actually control – cutting the costs. But that seems to fly against the entrepreneurial British business spirit. Better by far to add to the costs by hiring an ad agency and advertising your failing product on TV and in the press. The added sales will more than pay for the extra expense. Have you noticed that a sure precursor of a business collapse is a massive advertising campaign accompanied by a barrage of special offers and discounts? I do, of course, accept that it is better to go over the weir with a little hard cash in your pocket than to do so carrying 25 container loads of extinct stock. It weighs less for a start and makes swimming easier. But I am not referring to the 'closing down sale', 'everything must go' scenario. I am thinking of the moment months or years earlier when things were beginning to go wrong and the sales line had started its inevitable decline. That is the time when the blunder occurs – when the action that is taken is 180° in the wrong direction and its conclusion is inevitable.

Whilst many business blunders are dramatic and in retrospect hilarious, and therefore rightly featured in this book, by far the most common one, in the UK at least, is not brought about by doing something but by doing nothing. Maybe because success in business is a stranger to most of us, we conclude that if, at last, the business appears to be making a profit (even though small) and our lives enjoy a respite from the ceaseless rush from panic to catastrophe, we feel that at last we have cracked it. We're not greedy, we can just about exist and our fingers are no longer continually plugging holes in the dyke. So we do nothing, or, more specifically, nothing new. Why should we change a winning formula? Why spoil this happy streak? Ask IBM and General Motors who fell from grace at a stunning speed.

Business is a finely balanced art. In some ways, if we are not making mistakes we are not taking risks and making progress. The fine balance is in making affordable mistakes, or misjudgements, as we prefer to call them, and avoiding the atomic explosion of the true business blunder. This book, as well as being fun reading, does actually have a subliminal message for us all. I wish it luck and will, I hope, continue to make my own contributions to the second and ensuing volumes.

Chapter 1

Flawed Concepts

New Coke: Not the Real Thing

The American people have witnessed the demise of many national icons over the years. The reputations of Presidents, Hollywood stars and sporting heroes have bitten the dust with such regularity that some Americans would even greet stories that Mickey Mouse was bisexual with studied indifference. But tamper with their favourite soft drink and you're asking for trouble, as Coca-Cola discovered to its cost when, after 99 successful years, it decided to abandon its original formula and replace it with the new taste of New Coke. Such was the backlash from the American public that *Business Week* magazine called it 'the marketing blunder of the decade'.

Invented in 1886, Coca-Cola went on to establish itself as the United States' leading soft drink. Generations of Americans were raised on the great taste of Coke, backed by expensive advertising campaigns proclaiming that 'things go better with Coke', that Coke is 'the real thing' or simply 'it'. The drink became a global phenomenon, its position seemingly unassailable.

But naturally enough, Coca-Cola's great rival, Pepsi, was not prepared to accept defeat without a struggle. As the Cola wars intensified, Pepsi targeted younger drinkers and started making significant inroads into Coca-Cola's lead. It introduced its own imaginative advertising campaign, 'The Pepsi Challenge', with taste tests showing that consumers preferred

Pepsi to any other cola. By 1979, Coca-Cola's lead over Pepsi in the US soft-drinks market had been cut to just 4 per cent (23.9 opposed to 17.9) despite the fact that Coca-Cola was outspending Pepsi in advertising by something like $100 million. Clearly something had to be done.

The man in charge of Coca-Cola's destiny was Roberto C. Goizueta. Born in 1933, the son of a wealthy Havana sugar plantation owner, Goizueta arrived in the United States from Cuba at the age of sixteen. At the time, his command of the English language was minimal but, with the help of a dictionary and by watching movies, he soon picked up the basics. After graduating from Yale with a degree in chemical engineering, he returned to Cuba and started work there in Coca-Cola's research laboratories. In 1959, when Fidel Castro came to power, Goizueta fled to the US again with his wife and three children, arriving with the princely sum of $20. He proceeded to progress through the ranks of Coca-Cola until, in March 1981, he was appointed chairman and chief executive.

Goizueta was not afraid of making sweeping changes in the hope of boosting the flagging fortunes of Coca-Cola. As the company examined the reasons behind the decline (a slump that had taken place in spite of Coca-Cola's expenditure on advertising and its superior distribution network), executives began to think the unthinkable – that there was something unappealing about the taste of Coca-Cola. Stung into retaliation by the Pepsi Challenge campaign, Coca-Cola conducted its own taste tests. To the horror of the executives, these tests also revealed that most consumers preferred the taste of Pepsi.

The decision to change the taste of Coca-Cola after so many years was not one to be taken lightly, but Goizueta was determined to do whatever was necessary to put the fizz back into Coke. Fearful of incurring the wrath of the American public, the company opted for a 'softly softly' approach and sent its market researchers to test the water. In 1982, Project

Kansas was launched in which around 2000 consumers were asked a series of questions based on the premise that Coca-Cola had 'added a new ingredient' that would result in a smoother taste. The key element to the questionnaire was how the subjects would react to such a change. The results of the market research indicated that 11 per cent would be upset by a change to the taste of Coca-Cola but the company calculated that at least half of those would get over it in time. Significantly, however, no mention was made to the public at this stage of any plans to alter the actual formula of Coca-Cola.

Further research was conducted over the ensuing months. Company executives toured the United States, ostensibly to test potential commercials among local groups. At the end of each session, they suggested that a great new formula was being introduced for an unnamed, long-established product and asked whether people would want to buy this new variation. The answers were a resounding 'No' if the unnamed product was Coca-Cola.

Although this was scarcely the answer the Coca-Cola bosses wanted to hear, the technical division pressed ahead with developing a new flavour and in autumn 1984 finally came up with a new cola which they were confident would beat Pepsi. The need was never more pressing since Coca-Cola's advantage over Pepsi in the US soft-drinks market had now been further reduced to a mere 2.9 per cent. The new Coca-Cola was sweeter and less fizzy than the original and had a soft, sticky taste. This was principally because its ingredients included corn syrup sweetener which, being sweeter than sucrose, gave the new version a higher sugar content.

The initial signs were encouraging. Introduced in a series of blind taste tests (where the drinkers weren't told which brand they were sampling), the new Coca-Cola reversed the trend of previous similar blind tests by consistently outscoring Pepsi. In the biggest test ever conducted, 191,000 people aged between thirteen and fifty-nine, across some thirteen American cities, voted with their taste buds. A total of 61 per cent said they preferred the new Coca-Cola to the original and the new Coke also fared better than Pepsi. Not surprisingly, the researchers were greatly encouraged by these results and estimated that the new formula would boost Coca-Cola's share of the soft-drink market by 1 per cent, which would be worth an additional $200 million in sales.

Although $4 million and two years had been spent on researching the new flavour, one more crucial decision still had to be taken. Should the new Coca-Cola replace the original or should it simply be added to the range? Goizueta was wary about taking the original, much-loved Coca-Cola off the market altogether and proposed calling the new concoction Coke 2 or some other name. But the idea was rejected by his colleagues who argued that any product bearing the Coca-Cola name had to be number one, the best. Americans weren't a nation inclined to adopt anything that was second-best.

The new drink was to be called New Coke and, having made the decision to oust the original completely, Goizueta and his board proudly trumpeted their new baby. Supremely confident of the success of their product, they abandoned the cautious approach and went for the big kill. There was to be no low-key press conference in the hope of slipping New Coke almost unnoticed into the American consciousness. Instead they took over New York's Lincoln Center on 23 April 1985, inviting the media to 'the most significant soft-drink marketing development in the company's nearly 100-year history'. What the invitation lacked in grammar, it compensated for in impact. Over 700 journalists and film crews attended and there were satellite links to the media in Los Angeles, Atlanta and Houston. 'The best has been made even better,' Goizueta told the assembled throng, calling it 'the

boldest marketing move in the history of the packaged consumer goods business'. Employing a turn of phrase that would
come back to haunt him, he added that the decision to replace
the original 99-year-old formula with New Coke was also 'the
surest move ever made'.

Although nobly supported from the platform by his loyal
lieutenants – another Coca-Cola executive, Don Keough,
promised that the new formula would 'propel Coca-Cola into
this second century' (Coca-Cola's centenary was in May 1986)
– Goizueta and his team were given a rough ride at the press
conference. Instead of the world's media embracing the concept of New Coke with open arms, they bombarded the
platform with negative, even hostile, questions. The Coca-
Cola executives were taken aback and Goizueta became distinctly ruffled as he refuted insinuations that New Coke was
merely a clone of Pepsi. New Coke was nothing like Pepsi, he
insisted. He was also asked whether New Coke had been tested
against Pepsi in secret taste trials and, if so, how had it fared?
The truth was that New Coke had beaten Pepsi by a small
margin in the tests but Goizueta and his colleagues missed a
golden opportunity to score points at the expense of their great
rival by refusing to divulge the results of the trials. Instead,
Goizueta merely confirmed that New Coke had been tested
against Pepsi prior to introduction. As to the results, he
snapped: 'We don't have to show them and we don't want
to.' This immediately conveyed the impression to the media
that Coca-Cola had something to hide – that the results had
been disappointing – whereas in fact the opposite was the case.
It was not an auspicious start.

Sure enough, the media reaction to New Coke was mostly
negative. But the story was certainly big news and it was
estimated that within 24 hours of the press conference, a
staggering 81 per cent of the population of the United States
knew about the change – more than had been aware in July

1969 that Neil Armstrong had just walked on the moon. Bill Cosby was selected to promote New Coke and, amidst great pomp and ceremony, Coca-Cola launched a street sampling campaign with the call: 'Step right up to the greatest taste on earth'. In New York, the first cans off the production line were grandly delivered to workers renovating the Statue of Liberty in a fusion of American symbols.

As it dawned on the American public that New Coke was a replacement for, rather than an addition to, the original Coca-Cola, the complaints began to flood in. There were 450 calls from despairing Coke loyalists in the first four hours, but by the middle of May that figure had risen to 5000 a day. The widespread feeling was a sense of betrayal, that in changing the formula of Coca-Cola the company had destroyed something that was sacred to the nation. One caller declared that to change Coke 'is like God making the grass purple', while a columnist from the *Washington Post* predicted: 'Next week, they'll be chiselling Teddy Roosevelt off the side of Mount Rushmore!'

The outrage would have been less intense had the public liked the taste of New Coke. But they didn't. Complainants called it 'gross, disgusting and unexciting' and, in a reverse of the pre-launch market testing, a TV station commissioned a public opinion poll which showed that 59 per cent of drinkers preferred the old Coca-Cola, 25 per cent preferred Pepsi and just 13 per cent went for New Coke. It was a damning indictment. At the fateful press conference, Don Keough had promised that 'you're just flat going to enjoy it' but now his words were being twisted to say that it was hard to enjoy a drink that was so flat!

In addition to the abusive phone calls, there were some 40,000 letters of protest. Comments ranged from those that registered a wound to patriotic pride ('Changing Coke is just like breaking the American dream, like not selling hot dogs at

a ball game') to the less profound 'New Coke is absolutely
AWFUL . . . You guys really blew it.' Another correspondent wrote despairingly: 'I do not drink alcoholic beverages, I
don't smoke, and I don't chase other women. My only vice has
been Coke. Now you have taken that pleasure from me.' One
writer went further still and took the opportunity to wax
lyrical. 'My dearest Coke: You have betrayed me. We went
out just last week, as we had so often, and when we kissed I
knew our love affair was over . . . I remember walks across
campus with you discussing life and love and all that matters . . . I remember the southern summer nights we shared
with breezes leaving beads of water hanging delicately from
your body . . . But, last week, I tasted betrayal on your lips:
you had the smooth, seductive sweet taste of a lie . . . You
have become a prostitute, corrupted by money, denying your
ideals.'

These letters were by no means isolated and a psychologist
told the company that the emotions expressed by the public
were similar to those of grief-stricken parents mourning the
death of a child. In return, each writer received a standard
letter of reply from the company assuring them that 'our latest
research shows that . . . consumers overwhelmingly like our
great new taste.' If so, those fans of New Coke were keeping an
extremely low profile.

And so it went on. By the beginning of June, calls of
complaint were ringing in to Coca-Cola at the rate of 8000
a day. Gay Mullins, a hardened Coke drinker from Seattle,
founded a reactionary group, The Old Cola Drinkers of
America, and publicly dumped bottles of New Coke into
the city sewers. Mullins also attempted to put legal pressure
on Coca-Cola to revert to the old formula. Nashville song-
writer George Pickard got in on the act with a little ditty
entitled 'Coke Was It', parodying the Coca-Cola slogan of the
time, 'Coke Is It'. A retired air force officer revealed that his

will stipulated that his ashes be sealed in a Coca-Cola can but so disenchanted was he by New Coke that he was reconsidering the matter. Meanwhile in Alabama, a minister led his congregation in prayers for the return of the original Coke.

As people began stockpiling remaining supplies of the old Coca-Cola, a Beverly Hills wineshop owner obtained a consignment of the old formula and was able to sell bottles for three times their list price. Feelings were running high. In Marietta, Georgia, an irate woman assaulted a Coca-Cola delivery man with her umbrella as he tried to stock a supermarket shelf with New Coke and commercials for New Coke were roundly booed at sports stadiums.

There was even a hint of mutiny from within Coca-Cola itself. The company had anticipated that once the hullaballoo surrounding the changeover had died down, sales of New Coke would pick up steadily. But they had underestimated the damage done by the adverse publicity and when the June sales boost failed to materialize, Coca-Cola's own bottlers demanded the return of the old Coke. Even Roberto Goizueta's own father had spoken out against the change when it was first announced, telling his son that the move was a bad one and jokingly threatening to disown him. No one was laughing now, although Goizueta Jr did at least try to keep his sense of humour. 'I'm sleeping like a baby,' he told friends. 'I wake up every hour . . .'

Nor could the Coca-Cola bosses derive any comfort from their own market research. Whereas before 30 May, 53 per cent of consumers had apparently indicated that they liked New Coke, by June over 50 per cent said they no longer approved of it. And by the start of July, a mere 30 per cent of those surveyed admitted to liking New Coke. For an American at that time, it was rather like confessing to being a pen pal of Colonel Gaddafi.

With the nation up in arms, Coca-Cola chemists

desperately tried to salvage what was left of New Coke's reputation by increasing its acidity level to give it more 'bite'. But it was too late to chop and change the formula of New Coke. It had been universally rejected. All people wanted was the return of the original Coca-Cola and the despatch of the sugary imposter.

The company held fire as long as it could but with the situation worsening by the day, it decided that the Last Chance Saloon for New Coke was to be the holiday weekend of the 4th of July. When the sales figures for that weekend came through and were found to be poor, the decision was made to reintroduce the original Coke under the name of Coca-Cola Classic. On 11 July, less than three months after its axing, Coca-Cola executives admitted they had made a mistake and apologized to the public for prematurely ditching their favourite drink. Public pressure had won the day although New Coke earned a reprieve and retained its place on the soft-drinks stage, albeit in a supporting role. It certainly wouldn't have won many votes for Best Newcomer.

The news was greeted with joy throughout the land. ABC interrupted its afternoon soap *General Hospital* to relay the glad tidings, while on the floor of the Senate, Democrat David Pryor of Arkansas declared it to be 'a very meaningful moment in the history of America. This shows that some national institutions cannot be changed.' The following morning, the introduction of Coca-Cola Classic made the front pages at the expense of stories about President Reagan's cancer operation. Goizueta and Keough tried to put a brave face on things when they faced the press. Keough stated: 'Some critics will say Coca-Cola made a marketing mistake. Some cynics will say that we planned the whole thing. The truth is that we are not that dumb and we are not that smart.' Pepsi were in no doubt as to which category the whole episode belonged, describing the New Coke saga as a 'terrible mistake'.

It was, in truth, a monumental blunder – and a $4 million blunder at that. Nevertheless, many Coca-Cola executives still doggedly clung to the belief that New Coke would outperform Coca-Cola Classic. They were wrong again. By October 1985, despite the company spending far more on advertising New Coke than Classic, the latter was comfortably outselling the young upstart. It was no contest but, more worrying still for Coca-Cola, by the end of the year Pepsi had stolen the lead as the bestselling sugar cola in the United States. The presence of the two Coca-Colas had merely succeeded in dividing sales. The advent of 1986 did nothing to help the fortunes of New Coke. By the end of April, its market share had fallen below 3 per cent and the final blow was when McDonald's switched its massively influential account to Classic. It was the ultimate thumbs-down for New Coke.

Yet it was not all bad news for Coca-Cola. As New Coke continued to sink without trace, Classic quickly overtook Pepsi to regain its place as the leading soft drink in the United States. And out of the fiasco there came a veritable plus point – the nation's loyalty to, and love for, the original Coca-Cola was thoroughly reaffirmed. Nor should anyone underestimate the value of the mountain of publicity generated by the affair. It may have seemed crippling at the time but every word against New Coke was, in effect, a word in favour of Classic. So, unwittingly, Coca-Cola had achieved something of a publicity *coup* and Classic occupied a place in the nation's heart of which its rivals could only dream. Once again, everything was sweet in the world of Coca-Cola . . . sweet, but not too sweet.

The Sinclair C5: An Electric Shock

Sir Clive Sinclair is a man of vision. The pioneer of the pocket calculator and the pocket TV, he has always prided himself on being one step ahead of commercial technology. So when he announced the introduction of an electric car with the prediction that by the end of the century 'the petrol engine will be seen as a thing of the past', the motoring world took notice. But it soon became apparent that this time Sir Clive was on the fast track to failure.

Passionate about electronics, Sinclair left school at seventeen and embarked on a career in technical journalism. At the age of twenty-two, he set up his first business, borrowing £50 to form Sinclair Radionics through which he sold repaired radios by mail order. His inventive mind turned to grander things and in 1972 he came up with the pocket calculator, designing the whole thing from scratch to production in just nine months. At just six inches long, it was twenty times smaller than the most compact model then available and, by selling it through mail order, he was able to keep the price down to £79. However his success alerted overseas competitors. The Americans undercut his prices while the Japanese perfected a new improved silicon chip. As his profits plummeted, Sinclair realized he could not compete and moved on to his next scheme, a two-inch pocket television set, launched in 1977 at a price of £175.

After making his fortune by marketing a low-priced home computer, the highly intelligent (he is a former chairman of Mensa with a genius-level IQ of 159) Sinclair dreamed of an environment-friendly electric car, the vehicle of the future. It is a well-known fact that many inventors are slightly eccentric. How else do you explain the likes of Philadelphia's David Gutnam who, in the hope of reducing pedestrian casualties, invented a cushioned car bumper with a huge pair of claws to grab the pedestrian around the waist and prevent contact with the street? Or American Thomas J. Bayard, pioneer of the vibrating toilet seat, designed in the belief that physical stimulation of the buttocks would relieve constipation? Or

Earl M. Christopherson of Seattle who in 1960 patented a device to enable people to look inside their own ears? For all his intelligence, Clive Sinclair was no exception to the rule that innovation is often accompanied by a degree of eccentricity. This explains a lot about the C5.

Sinclair originally envisaged a conventionally shaped four-seater family saloon but a law introduced in Britain in 1983 made it possible to run small electric vehicles on the highway without road tax, a licence or compulsory insurance. He immediately saw the potential for some form of electrically assisted cycle which, because of the new legislation, could be driven by fourteen-year-olds, would not require Department of Transport approval and would not be subject to the usual parking regulations. A fume-free, low-cost, easy-to-park vehicle that anyone could drive held an obvious appeal and seemed a likely money-spinner. That same year, Sir Clive sold a £13.6 million stake in his successful computer business, Sinclair Research, to various institutions and used part of the money to set up a new company, Sinclair Vehicles, to develop his electric car. It was very much his own private venture, funded by his own money.

The C5, as it came to be known, was made under contract by Hoover at Merthyr Tydfil, a factory more commonly associated with the manufacture of washing machines. This was not as bizarre as it sounded since the C5 boasted a washing-machine motor. Huge secrecy surrounded the development but the C5 eventually emerged as an open-top, single-seater, lightweight three-wheel buggy, powered by a conventional lead acid battery and foot pedals – a dream machine . . . for Fred Flintstone. Its body was made from a single plastic moulding and it measured just 31 inches in height, thus adhering to Sir Clive's conviction that small is beautiful. There was no steering wheel and the vehicle was manoeuvred by a handlebar that lay beneath the driver's thighs and from where it was operated by the driver's left thumb. The accelerator was a simple on/off button. Sinclair Vehicles claimed a top speed of 14 mph and that the battery would give a range of around 20 miles before it needed recharging. Optional extras included waterproof clothing.

The Sinclair C5 was unveiled at Alexandra Palace, London, on 10 January 1985 – hardly the most auspicious time of year to launch an open-top vehicle. Forty-four-year-old Sir Clive described the C5 as 'a cultural shock for the motorist' and announced that he hoped to sell 100,000 in the first year at £399 each. It was to go on sale at electricity board showrooms, chain stores and through mail order. Delivery would be in a huge cardboard box but any stores wishing to sell the C5 had to prove to Sinclair Vehicles that they had enough space to give demonstration rides to purchasers and, of course, their staff had to be familiar with the vehicle's workings. Much was made of the C5's compact nature, the fact that it didn't give off any fumes and that it was considered to be safer than a moped. Sir Clive was typically optimistic and hinted that a production capacity for 200,000 vehicles a year would be available by June.

However, not everyone shared his enthusiasm. The day before the launch, James Tye, Director General of the British Safety Council, said after testing the C5 at Sinclair Vehicles' Coventry headquarters: 'I am astonished that within a few days fourteen-year-old children will be able to drive on the road in this without a licence, without a crash helmet, without a seat belt, without insurance and with no form of training.' The Automobile Association also expressed considerable concern. 'We have reservations on two counts: the desirability of allowing the vehicle on the road without insurance cover and because it seems to have moved from the concept of a motor-assisted bicycle to a road vehicle. It could, due to its size and inconspicuousness, present a hazard to its occupant and other road users.'

And therein lay part of the problem. For the C5 wasn't quite sure what it was supposed to be. It was described as a bicycle that thought it was a car, but it turned out to be neither. Motoring journalists were equally puzzled. The motoring correspondent of *The Times* hailed it as a major breakthrough in electric motoring but a fellow scribe called it a 'fun machine that can hardly be regarded as serious, everyday, all-weather transport'. Newspaper photographs of vulnerable-looking C5 drivers peering up apprehensively at huge lorries did little to convince the public that it was safe to venture out in a C5 in busy traffic. Next to a juggernaut, the little C5 looked like a mouse at the mercy of a voracious lion – an image that was quickly seized upon by the satirical TV puppet show *Spitting Image* which featured a sketch where brutish lorry drivers slapped stickers on their windscreens for every C5 they managed to hit.

In spite of any misgivings, an expensive promotion campaign ensured an initial surge of orders. Barrie Wills, the Managing Director of Sinclair Vehicles, enthused: 'The reaction from retailers and the public has been absolutely overwhelming. We opened a special mail order telephone line at our Camberley distribution centre and it is so busy we cannot get through ourselves!' When, four weeks after the launch, it was announced that there were 5000 C5s on the road (a figure that subsequently proved to be a trifle exaggerated), Wills described the news as 'very encouraging . . . a broad acceptance of our revolutionary new product'.

But storm clouds were gathering. Customer dissatisfaction was rife with buyers complaining about the poor technology and lack of sophistication in the C5. A worrying number were returned to the dealers. The most common complaints were that it was too low, too slow and too limited in range. Far from the claims of being able to do 20 miles without recharging the battery, most drivers were lucky to get a dozen miles from a single charging. Newspapers carried the story of a sixty-four-year-old disabled man from Devon who, excited at the arrival of his C5, took it out on its first journey, only to be forced to retrace his steps because it was unable to negotiate a nearby hill. Sinclair Vehicles had claimed that a C5 could tackle a one in 12 hill and, with pedal assistance, a one in seven gradient, but the adverse publicity merely served to enhance the hapless vehicle's position as a national laughing-stock. One critic described it as a 'Formula One bath-chair'.

There were other difficulties. Drivers found the C5 particularly uncomfortable after any more than a mile's travel and questions were raised about its accountability. Since it didn't need to be insured, if a C5 caused an accident, who would pay? In February, Nicholas Botting, a twenty-one-year-old student, became the first person to appear in court for being drunk in charge of a C5. He had won the C5 at a Valentine's ball but because nobody knew how to start it, he decided to pedal home, allegedly along the pavements of Whitehall. The case raised a legal question as to whether the C5 was a pedal cycle, a motor vehicle or something completely different. As confusion spread at a rate considerably faster than the C5 itself, the case against Mr Botting was dropped.

The lack of speed of the C5 was proving an enormous handicap to sales. Few people wanted to travel in something that was slower than a milk float and which succeeded in making a Reliant Robin look cool. In a bid to overcome its sluggishness, some C5 drivers bought special conversion kits which, for less than £10, would double the speed to nearly 30 mph by connecting a second battery. Sinclair Vehicles were alarmed by this development and warned: 'By doubling the battery power you would quadruple the heat generated and the motor would probably blow up. In any event, 15 mph is the maximum permitted for an electrically assisted cycle. Anything above that would make it illegal.' A further complication arose with plans to sell the C5 to the Isle of Man and the Channel Islands where, because of different vehicle regulations, the C5 was still classified as a moped. To run there, it needed a minimum speed of 15 mph and to weigh more than 60 kg, both of which were the legal maximums for the C5 in the rest of Britain. To qualify as a moped it also needed to have such additions as a horn, indicator lights, a rearview mirror, illuminated registration plates and a better braking system. So Sinclair Vehicles announced plans to launch a modified version for sale on the Isle of Man and the Channel Islands. They also hoped to launch the C5 in ten European countries for the autumn but there, too, changes had to be made to bring the vehicle in line with European laws. Given the C5's reluctance to climb hills, the manufacturers wisely targeted Holland as a possible sales outlet but the Dutch were particularly vociferous, demanding major alterations to the braking system and improvements to the lights and reflectors at the rear of the C5. All of these amendments would take time and money.

By March, just two months after the launch, the Sinclair C5 was desperate for some good publicity. After the initial rush, sales had slowed to a trickle, a situation that Sir Clive blamed on that familiar scapegoat, the press, for its lack of foresight and pessimistic reporting. Even the chance to earn some favourable column inches was scuppered when the workforce at Merthyr went on an unconnected pay strike on the very day that the Prince and Princess of Wales were to have been driving a C5 at the Hoover plant. By the end of the month, Sinclair had resorted to hiring teenagers to drive around the streets of London in C5s in a bid to give sales a much-needed boost. The Minister of Transport, Lynda Chalker, did her best by declaring the C5 to be safer and more stable than a bicycle, insisting that it was clearly visible on the road in its standard white bodywork. No sooner had she issued her vote of confidence than, on 29 March, production was halted at Hoover 'to rectify a minor fault'.

The C5 production line reopened three weeks later but with only ten of the original 100-strong workforce (the rest having been transferred to the more lucrative washing-machine manufacture). The declining sales figures had meant that production of the C5 was being cut by a staggering 90 per cent. Instead of 1000 vehicles a week, the factory would now be producing just 100 and, with unsold vehicles mounting by the day, even that number was more than sufficient to meet demand. The C5's only hope of survival appeared to rest with the notoriously unpredictable British summer as Sinclair Vehicles prayed that an upturn in the weather would be reflected in the sales.

By May there were in the region of 6000 unsold C5s at Merthyr. Sir Clive came up with another reason for the slow sales, saying it had taken longer than expected to organize retail distribution of his brainchild. He explained: 'The product sells to the customer but the customer cannot get it at the moment because the shops have not got it in. It was over-optimism if you like.' Meanwhile, all was not well at his computer firm, Sinclair Research, with sales of the new QL computer reaching only half of the anticipated number. Rumours abounded that Sinclair Research was in financial difficulties. Although the two companies were entirely separate, the stories did little to inspire confidence in Sinclair Vehicles and its ailing product.

Just when it seemed that things couldn't get any worse, they did. Instead of bringing a boost to sales, the summer of '85 brought further official condemnation of the C5. The Advertising Standards Authority had received complaints claiming that advertisements for the C5 exaggerated its safety features, aerodynamic design and general benefits in relation to bicycles and mopeds. After investigating the complaints, the Authority ordered Sinclair Vehicles to withdraw certain claims about the C5's speed and safety. Far more damning was a report from the Consumers' Association which concluded that, in its present form, the C5 was of limited use, potentially dangerous and represented poor value for money. *Which?* magazine carried out extensive tests on three C5s, all of which broke down with 'a major gearbox fault'. The battery was also found to offer much less mileage than had originally been hoped. The longest run achieved on the tests between battery charges was only 14.2 miles (compared to the manufacturer's claim of 20). Furthermore, *Which?* calculated that a realistic range was between a miserly five and ten miles, but even then only if the driver pedalled a lot. The vision of a C5 driver being able to sit back and enjoy the ride was becoming something of a myth. The tests also revealed that the visibility masts, introduced to make the little C5 easier to spot by other vehicles in traffic, had a tendency to snap. But the most worrying part of the survey concerned the safety of the C5. It voiced the fears of many people by stating the belief that the C5 was dangerous because it was so low. It was found to be easily hidden behind other vehicles, thus making it extremely vulnerable in heavy traffic, and the driver's seating position was actually at bumper height. In the event of an impact, the poor C5 driver was a sitting duck. Nor did the *Which?* team consider the C5 to be a bargain. The manufacturers made great play of the fact that it cost less than £400 but, as the report pointed out, by the time essential extras such as mirrors, indicators and a horn were added, the basic price increased to £441.85. And you could buy a second-hand car, albeit not exactly top of the range, for £500. This was by no means the finest hour in the short, turbulent history of the Sinclair C5.

In July, the inevitable happened, although not for the most widely predicted reasons. Production of the C5 was halted at

Merthyr as Hoover became locked in a financial dispute with Sinclair Vehicles. With retailers blaming the vehicle's failure on a lack of advertising, they embarked on a price-cutting spree in a bid to stimulate sales. In August, Comet lopped nearly £150 off the basic price, reducing it to £259.90, while other retailers went further still, selling the C5 for £199, half its original figure. Even with such discounts, the C5's summer sales weren't much better than those for snowmobiles.

In October, Sinclair Vehicles was put into receivership. It emerged that only 14,000 C5s had ever been made and that a mere 4500 had actually been sold – a far cry from Sir Clive's hopes of selling 100,000 in that first year. In the run-up to Christmas, 4000 vehicles from the unsold C5 mountain were bought by a surplus goods firm for a knockdown £300,000 and in stores it was being sold as a toy at a quarter of its original price.

And that became the fate of the C5 – a curious novelty. Lord Beaulieu took one to his motor museum in Hampshire and another became an exhibit at a museum in Wales. Some ended up as means of transport on golf courses, fairgrounds, holiday camps or leisure parks while others even served as exercise bicycles. Indeed, a chain of North London fitness centres used the C5 in its advertisements. Basically, the C5 performed a variety of functions and fulfilled an assortment of needs – but unfortunately they did not include its intended function as a road vehicle.

So what went wrong? There is no doubt that the C5 was patently unsuitable for use in heavy traffic, to the point of being downright dangerous. Its lack of speed and range (the battery technology singularly failed to match the vision of the designer) rendered it impractical for everyday motoring as did its inability to climb hills. That better results could be achieved by furious pedalling was scarcely a recommendation. Maybe, like so many failed innovations, it was simply ahead of its time. In a country with no traffic and no hills, it could have been a winner.

The venture cost Sir Clive an estimated £8.6 million of his own money. He remained philosophical in the wake of the demise of the C5. 'No regrets. None at all,' he said. 'I think part of the trouble was that most species of animal, including man, are suspicious of change. They regard it as a bad thing and tend to reject it unless it is introduced very carefully . . . If you can't have a failure once in a while, it probably means you don't possess the will needed for the successes.'

In April 1986, Sir Clive sold his computer business to Amstrad boss Alan Sugar. Sir Clive bounced back; the C5 didn't.

IBM: The Byter Bit

International Business Machines Corporation has been one of the giants of the technological world for over 30 years. Developing an unrivalled reputation in the lucrative field of large mainframe computers, IBM was frequently held up by industry analysts as a supreme example of the right way to run a prosperous company. For years, its rivals could only look on with envy. The largest computer company in the world, IBM boasted profits to match. In 1984 it reported an awesome profit of $6.6 billion, paving the way for the years to come. Its 1990 profits also stood at $6 billion but within two years this was converted into an equally astonishing loss of $4.97 billion, at the time the biggest annual loss in American corporate history. A total of 43,000 employees were laid off during 1992 and IBM's share price crashed from over $100 in the summer of 1992 to $48.375 when the massive loss was announced six months later. IBM was suddenly a company in crisis.

Yet although the 1992 figures shook the corporate world, in

truth the writing had been on the wall since the early 1980s when a succession of blunders coupled with a large dose of complacency served to undermine IBM's seemingly unassailable position at the head of the computer business.

IBM were the fat cats of the industry, a worldwide success story and one of the largest US-based employers. The company operated a strict dress code, employees wearing a uniform of blue suit, white shirt and dark tie. Consequently, it acquired the nickname 'Big Blue'. As well as its appearance, IBM prided itself on its vast research laboratories, the staff of which included no fewer than three Nobel Prize winners. Not surprisingly, the company saw itself as being at the cutting edge of technology. Traditionally, IBM had set the standards for others to follow.

IBM's position of strength had been built around mainframe computers – a market worth around $50 billion worldwide – but times were changing. The trend was towards smaller, personal computers, the increasing popularity of which was to undermine the company's core mainframe business. As mainframe profits diminished, IBM squandered a succession of opportunities to make the PC an equally successful enterprise. The result was that by 1993, IBM had little money coming in from either mainframes or PCs. Quite simply, the vast IBM structure, heavily bureaucratic, seemed unable or unwilling to react to the changes with sufficient speed. Consequently, much smaller rivals were able to steal a march on IBM and establish themselves in the market-place before the slumbering giant was roused.

Of all the management mistakes that contributed to IBM's decline, one stood out head and shoulders above the rest: two embryonic West Coast firms, Microsoft and Intel, were allowed to become major players at the expense of IBM. In 1982, the *combined* stock value of Intel and Microsoft added up to about one-tenth of IBM's; by the end of 1992, the *individual* market value of both companies was almost the same as IBM's (IBM was valued at £30,715 million, Intel at $24,735 million and Microsoft at $23,608 million).

Around 1980, IBM had 340,000 employees, $27 billion of assets, $26 billion of sales and profits of $3.6 billion, whereas Microsoft had just started out with 32 staff and very little else. IBM was preparing to enter the brave new world of personal computers and had been involved in discussions with Bill Gates, the dynamic young boss of Microsoft. IBM had the option to buy the operating system that would become DOS (disk operating system) and would ultimately make Gates a fortune. Instead it passed up the chance, allowing Gates to buy the system for just $75,000. IBM reasoned that Microsoft would be left to solve all the teething troubles with the new system, but the effect of the decision was to put IBM at a huge disadvantage in the personal computer stakes because it enabled Microsoft to set and own the standard. The decision also put IBM on a collision course with Microsoft – a battle that would eventually force IBM to spend billions of dollars in an attempt to reclaim a standard that Microsoft had bought for $75,000. While Gates was on his way to becoming the richest man in the United States, IBM executives were left counting the cost of their error.

IBM and Microsoft did sign a joint development agreement in 1985, but the agreement did not cover Microsoft's new software project, Windows. Since it considered itself to be the world leader in technology, IBM thought it had nothing to fear from competitors. But its PC software left a lot to be desired. Unfortunately nobody at the company seemed prepared to admit just how inferior its software was and IBM kept ploughing millions of dollars into poor concepts. In 1984, it launched Top View which was rapidly christened 'Top Heavy' by customers because it was dull and operated too slowly. People wanted software with pretty colours and smart graphics but Top View was decidedly uninspiring. It was so unpopular that IBM ended up giving away most of its copies. Meanwhile Gates was busy evolving the more complicated and ultimately more successful Windows. If Windows had been included in the joint development agreement with Microsoft, IBM might have been able to salvage something from its previous *faux pas* but the agreement not only failed to tie IBM and Windows together, it also did nothing to remove Windows as a competitor to IBM's own inferior software. With it went any chance of IBM maintaining its leadership of the PC market.

It took Gates something like nine years, until 1990, to perfect Windows, but IBM's response was so slow that he had all the time he needed to establish it in the market-place. By the time IBM produced software of a quality to rival Windows, the money that Microsoft had earned from royalty payments from DOS sales to other manufacturers of PCs (such as Compaq and Tandy) had made it strong enough and wealthy enough to be able to stand up to the might of IBM.

The uneasy alliance between IBM and Microsoft continued and IBM continued to toss away opportunities to secure its niche. As late as the middle of 1986 Gates was offering to let IBM buy a stake in Microsoft. Once again, IBM rejected the offer. It was to prove an expensive mistake. To have purchased 10 per cent of Microsoft would have cost less than $100 million but would have earned handsome dividends in the long term.

It was a similar story with Intel. Just as IBM encouraged the development of Microsoft without reaping the rewards, so it signed up another small company, Intel, to make the chips for its PCs. And like Microsoft, Intel flourished under the IBM wing until it was strong enough to stand on its own two feet. By appointing Microsoft and Intel as its suppliers, IBM surrendered its chances of controlling the PC industry. Instead it allowed both companies to grow and dominate their respective fields – Intel in microprocessors and Microsoft in operating-systems software. Far from ensuring that such innovations came from within IBM itself, the company's attempts to save developmental time and let others sort out any teething difficulties passed the initiative to these hungry youngsters. As one commentator wrote: 'IBM gave these two small firms a golden opportunity, which both grasped to the fullest.'

In particular, IBM dallied over adopting the Intel 80386 chip. This not only cost them additional influence over Intel, the only other company likely to challenge Microsoft as the standard-setter of the PC business, but it also lost them sales. In September 1986, another small firm, Compaq, announced the introduction of a PC that incorporated the new Intel 80386 chip and therefore operated several times faster than IBM's most powerful machine. IBM had missed the boat again. These blunders with Intel and Microsoft meant that IBM could not rely on its PC business once the mainstay of its income, the mainframe business, ran into difficulties. And that was to prove disastrous.

There was little doubt that IBM had the expertise. Its vast – and extremely costly – research and development department was capable of remarkable inventions yet these skills were cancelled out by an inability to translate laboratory discoveries to the market-place as quickly as its smaller rivals. IBM invented the technology for both floppy disks and hard-disk drives but because it saw itself primarily as a seller of whole systems, rather than a supplier of individual parts, it chose not to get involved and allowed other companies to make their fortunes by selling disk drives. IBM was also the biggest chip maker in the world but Japanese firms were able to establish themselves by selling memory chips to manufacturers and in the process learning how to make them more cheaply than

IBM. So IBM's competitors were continually able to undercut its prices. IBM did try to build a modem and sell it through dealers but it was unsatisfactory and did not sell well. And in 1985 plans to make a mini-computer with a new chip were dropped after $1 billion had been spent on the project.

At first, the PC and IBM seemed genuinely compatible. Under the guidance of middle manager Don Estridge, IBM launched its first personal computer in 1981. It was an enormous success and helped IBM to announce record annual profits for any company. It also gave the PC credibility with IBM's all-important senior management, the people responsible for making the decisions. But Estridge's success did not meet with wholesale approval and some IBM executives became resentful of the amount of publicity he and his 'baby' were receiving. The first IBM PC worked because the company's huge, cumbersome set-up gave it a free rein. However once petty bureaucracy and internal politics reasserted themselves, it was doomed to failure.

During 1982 and 1983, Estridge and his team planned a series of expansions which could have proved invaluable. They attempted a home computer and wanted to build a faster processor into the PC, but everything foundered in a sea of red tape. The result was that IBM's new PC for 1983, the PC jr, aimed specifically at the home market as opposed to IBM's traditional business outlet, was hopelessly inadequate. It was supposed to come out in July in time for the Christmas season but IBM bosses insisted on a number of changes which not only had an adverse effect on the product itself but also caused inevitable delays. Notably, they introduced an inferior keyboard and scrapped plans to sell the PC jr in department stores. Consequently, instead of a good quality, relatively cheap product sold through mainstream stores, the PC jr finished up as an inferior, expensive piece of equipment sold through the same outlets as mainframes. To rub salt into the wound, it was launched too late for Christmas. It was a disaster. Realizing their error a year later, IBM reduced the price, improved some features and finally allowed it to be sold via department stores, but by then IBM's competitors had come out with more appealing lines. The ill-fated PC jr was scrapped in 1985.

This echoed the fundamental problem throughout the early 1980s – IBM could not rid itself of its mainframe mentality. Everything was still geared towards producing the ailing mainframes, the company being painfully slow to embrace new ideas. IBM was convinced that the growth of PCs would stimulate the demand for mainframes. In fact, the opposite was true. Mainframes had long been the principal source of profit for IBM, and company executives, riddled with conservatism, could not accept the fact that they were in danger of becoming a thing of the past, particularly as they offered greater profit margins than desktops. Although there was still a market for the big mainframes, it was declining steadily. And when they were eventually ousted by PCs, IBM was caught napping. It had nothing with which to replace the mainframe, having managed to throw away all its strategic advantages in the PC field. In 1992, Microsoft and Intel, seizing the initiatives that IBM had offered them, together earned nearly $2 billion while IBM's PC business lost $1 billion.

IBM executives actually foresaw many of the problems that lay ahead. They commissioned long-winded task forces which accurately predicted the changes in the market that would ultimately damage IBM, but the company top brass still could not bring themselves to make the necessary adjustments. In some respects, this resistance to change was understandable. After all, at the time, IBM was the most profitable, most revered company in the entire world. Why should there be any need to change, thought the decision-makers.

IBM's management structure meant that all decisions had

to be made from the top rather than lower down the line. This had the dual effect of slowing down the very process of decision-making (since executives not familiar with the project under discussion would feel the need to familiarize themselves with every aspect before committing themselves to a decision) and of reducing the drive and enthusiasm of lower-level managers. Consequently, some middle managers with bright ideas were reluctant to put them forward for fear of rocking the boat. Nobody was prepared to take a chance. What should have been an environment of innovation became one of 'safety first'. And any far-reaching decisions that were made took too long to incorporate, allowing IBM's smaller, leaner rivals to snatch first bite at the cherry. Time after time, IBM was too late bringing new machines on to the market or was too slow in reacting to the climate of change that was rife in the computer industry during the 1980s and early 1990s.

Much of this was down to IBM's own top-heavy corporate structure. In 1985, chairman John Opel revealed: 'If I were to take IBM and divide it up into a lot of little companies and put them on the market and offer investors the opportunity, I could probably quadruple the market value of IBM.' But he added quickly, almost by way of apology: 'It's just a thought I had.' In the end, he was unable to summon up the courage to follow his instincts. It was not until 1991 that the new chairman, John Akers, announced plans to split IBM into 13 divisions, each with its own autonomy, thereby pushing the company power base downwards, away from the very top. But these radical measures were too late to prevent the slump that had been building up for the past decade.

IBM's initial resistance to change was partly due to complacency. And that complacency was partly brought about by another dubious decision – that of switching to a policy of selling, rather than leasing, the giant mainframe computers. Ironically, the policy shift itself was as a result of a rare sense of fallibility within IBM. The company had been worried about its leasing policy for some time, fearing that a rival firm might develop a technology that would surpass that of the IBM mainframes. Alarmed that customers, seeing a superior alternative, might cancel their rental agreements, thus leaving IBM with a pile of second-rate, obsolete machinery, IBM decided to encourage its customers to buy mainframes outright. The immediate impact was a boost to profits. Revenue and earnings rose dramatically in the short term, enabling IBM's profits to double from $3.3 billion in 1983 to £6.6 billion the following year. Similarly, IBM's stock-market value more than doubled, reaching around $72 billion at the end of 1984, making it the most valuable company in the world. However, these figures merely served to give IBM a false sense of security and the loss of leasing left the company particularly vulnerable when the mainframe bubble burst.

Another effect of the phasing out of leasing was to damage the relationship between the IBM sales force and some of its customers. While it had been obliged to rely on rentals for commission, the sales team went out of its way to keep regular customers happy on an ongoing basis, but now there was no leasing, it had to start from scratch each January and go out and look for new sales. With the emphasis switching towards finding fresh outlets, the tendency was to neglect some existing customers. Thus people who had been used to IBM's finest sales service suddenly found themselves treated less satisfactorily.

Indeed, IBM's sales policies of the early 1980s did little to ease the company's wider problems. Salesmen were told that they would lose their commission if any product they sold was ever replaced by something else. So they strove to ensure that customers kept existing equipment, even if that meant ignoring new IBM products like the PC which were vital to the company's future. Nobody was willing to surrender the commission on an expensive mainframe in exchange for a cheaper personal computer or mini-computer. It all served to impede the flow of IBM's lifeblood – the PC.

One of the problems with the PC was that IBM got it wrong so often. The company went through an unhappy period of putting the wrong products on the market or bringing out good ones too late. Those delays that weren't caused by IBM's dinosaur-like bureaucracy were the result of the company's labour cutbacks, instigated in a bid to compete with the cost-effective Japanese. To match the Japanese prices, IBM tried to cut back on its own expenditure, but this meant that the quality of the product sometimes suffered. The unlamented PC jr was just one of a number of flawed products brought out by IBM in a vain bid to make up for lost time and break new ground. In 1986, it introduced the convertible laptop, a machine that was virtually obsolete as soon as it hit the market-place. Among other things, it was too heavy, it didn't have sufficient processing power and it featured a screen that was extraordinarily difficult to read. It didn't even contain a modem, despite the fact that the principal advantage of a portable computer is for the user to travel with it and communicate with work colleagues via a modem. As a result of this ineptitude, IBM missed the chance to establish a footing on the lucrative laptop ladder. It tried again in 1991 but with a model that was $1000 more expensive than rival brands of equal quality. Desperate to compete, IBM kept slashing the prices of its new laptop but customers merely perceived this action as a sign of failure and gave it a wide berth.

Competitive price-fixing had been a constant difficulty to IBM – another legacy of its cumbersome organization. As customers became increasingly knowledgeable and more confident about computers, they were able to choose for themselves which model they wanted without the assistance of a heavy-handed salesman. And, as in any walk of life, they wanted value for money and a good deal. All too often, IBM products were considerably more expensive than the competition. When IBM held sway in the mainframe field, it could afford to charge what it liked for it was widely regarded as being the only reliable mainframe producer. But as competitors caught up, rival mainframe firms – notably the Japanese – developed good reputations with lower prices. The only way IBM could compete was to reduce its prices to match. And in a dwindling market, this was a dangerous game. When IBM mainframes did sell in 1992, it was at a 50 per cent discount. By early 1993, the discount had risen to 70 per cent.

It was in 1990 that IBM first felt the consequences of its blunders. Its share in the PC market dropped alarmingly as new competitors offered their own PCs at lower prices than IBM. Furthermore, these 'clone' products were said to be every bit as good as IBM's in terms of quality. As a full-scale computer price war broke out, IBM lost further ground. In June 1992, IBM endeavoured to counter Compaq's latest price cuts with a further round of reductions, but IBM prices were still as much as one-third higher than those of its competitors. And having already announced its new autumn range, IBM found it difficult to sell the current models – all this at a time when it was also being forced to slash its mainframe prices. The crisis cost IBM some $75 billion of stock-market value, not to mention the thousands of jobs.

But there is a happy postscript to the story. IBM did not achieve greatness by accident and was not about to relinquish its reputation overnight. The necessary changes to company structure were implemented and by June 1994 the company had rallied. The disastrous figures of 1992 had been just a temporary blip – but one that nobody at IBM would be allowed to forget.

The Irish Canal: Flowing in the Face of Nature

In 1840, an unnamed English canal designer planned to link Lakes Corrib and Mask in western Ireland. The construction work was undertaken by a local company but since the men built the canal entirely on porous limestone, no sooner had the water been poured in than it drained away again. Not surprisingly, this set the project back several months but a solution appeared to have been found by the laying of a clay bed at its base.

Thereafter everything progressed smoothly until, with the canal almost completed, it was discovered that one of the lakes was several feet lower than the other. It suddenly dawned on the workmen that they were asking water to flow uphill. At that, the entire project was abandoned.

R101: The Wreck of a Dream

In the period immediately after the First World War, a gaggle of aviation experts and influential politicians expressed the opinion that the future of long-distance air travel lay not with aeroplanes but with airships. With the benefit of hindsight, it is easy to expose the folly of such a view but, in truth, sufficient evidence was already available at the time to indicate that airships would never be able to provide a reliable, safe, cost-effective service.

Any passenger service – be it air, sea, rail or bus – has to operate according to some form of timetable, even if, like the British Rail volumes of the 1980s, they were largely works of fiction. Yet the problems with airships were so fundamental that it should have been obvious from the outset that, whatever their virtues as a means of transport, they could never aspire to offering a regular, reliable service. The most glaring deficiency was their speed . . . or rather, lack of it. The average speed in tests of the two British airships of the late 1920s – R100 and R101 – was a less than supersonic 44 mph and even that was dependent on benevolent winds. Flying in the face of just a normal-strength wind could double the journey time of an airship, thereby making any attempt at punctuality impossible. Gales – or worse – simply didn't bear thinking about. A contributory factor in the general sloth of airships was the seeming eternity it took for them to pick up speed after lift-off. On its fateful flight to India in 1930, it took R101 13 minutes to attain a speed of 40 mph. This inability to accelerate meant that the productivity of an airship in terms of miles per annum was extremely low. Moreover, the costs of construction, maintenance and flying were high. In short, the airship was a bad business proposition.

There were further difficulties to be taken into consideration – matters of safety rather than economy. Airships were forced to fly low in a bid to conserve gas and were thus always at the mercy of low-level turbulence. This not only subjected passengers to a bumpy ride but increased the risk of airships being buffeted into trees or hills. Mooring an airship in anything other than the lightest of winds was fraught with problems, while the structures themselves were notoriously vulnerable to any change in climate. In cold weather, there was the constant danger of ice forming on the fragile outer covers; in the tropics, there was the terrifying risk that the airship's petrol engines would explode. An airship filled with hydrogen constituted a continuous fire hazard. Small wonder that a lot of people had serious misgivings about airships as a form of passenger transport.

Nevertheless several nations – the United States, Germany, France and Britain – enthusiastically pioneered airship travel in the 1920s. The early signs were not good. On 24 August

1921, making its fourth test flight over the River Humber, Britain's R38 broke up in mid-air. Forty-four of the 49 people on board were killed, many of them perishing in burning pools of petrol. Two years later, the French airship *Dixmude* was struck by lightning off Sicily. But these disasters did nothing to quell the determination of airship advocates, of whom the leading light in Britain was Brigadier-General Lord Thomson of Cardington.

The huge German Zeppelins had been a formidable adversary during the 1914–18 war but the idea of using them for passenger transport was a new departure. Hoping to learn from the R38 tragedy, Vickers, the most experienced builders of airships in Britain, suggested the notion to the Conservative government in 1923. Vickers envisaged building airships to fly to the distant corners of the British Empire, but before the government could reach a final decision, it was ousted from power and replaced by the country's first Labour government, under the leadership of Ramsay MacDonald. Labour swept to victory on promises of nationalization and state control and Lord Thomson, its Secretary of State for Air, moved quickly to prevent any possible monopoly of airship-building by the capitalist Vickers. Thomson perceived airships to be the future of aviation. His airship programme was based on the premise that aeroplanes would be developed to fly over distances of up to 700 miles non-stop and that airships would cater for longer, transcontinental flights of up to 3500 miles. In order to stifle Vickers' ambitions, he proposed that two craft of similar capacity should be built – one by Vickers and the other by the Air Ministry. The government would then determine which of the pair was the superior.

In reaching this decision Thomson rejected the proposals put forward to the previous government by Commander Dennistoun Burney, MP, whose scheme was for six new airships from Vickers at a total cost of around £4,800,000.

Thomson veered away from this plan for two reasons: Vickers would have ended up having a monopoly of airship-building in the UK and the government would have been expected to provide most of the finance. On 21 May 1924 he told the House of Commons: 'My immediate object is to enlist the co-operation of private enterprise in these early stages, not so much in competition with the Air Ministry as, rather, in a spirit of emulation. The history of aviation is largely based on combinations of this sort as the efforts of the early pioneers proved. They wanted to make money, but they also made sacrifices. They tried and failed and tried again, while the world looked on. The pioneers not only proved their case, but many of them made their fortunes.' In a statement scarcely guaranteed to soothe the nerves of those wary of the safety record of airships, he added: 'Under the Burney scheme, if one airship crashed, there would be £400,000 gone. Now, if one of the first two ships crashed, we would still have the experts in government employ. We would still have the air highway and we would still have the power of employing people and giving out contracts. We would still have the determination to go on with the resources of a government behind the plans and the endeavours.'

The two airships were to be called the R100 and the R101. The former was to be built by the Airship Guarantee Company, an offshoot of Vickers, at an old hangar at Howden in Yorkshire. The Vickers team's designer was Barnes Wallis (later to achieve fame for his dam-busting bouncing bomb of the Second World War) and the chief calculator was Nevil Shute Norway who went on to become better known as the novelist Nevil Shute. The R101 was the government project and was to be built at Cardington, near Bedford, designed by Lieutenant-Colonel Victor Richmond under the watchful eye of Lord Thomson. The set-up at Cardington was less than ideal since many of those responsible for the design of R101 were new to the job and had little experience of airships. The leading government experts had been killed in the R38 crash.

Following the R38 disaster, the Air Ministry insisted from the outset that R101 should be powered by diesel engines instead of petrol. This stipulation was good news for those who feared the formation of petrol vapour with its dangerously low flash point in tropical conditions, but it was in fact to present greater problems. Those difficulties were foreseen by members of the actual design team who argued against the decision but their pleas were disregarded. Diesel engines it was. But beyond that the Air Ministry seemed to have little idea. As late as 1926, it was still acting on theory rather than fact when reviewing the strains and stresses placed on an airship in flight. Nearly a quarter of a century after Count Zeppelin had launched the first practical rigid airship, the Air Ministry had no figures to show whether its ships would disintegrate in mid-air or survive.

Initial design work on the two airships began in the summer of 1924 but in November of that year Labour were kicked out of office and the Conservatives, who then governed until June 1929, were considerably less enthusiastic about the twin projects. Work continued but at a much slower pace than anticipated and the original date for R101's maiden flight – January 1927 – came and went without a murmur. But with Labour back at the helm in 1929, it was full steam ahead again even though there had been another international airship disaster with the loss of the United States' *Shenandoah* which broke up in the air over Ohio in 1925.

By the time R101 was finally unveiled in 1929, the Air Ministry was facing widespread criticism of the airships, particularly regarding the repeated delays and rumours about excessive weight. Colonel L'Estrange Malone, the Labour MP for Northampton, ridiculed the entire airship policy and suggested that the Air Ministry should cut its losses and scrap both R100 and R101. He said that to continue would be to throw good money after bad and 'increase a cost of £2,000,000 to more than £2,500,000 without results, while £20,000,000 would be needed before regular services could be mounted with a fleet of airships'. He added that aeroplanes would be a much more viable alternative and quoted the views of noted naval architect E.F. Spanner regarding the dangers of airships. Give up now, urged Malone, rather than face inevitable disaster. His words fell on deaf ears.

The rumours surrounding the weight of the R101 were not without foundation, although the Air Ministry did its utmost to keep any developmental hiccups secret from the general public. R101 was very much an experimental craft and thus incorporated a number of devices new to airship construction. The most catastrophic were the five huge, heavy eight-cylinder railway diesel engines which the Ministry had insisted upon . . . as a safety feature. These engines (which weighed twice as much as the R100's petrol-powered units, the Vickers team having rejected the idea of diesel) were not only much heavier than the designers had originally estimated but they also provided considerably less power than anticipated. For good measure, they had a tendency to vibrate violently at higher speeds.

It doesn't take an engineering genius to appreciate that a key function of an airship is an ability to lift off the ground. An airship that can't actually get airborne is about as much use as a chocolate teapot. But R101's engines were so heavy that, far from being a safety device, they hindered lift-off. It wasn't as if all five engines were in constant use. In fact, only four were needed for the purposes of flight, the fifth being added to provide reverse thrust when mooring the ship since the design team had been unable to produce an effective reversing propeller. Weighing a hefty 113.4 tons instead of the 90 tons of the original specification, R101 was in danger of resembling a giant dodo.

The diesel engines weren't the sole contributory factor to the excess weight. The structure of the airship was unnecessarily heavy while nobody seemed to have taken into account the effect of all the advanced equipment which was added on a regular basis. Incredibly it was not until the R101 was inflated and tested for the first time that it was discovered that its lifting power was somewhere around half what it should have been. Trying to compensate, the designers immediately set about ordering the removal of all the extra gadgets such as the complex controls which had been installed to operate rudders and elevators. R100 had none of these devices and handled perfectly. All the chopping and changing simply served to unbalance R101.

If only Lt-Col. Richmond had taken the trouble to consult Barnes Wallis and the Vickers team, many of the R101's problems might have been overcome. But whilst Wallis was more than willing to share knowledge with his rivals, the government team was not and made no attempt to liaise with its opposite numbers during the entire five-year construction period. The airship programme had become a matter of pride. One particular problem which the Vickers team had managed to surmount was another decree from the Airworthiness of Airships Panel – namely, that the German system of attaching the hydrogen gasbags to the airship's girders was on no account to be used in either ship. Barnes Wallis successfully solved the puzzle but the Air Ministry team employed a complicated system of wires to hold the gasbags and when these had to be let out subsequently in another desperate attempt to acquire more lift, the bags lurched around inside the outer covering and also rubbed against bolts and other sharp protrusions which stuck out in every direction. The resulting leaking hydrogen scarcely inspired confidence.

But of course all of these trifling inconveniences were kept from the public who instead were informed by the 1920s equivalent of government spin doctors that everything was going absolutely swimmingly. When R101 was finished, VIP guests were invited to Cardington to admire its sleek lines as it drifted gently in the breeze while anchored to its mooring tower. At 200 yards long and filled with five and a half million cubic feet of hydrogen, it was the biggest airship in the world . . . and by far the heaviest. Lord Thomson gushed: 'People are always asking me to give a name to R101. I hope it will make its reputation with *that* name.' How right he was!

R101 made its maiden trial flight on 13 October 1929. Taking off from Cardington on a five-hour, 300-mile journey over south-east England, the mighty airship brought London's traffic to a standstill as crowds stopped and looked skywards to watch it glide effortlessly above the capital. On board, the 52 passengers enjoyed a four-course lunch in the dining saloon and marvelled at the airship's quietness – they could even hear the sound of car horns and trains on the ground below. In case of emergency, the crew were provided with parachutes and knives for the canvas.

Despite outward appearances, all was not well with the R101. The lack of lift was proving a major headache. However, the men from the Ministry were not prepared to admit defeat and, on 28 June 1930, the R101 was hauled out to attract some favourable publicity at an air show at Hendon. Of all the wonderful craft on display that day, none was more eagerly anticipated than the R101. And the giant airship did not disappoint with a spectacular sky-diving performance worthy of today's Red Devils. First, it suddenly dipped its nose and plummeted towards the ground dramatically before righting itself. The 100,000 crowd had barely regained their breath before the airship, already flying worryingly low, repeated the feat, this time pulling out of its headlong descent just 500 ft above the captivated spectators. They all went home singing the praises of the R101 and expressing amazement at how manoeuvrable it was for its size. Little did they know that none of this was intentional. Far from showing off the airship's versatility, the beleaguered coxswain had been frantically trying to control the beast to avert disaster. Nor were the public told that, when examined after the air show, R101's gasbags contained over 60 leaks so that highly inflammable hydrogen was seeping out all over the airship.

An Air Ministry inspector pronounced: 'Until this matter is seriously taken in hand and remedied, I cannot recommend the extension of the present permit-to-fly or the issue of any further permit or certificate.' This was not what his superiors wanted to hear. So they ignored his report.

In a desperate bid to put things right, the Cardington team cut the airship in half, inserted an additional section in the middle, put in an extra gas tank and reassembled the whole thing. It was led back to its mooring tower but in a matter of minutes the entire outer skin started to ripple in the wind and a massive 90 ft gash opened up along one side. This was not a good sign.

Other defects became apparent. The beautifully shaped fins developed a nasty habit of stalling and serious weaknesses were observed in the airship's outer cover. The cover split repeatedly until the Cardington team realized they had no option but to replace it with a stronger material. However, for some unaccountable reason two areas were left untouched, including the region of maximum stress just aft of the nose. Even the areas that were repaired were treated with a rubber solution which did not mix with the fabric of the cover, which then became brittle and broke up. Furthermore, the failure of an oil cooler during the final trial flight on 1 October 1930 meant that the projected full-speed trial on all engines was never actually carried out. Thus the outer cover was never exposed to its likely level of stress, especially at the unrenewed nose portion. If it had been, it is highly probable that the nose section cover would have split and any grandiose plans to fly R101 to distant climes would have been postponed, if not reconsidered altogether.

As it was, Lord Thomson was still planning to fly to India in R101 as soon as possible, partly to further his hopes of becoming Viceroy of that country and partly because his great airship programme was in danger of falling apart before his very eyes. His designers were less convinced and, prior to R100's departure for Canada in July 1930, had requested that both trips be postponed. But the Vickers team, knowing that they were winning the race, refused and R100 duly set off for a successful flight. After the transatlantic crossing, one of R100's engineers found his watch, which he had removed while working on a top girder, still safely balanced on the airship's outer hull. With R101, it would have been smashed to pieces within seconds of lift-off.

R100's triumph increased the pressure on the Air Ministry whose own device was now seen to be lagging badly behind. Fearful of R101 being branded a failure, Lord Thomson forged ahead with his plans despite the fact that the airship had yet to fly at full power or undergo 'poor weather' tests. These were absolutely essential since the lightest of rain would add up to 3 tons to the weight of the cover while heavy rain could add as much as 7 tons. This was a daunting prospect on a craft that was already seriously overweight and facing a constant struggle to stay airborne. Nor had R101 been granted its airworthiness certificate, issuable only when all trials had been completed satisfactorily. The Air Ministry circumnavigated this little snag by writing one out for themselves, deciding that the full-speed trials could be carried out in the course of the voyage . . . with a ship full of passengers. Observing the fiasco from the sidelines, Nevil Shute described the decision to fly to India that autumn as 'sheer midsummer madness', adding of Lord Thomson: 'Under his control, practically every principle of safety in the air was abandoned.'

On 2 October, Lord Thomson announced that he wanted to set off for India the following day. 'The R101 is as safe as a house,' he said, 'at least to the millionth chance.' His staff protested but his Lordship would agree to only the briefest of postponements. R101 was to leave for India on the evening of 4 October. To depart at night compounded the previous errors since flying low in the dark was a tricky enough exercise in any airship but with one as ill-prepared as R101 it was nigh on suicidal.

The airship was to be captained by Major G.H. Scott who had taken the R100 on its epic journey to Canada and back. Scott, a man with a reputation for pressing on regardless, whatever the weather conditions, had heard all the stories about R101's instability but decided to go along 'for the ride'. Also on board was Air Vice-Marshal Sir Sefton Brancker, director of civil aviation. He was extremely wary about R101 and expressed grave misgivings about its safety record. Lord Thomson challenged him to stay at home if he was scared. Sir Sefton accepted the bait and joined the other 53 passengers and crew as R101 took to the skies in the evening rain.

The fate of R101 has been well documented. Shortly after two o'clock on the morning of 5 October, it was flying dangerously low over Beauvais in northern France when the nose suddenly dipped. In an action replay of Hendon, it righted itself before dipping again. This time there was to be no last-ditch reprieve and it plunged into a wood on the outskirts of the town. The fabric around the ship's nose had split and hydrogen was pouring out from the leaking gasbags. Almost immediately, there were three mighty explosions and within seconds of the crash R101 was reduced to a skeleton of twisted steel. The 'safe' diesel fuel burnt almost as fiercely as petrol would have done. Only six people – all crew members – survived. Lord Thomson, Major Scott and Sir Sefton Brancker were among the 48 killed.

In the aftermath of the disaster, the finger was pointed in a number of directions. Major Scott's decision to drive R101 for the entire seven and a quarter hours of its flight as the 'fast cruise regime' to make progress against fierce headwinds exposed the airship to more severe conditions than it had ever before encountered for such a long period of time. Previous successful airship flights (such as the R100 trip to Canada and Germany's Graf Zeppelin which had circled the earth in 21 days in August 1929) had been across oceans during the summer months whereas R101 was travelling across land in late autumn. The Cardington team failed to make sufficient allowances for the change in the weather and to take into account the greater turbulence usually found over land compared to the sea. But wherever blame may be apportioned, the bottom line is that the R101 was not fit to fly.

The demise of the R101 effectively signalled the end of the British government's airship programme. R100 was broken up and in August 1931 the government formally announced that British airship development should be abandoned. The cost of producing the two airships was £2,400,000. That money brought just 424 flying hours – 297 from R100 and 127 from R101, working out at a cost of £5,653 per hour. And there was the small matter of the loss of 48 lives. The airship had been exposed as a fraud. It was not cost-effective, it could never hope to achieve a regular, reliable passenger service and it was not even an all-weather craft. To have pumped that amount of money into such a project – despite the warnings *en route* – was sheer government folly. It is of no consolation that the British government was not alone in its folly. Between 1921 and 1937, the great rigid airships – R38, *Dixmude*, the *Shenandoah*, R101, the *Akron*, the *Macon* and the *Hindenburg* – all met with disaster, at a total cost of 266 lives. As well as Britain, France, the United States and Germany all lost airships and all abandoned their construction programmes. It was time for the aeroplane to take centre-stage in the fight for air passenger travel. The airship had been found wanting. It had been an expensive lesson for all concerned.

AC Gilbert: Toy Story

The AC Gilbert Company had a reputation for making quality toys to meet the educational needs of America's children. True, they produced train sets but their most popular lines were chemistry sets, microscopes and, the bestseller of all, the Meccano-like Erector engineering sets that had enthralled youngsters for half a century. Parents and children alike knew where they were with a Gilbert toy. It wouldn't be cheap, but neither would it fall apart after a few minutes' play. The name was a byword for solid craftsmanship. Yet in a desperate bid to 'dumb down' to meet the changing markets of the 1960s, the company opted for a disastrous strategy of producing low-cost, low-quality toys. The hard-earned reputation of the previous 50 years went out of the window but the new policy backfired anyway and the company went out of business in February 1967. For young Americans, it was the end of an era.

Alfred Carlton Gilbert had founded the Mysto Manufacturing Company back in 1909, primarily for the manufacture of his latest invention, the Erector engineering set. Seven years later, Mysto became the AC Gilbert Company which went on to establish itself as one of the United States' leading toy makers. Its heyday was the 1950s when annual sales regularly topped $17 million – a remarkable achievement for a relatively small company.

Flawed Concepts

A. C. Gilbert senior died in 1961 and his son, A. C. junior, took over the reins. A. C. junior inherited a traditional firm in a rapidly changing market, a potentially incompatible mix. The world as a whole was changing in the early 1960s. It was the time of *Lady Chatterley's Lover*, the Twist and the Pill. Old-fashioned values were eschewed in favour of new moral freedom and the greyness of the fifties was replaced by the bright, vibrant, swinging sixties. Everything was more colourful, more daring – clothes, music, American Presidents. And this dramatic shift in trends was reflected in western toy markets. Barbie and Sindy were all the rage (with Action Man lurking in the bushes for 1964). Girls no longer wanted baby dolls with feeding bottles and cots – they wanted dolls that were a mirror image of their older selves, complete with square-jawed boyfriends, fast cars and a wardrobe to die for. For their part, boys were shifting from that old favourite, the train set, to exciting new slot-car racing sets. Who wanted to drive a plodding goods train when you could corner Indianapolis at 160 mph?

All of these brave new products benefited from another sixties' phenomenon – the relentless TV advertising campaign. Whereas toy advertising had previously relied mainly on gentle magazine promotions, this was the dawning of the age of the hard sell so that in the months leading up to Christmas, families were bombarded with commercials for the new lines. It took a Scrooge of a parent to resist. Retail outlets were changing too. In the US, small toy shops staffed by kindly old men who could spot a toy soldier at 100 paces were closing down and being replaced by huge, faceless discount stores staffed by acne-ridden youths. These stores didn't want to know about expensive, upmarket products for selective buyers – they were solely interested in low-priced, fiercely advertised toys that they hoped to be able to shift by the thousand.

Without the resources available to larger companies, AC Gilbert was slow to react to these changes. Either it hadn't seen them coming or it was simply content to continue as before, trading on its good name, not realizing how fickle youngsters can be. Indeed, the company didn't even realize that there might be a problem until the end of 1961 when that year's sales figures came in at $11.6 million, a drop of $1 million on the previous year.

The slump in sales triggered a fall in Gilbert's share price and in the early months of 1962, the company caught the predatory eye of businessman Jack Wrather. An independent TV producer who had struck gold with the hit shows *Lassie* and *The Lone Ranger*, Wrather was on the lookout for a likely company and saw AC Gilbert as the perfect opportunity to flex his purchasing muscles. So he spent around $4 million in acquiring 52 per cent of AC Gilbert. From his knowledge of what the children of the day wanted, he concluded that the company had been stuck in a time-warp and immediately set about replacing the top AC Gilbert executives with his own people. A. C. junior did stay on as chairman but his influence was markedly reduced.

Wrather knew all about the power of television and decided that the 1961 sales decline was partly a result of inadequate advertising. Now whilst lack of advertising is almost certainly a recipe for disaster, a flood of advertising does not necessarily guarantee success, as another product of the time demonstrated only too well. A new brand of cigarettes – Strand (3s 2d for a packet of 20) – marketed by Wills, was heavily advertised on British television from 1960. The commercial depicted a stranger in hat and raincoat lighting up on a deserted street corner while staring at the window opposite that was sparkling with Christmas fairy lights, and promised: 'You're never alone with a Strand'. The slogan caught on, the actor playing the mystery man became an overnight celebrity and the music from the commercial reached number 39 in the UK charts. But nobody bought the cigarettes. For this was a case of advertising having an adverse effect on sales. Whereas the thinking behind the commercial had been to capture the mood of loneliness and defiance that prevailed among young people at the time, most thought that if they bought Strand, they would end up as lonely as the chap on television. The result was that within a couple of years. Strand cigarettes were discontinued, killed off by their own advertising.

But Jack Wrather had no qualms about excessive advertising. He increased the sales staff by 50 per cent and encouraged them to instigate a far more aggressive sales approach in future. His executives also felt that, at a time of such sweeping changes in toy trends, AC Gilbert was not coming up with enough new ideas. Every other company seemed to be marketing something new whereas Gilbert appeared to be relying on the tried and tested, the old faithfuls. With a range of new lines, Wrather hoped to boost sales to the $20 million mark for 1963.

But miracles don't happen overnight and before the benefits could be reaped from the 1963 season, there was the small matter of 1962 to deal with. It turned out to be another bad year for the company with sales dipping to $10.9 million. More alarmingly, this was part of an overall loss of $281,000, compared to a profit of $20,011 from the previous year. These figures weren't entirely unexpected since preparing the new range was an expensive business and, by its very nature, it meant that some obsolete materials had to be scrapped. The 1963 Gilbert catalogue was certainly impressive on paper – a new beginning in every respect. More than 50 new items were included, raising the line to 307, comfortably the biggest in the company's long and distinguished history. Whereas hitherto the firm had concentrated on producing boys' toys, the new range included, for the first time, playthings for pre-school children as well as dolls and other toys aimed at girls aged between six and fourteen. Old favourites like the Erector sets were also given a new look, packaging that had remained unchanged for years being altered to stand out in crowded discount stores and supermarkets. The feeling was that the old Gilbert toys looked too dull and staid when stacked alongside competitors with colourful boxes. It cost the company over $1 million to repackage the entire line but everyone in the firm was convinced that the bright new Gilbert image would be a winner.

Perhaps the new Gilbert executives had underestimated their market, for it takes more than pretty packaging to win a child's approval. If the product is inferior, the toy is left to gather dust in a corner. Meanwhile, word soon spreads via the school playground that it is not a good buy. Sadly, some of the new range *was* of disappointing quality, most notably the girls' dolls which, in addition to being poorly made, were overpriced. And, inexcusably, there wasn't even a change of dolls' clothes, thereby depriving the buyer of much of the pleasure that should have come with the purchase. One of the main reasons for buying a doll was to add to its wardrobe; with the Gilbert doll, this wasn't possible. The sense of public disappointment was reflected in the sales figures which, for all the advertising and new packaging, slipped yet further to $10.7 million. Yet the really disconcerting news was that the company had made a loss of $5.7 million for 1963. This enormous loss was mainly due to another company innovation. In an attempt to establish the company name in the competitive field of discount stores and supermarkets, AC Gilbert made a number of concessions to these outlets, including providing goods on a sale-or-return basis. Naturally, the stores were only too happy to display Gilbert's toys under such an arrangement but the move proved to be an economic disaster for the company. Any goodwill that it gained from its deal with the supermarkets was more than offset by the returns of many of the low-priced toys. The result was a thumping loss and Gilbert was left with a mountain of unsold toys after Christmas, to the value of $3.5 million.

Wrather wasted no time in deciding where the blame lay and promptly fired most of the top management team that he had appointed just two years earlier. A. C. Gilbert junior was reinstated as president while Anson Isaacson, formerly with the Ideal Toy Company, was brought in as chief operating officer and chairman of the executive committee. Neither man was in any doubt as to the gravity of the situation. Over the previous two years the company had lost nearly $6 million – a terrible burden for a firm whose annual sales income only amounted to around $10 million. To dig itself out of its hole, the company was forced to renegotiate loans at higher interest rates. It also managed to persuade its principal creditors to agree to payment being delayed.

The company was in crisis with drastic measures following one another like a row of buses. Many of these sweeping moves totally reversed previous decisions, leaving insiders and outsiders alike wondering exactly what was going on at AC Gilbert. Following Wrather's sacking of his own hand-picked senior executives, Isaacson fired the entire sales staff, most of whom had been hired less than two years earlier as part of the great sales expansion. Now, instead of expansion, there were huge cutbacks with Isaacson opting to channel sales through independent manufacturers' reps. Independent reps had the advantage of being considerably cheaper than a proper company sales force although they did charge a fixed commission on all sales. The idea sounded fine in theory but the company soon realized that it had little control over its new sales team. And dealers didn't like the arrangement at all because it meant that there was no personal liaison with a Gilbert salesman. Long-standing relationships became soured as the reps were accused of being only concerned with landing orders. The human touch, which had been such a key ingredient in Gilbert's past success, had fallen by the wayside in the battlefield of big business.

Isaacson wasn't merely content with wielding the axe on the sales staff and announced further redundancies to reduce administrative and operating costs from $10 million to a more manageable $4.7 million for 1964. Although the need to save money in all areas was blindingly obvious, the severe staff cutbacks did not go hand in hand with a company trying to produce new lines in a hurry. It was a move that was to play a significant part in the company's eventual downfall.

In June 1964, A. C. Gilbert junior died. Wrather became chairman and Isaacson assumed the post of president. For Christmas of that year, the company got rid of many of the previous year's failed products and added 20 new items to the range. Sales rose to $11.4 million and, briefly at least, the outlook appeared brighter.

For 1965, AC Gilbert sought to capitalize on some of the crazes that were prevalent at the time, particularly that for spies and secret agents. James Bond and *The Man From UNCLE* were the talk of the playground and so the company brought out a range of figures for Christmas. The only problem was that they didn't reach the shops until after Christmas Day. The swingeing company staff cutbacks of 1964 had seen to that. By operating with a skeleton workforce, AC Gilbert no longer possessed the manpower to facilitate quick introductions.

For a company in such dire straits financially, Gilbert spent a lot of money that Christmas in what amounted to a last throw of the dice. A total of $2 million was spent on TV advertising centred around the Saturday morning Beatles cartoon shows and $1 million was spent on an ambitious point-of-purchase display programme, some 65,000 animated displays being supplied to dealers free of charge. On the one hand, the gamble worked as sales rose to an impressive $14.9 million (the company's highest since the halcyon days of the 1950s) but on the other hand, the exercise proved disastrously expensive as the year-end produced an overall loss of $2.9 million. Much of the loss was attributable to heavy returns on the company's new 007 car racing set, once again bringing into question the soundness of the sale-or-return operation. These sets suffered from poor engineering, shoddy construction and bad packaging. And they were woefully overpriced.

The 1965 financial results plunged AC Gilbert back into the mire, deeper than ever. The company was facing an uphill battle just to stay alive. Isaacson sought financial help to raise sufficient money to carry on trading for another year and managed to obtain a loan of $6.25 million, granted on the condition that AC Gilbert made a profit in 1966. If the results produced another loss, the loan would be called in and the company assets liquidated. In the event, Isaacson's money-raising efforts were just delaying the inevitable. The year of 1966 was an unmitigated disaster for the company, ending in a calamitous loss of $12,872,000. There was no way AC Gilbert could continue and the following February the old family firm went to the wall.

So where did it all go wrong? There were a number of contributory factors but the major charge that can be levelled against the company was that it was guilty of failing to recognize the shift in the toy market until it was too late. For example, slot-car racing sets, which were in their infancy in the late 1950s had, in the space of six or seven years, grown in popularity to the point where they were outselling train sets. Yet Gilbert continued to concentrate on train sets, neglecting slot cars until it was almost too late. And when they did finally join the slot-car market, they did so in a panic and did not allow themselves enough time to perfect the product. The outcome was the poor-quality 007 set, the failure of which did much to precipitate the company's downfall.

Having been initially slow to react to market moods, Gilbert executives suddenly started running around like headless chickens, making wholesale changes. Complete new ranges were introduced at a moment's notice without sufficient thought and consideration. The company's engineering and production departments, which had been used to manufacturing science sets and trains, were suddenly confronted with dolls and figures. The expertise wasn't there, as a result of which many of the new toys were poorly designed and of inferior quality. Not only did these toys fail to find favour with a mass market but they eroded the company's good name. AC Gilbert had a deserved reputation for making high-quality educational toys. Through years of hard work, it had carved out a niche for itself at the top end of the market. Then it surrendered everything in a headlong dash to join the fiercely competitive mass market in which it was up against more experienced and much larger rivals. The company was out of its depth, particularly since it had done away with its sales force. As changes continued to come thick and fast, it decided the only solution was to spend more on advertising. For a firm on the verge of bankruptcy to splash out $3 million on advertising and promotional displays was foolhardy in the extreme. Perhaps nobody at the company had ever smoked Strand.

The toy-buying public perceived a general decline in Gilbert's products in the 1960s. It was a period of some prosperity yet the company decided that people would no longer pay high prices for a toy, no matter how good the quality. Erector sets, which once cost as much as $75 but boasted sturdy parts and came in long-lasting metal boxes, were taken downmarket so that by 1966 they cost only $20 but had brittle parts and came in cheap cardboard boxes. Buyers were not impressed. It was much the same with the company's prestigious chemistry sets. The quality of those suffered and they were encased in cheap gaudy packaging that was wholly inappropriate for an educational toy. One of the new items in the Gilbert range was the All Aboard landscaped train accessory with panels that fitted together to create a scenic layout. The idea was sound but once again the quality was poor and it never achieved the anticipated sales.

For AC Gilbert, initial tardiness was followed by a succession of hasty, misguided decisions as the company attempted to alter its whole image almost overnight. It was a recipe for disaster, and so it proved.

Fonthill Abbey: A Supreme Folly

William Beckford was no ordinary eighteenth-century landowner. The death of his father in 1770 left William with an estate worth £1 million, making him just about the wealthiest ten-year-old in England. He subsequently used the money to satisfy his own eccentricities. Wherever he travelled, he was accompanied by his personal doctor, cook, valet and baker, plus two dogs, three footmen, 24 musicians and a Spanish dwarf. It is said that for one particular trip to Portugal he even took with him a flock of sheep – to improve the view from his window. Similarly, wherever he stayed, he supplied his own bed, cutlery, crockery and wallpaper. Indeed, he refused to occupy any bedroom until it had been redecorated to his taste. But his greatest – and most costly – eccentricity was the construction of Fonthill Abbey in Wiltshire.

In 1795, Beckford employed a team of labourers to build the abbey on the family estate near Hindon. It was to be a folly and was to reach a height of 300 ft in order to compete with the spire of Salisbury Cathedral. Beckford poured a great deal of money into the project but paid an even higher price for his impatience. His first mistake was in refusing to wait for proper foundations to be dug, insisting instead that those that had already been laid for a small summerhouse would suffice. Ignoring the architect's plans and the protests of the builders, he pressed ahead relentlessly, boasting that he would soon be living in the tallest private residence in England.

The 500 labourers worked day and night. To encourage them in their work, Beckford increased their ale ration but this had the unfortunate effect of making most of them too drunk to know what they were doing.

Five years later, the building was still not finished and Beckford was growing increasingly frustrated. Even though the kitchens were by no means ready, he was determined to eat his Christmas dinner there. The beams had not been secured and the mortar was not yet dry, with the result that as Beckford dined, the kitchens caved in around him and had to be rebuilt.

In 1801, Fonthill Abbey was finally completed – or so it seemed. For at the first gust of wind, the tower swayed, crumbled and crashed to the ground. Undaunted, Beckford immediately ordered the construction of a new tower on the rubble of the old. Additional stone was brought in to strengthen it and, after another seven years' hard labour, Beckford's dream was realized at last. By then, however, he had grown weary of the folly and sold it in 1822 at a considerable loss. He was fortunate to find a businessman almost as incompetent as himself: one night in 1825, another gale sent the whole thing tumbling down again.

The Bristol Brabazon: Sold for Scrap

For the Allies, the summer of 1941 was one of the darkest periods of the Second World War. London suffered from heavy German bombing (1400 people being killed on one May night alone), the Nazis invaded Crete and Russia and the Japanese swept west towards Thailand and Cambodia. Pearl Harbor was on the horizon.

In August of that year, as part of the ongoing battle to increase Britain's military capacity and devise new weaponry to crush the enemy, the Ministry of Aircraft Production issued a specification for a heavy bomber capable of carrying a 10,000 lb load over a range of 4000 miles at an average speed of 300 mph. This represented a formidable challenge for any aeronautical designer, yet surprisingly the Ministry only saw fit to send the specification to the three firms in the country that were already building four-engined bombers.

One of these was the Bristol Aeroplane Company. In 1942, the company was busy working on designs for the new Buckingham bomber (which had an initial order of 580) but then a decision by the British and American chiefs of staff rendered the Buckingham redundant and left the Bristol design office looking decidedly underemployed. Seizing the opportunity, Captain R. N. Liptrot of the Ministry asked Bristol's technical director Leslie Frise whether he would like the design contract for the proposed monster bomber. Frise accepted and set to work on a project that became known around the site as 'the 100-ton bomber'. Soon he had come up with designs for a giant aircraft with a colossal wing span of 225 ft and an area of 5000 sq. ft. The Germans were already quaking in their jackboots.

By the end of 1942, the British government was in a more optimistic frame of mind. The Americans had joined the war effort, the Germans had been defeated at El Alamein and were also on the point of surrender in Stalingrad. As a result, thoughts began to turn to the end of the war and a special committee was formed to consider the post-war prospects for civil aviation, with particular regard to the types of aircraft that should go into development. The first meeting of the committee took place on 23 December 1942 but, in another curious oversight, most of the chief designers who had first-hand experience of working on civil aircraft were not invited to attend. Those who were present discussed five types of civil aircraft of various size and for use on different routes. Captain Liptrot suggested that the huge Bristol 100-ton bomber (still unbuilt) could fulfil the requirements for the first and largest aircraft on the wanted list – a plane capable of flying 100 passengers in luxury non-stop from London to New York.

Chaired by the Minister of Aircraft Production, Lord Brabazon of Tara (the first Englishman ever to have piloted an aeroplane), the committee met again on 14 January 1943. Representatives from Bristol, who had been absent from the first meeting, had heard about the new committee and made certain they were present this time. Their reward was a formal government announcement on 11 March that the Bristol Aeroplane Company was to be invited to design the new flagship of civil aviation, on condition that it did not interrupt essential war work at the base. In honour of the minister, the plane was to be called the Brabazon.

The government envisaged the Brabazon as being more than just another aeroplane – they saw it as a symbol of Britain's greatness. And, naturally enough, the greatest nation had to have the largest airliner. 'Financial considerations must necessarily be secondary,' boomed the Ministry, meaning that money was no object in creating this embodiment of magnificence. Meanwhile plans for the 100-ton bomber were scrapped because it was thought that by the time it came into service, the war would probably be over. So more Lancasters were ordered instead. That was one thing the Ministry did get right.

As well as flying non-stop to the United States, it was envisaged that the Brabazon would also link the far-flung corners of the British Empire. It needed to be designed in such a way as to utilize the short runways and remote airfields of Africa and the Far East; it not only required a huge range to get to these places, it also had to have a low speed for landing and take-off. But it was here that a minor contradiction arose. To achieve a vast range, you need a big plane; for a low landing and take-off speed, you need a small plane. It was not thought possible to match both criteria in one airliner.

The Bristol designers solved the problem by making the Brabazon very big but very slow. Adapting the plans for the 100-ton bomber and adhering to the theory that bigger means better, they came up with a passenger-carrying aircraft which, for sheer size, surpassed anything seen before. Unfortunately, the problems it created were also of a size rarely encountered previously. Among the ideas rejected were for a double-decker 50-berth 'flying hotel'. In the end, the designers settled for a plane which at least looked conventional. With money no object, they built an obscenely expensive full-scale mock-up of the aircraft, right down to the last detail – the soap dish in the ladies' powder room.

At first, Bristol was instructed to order the materials for building two prototypes on the understanding that a further ten Brabazons would later be ordered for full production. In March 1946, by which time most of the design work had been completed and the construction of the first plane was under way, Bristol received a firm contract. It was for four Brabazons – the first, a Mk I, to fly in April 1947, with the other three Mk IIs to follow in 1948. To put it mildly, the schedule was optimistic. Even apart from the design of the plane itself, there were so many other factors to be taken into consideration given the scale of the project. The existing facilities at Filton, outside Bristol, were woefully inadequate for a plane of that size. An enormous new seven and a half acre assembly hangar had to be built specifically for the Brabazon and the runway had to be extended to 8176 ft (twice its original length) just to get the 140-ton monster into the air. This necessitated demolishing the nearby village of Charlton and scrapping plans for a dual carriageway.

Perhaps these sacrifices would have been worthwhile if the Brabazon had lived up to its promise. But it didn't . . . not by the length of the Filton runway. The most glaring handicap was that pilots found it difficult to keep the Brabazon's wings off the ground, a fairly rudimentary requirement for a flying machine. Quite simply, the wings were too big and too heavy so that, particularly in poor weather, they had a tendency to scrape on the runway during landing. The final wing-span worked out at 230 ft (even longer than the aborted bomber) and the wings were so thick that a man could walk around inside them. However they were also so stiff that the Ministry of Transport refused to grant the Brabazon a certificate of airworthiness to operate above an altitude of 25,000 ft, an absolute essential for practical airliner traffic. The structure of the rest of the aircraft was made as light as possible but, whilst it was found to have good lift at low speeds, it also suffered from considerable drag at higher speeds. Not that it was capable of much by way of speed. It boasted a maximum cruising speed of 250 mph, a landing speed of 100 mph and a take-off speed of 85 mph – not much more than the sort of figures attainable by some 1930s biplanes. The lack of power was attributable to the Bristol Centaurus engine. Bristol installed eight of its Centaurus engines driving contra-rotating propellers but they left the Brabazon Mk I hopelessly under-powered. For the Mk II planes, it was proposed to replace the Centaurus piston engines with Proteus turboprops but the latter were proving a nightmare in development. Instead of being fêted, the Brabazon seemed somehow fated.

Its cause wasn't helped by continual delays which meant that the Mk I wasn't completed until December 1948 and, after nine months of ground testing, didn't make its maiden flight until 4 September 1949 – over two years behind schedule. Featuring no fewer than 1000 automatic recording instruments and with its fuselage and wings secured by 1,500,000 rivets (which, *The Times* helpfully pointed out, equated to 11 miles of single-line riveting), the Brabazon soared into the air from Filton at the start of a 25-minute journey to the accompaniment of cheering and applause from enthusiastic onlookers. As the mighty nose rose from the runway, well-wishers shouted, 'She's off!', perhaps as much in surprise as anything since it was the largest plane ever to take off from a runway anywhere in the world. At 177 ft, it was 15 ft longer than the United States' Convair B-36 bomber. It had an area of 5317 sq. ft, although some of this was oddly proportioned. At the front and rear of the aircraft, the low floor left a vast area of unoccupied space above passengers' heads whereas in the area above the wing, headroom was severely restricted. So much for travelling in luxury.

The maiden flight went satisfactorily and prompted a message of congratulations from Mr Strauss, the Minister of Supply. 'This is a proud day for British civil aviation,' he gushed. 'It confirms our faith in this great enterprise and is an inspiration to us all. The successful first flight foreshadows the time when Britain's civil aircraft will lead the world. Best wishes for continued success in the trials. Good luck Brabazon, bravo Bristol.' At least he had a nice line in alliteration.

But others were less enthusiastic and serious doubts were being raised about the wisdom of building big aircraft. For not only was the Bristol Brabazon almost capable of being overtaken by seagulls, it had certainly been overtaken by events. By the time it took to the skies for the first time, it already belonged to a bygone age. The move was towards faster, sleeker airliners. The air routes were being filled with Boeing Stratocruisers and Lockheed Constellations and the whole concept of the Brabazon was now obsolete since the majority of airports were extending their runways anyway to accommodate US long-distance airliners. The Brabazon had taken so long to design and build that by the time it was ready there was no demand for it.

The delays on the Mk I inevitably had a knock-on effect on the Mk II. Irked by the lack of progress, the government cancelled orders for the last two Mk IIs in 1950 before much work had been done on them. And the Proteus engine was still nowhere near ready. As one observer noted: 'Even though the Mk II was years late, it still looked like arriving before its engine!'

Then the Brabazon Mk I suffered another blow – this time fatal. After just 400 hours of flying, dominated by problems with propeller mounts and gearboxes, the much-vaunted machine was found to be suffering from metal fatigue. Cracks had started to appear around the engines and scientific analysis revealed that most of the structure would only last 5000 flying hours. The end of the road was nigh.

By 1952, the jet age had dawned. The heavy, clumsy Brabazon couldn't hope to compete with the new long-range jets. Within a few years, they would be carrying 50 per cent more passengers than the Brabazon in half the flying time. The task for which the Brabazon was originally intended could now be performed by smaller, more economical planes such as Bristol's own Britannia. The government, already uneasy, began to get cold feet about the cost, the seemingly endless development delays and the increasing lack of interest from both BOAC and the RAF. The Air Registration Board insisted that the still-unfinished Mk II should be able to fly at cruising speed through severe vertical atmospheric gusts. The Bristol designers made strenuous attempts to develop a gust-alleviation system but met with no success. Rather than continue wasting time and money on a project dogged by apathy, it was decided to give up.

In July 1953, the new Minister of Supply, Duncan Sandys, announced the decision to terminate the Brabazon project, commenting grimly that 'neither the civil airlines nor the fighting services can foresee any economic use for the Brabazon.' The completed but flawed Mk I and her half-finished sister were declared surplus to requirement and were cut up and sold for scrap for £10,000. The project had cost £12.5 million for one plane which never carried a single fare-paying passenger. Filton was left with a massive assembly hangar which proved inconvenient for subsequent use and an extra-long runway that was rarely needed. Those two constructions alone had cost a staggering £6 million. All that remained of the poor old Brabazon was its nose-wheel which ended up in the Science Museum in London. There, small boys used to push a button and make the nose retract . . . until the mechanism broke down. Somehow that was a fitting end to the short career of the Bristol Brabazon.

Ford Edsel: A Name to Forget

For all the glorious 96-year history of the Ford Motor Company, with decade after decade of worldwide triumph, there is still one name guaranteed to bring the most hardened Ford executive out in a cold sweat: the Edsel. When a company is accustomed to almost unbroken success, failure becomes all the more difficult to contemplate, but just as the White Star Line had the *Titanic* and the Bond films had George Lazenby, so Ford had the Edsel.

It was in the late 1940s that Ford first recognized the need to introduce a new model in the medium price range. The company already catered for the upper and lower ends of the American automobile market but something was sadly lacking in the middle. All too often, people would start out with a cheap Ford but then, when they were ready to move a little more upmarket, they would switch to a different make of car. Ford had nothing worthwhile for that middle ground. As one executive lamented: 'We have been growing customers for General Motors.'

Ford's internal research also indicated a definite trend towards middle-of-the-range motoring. The company's forward planning team predicted that the 1950s would be a period of prosperity and that customers would be able to afford, and be eager to buy, slightly more expensive cars than in the immediate post-war period. The feeling from within the company was that if Ford failed to bring out an exciting new model for that market, then it would miss out badly. Reacting to the recommendations, Henry Ford II authorized the setting-up of a new division, christened Special Products, to be headed by one of his leading managers, Richard Krafve.

Henry Ford II wanted to see Ford compete with General Motors, whose Pontiac, Oldsmobile and Buick, along with the Chrysler Dodge, were dominating the middle ground of the American market. All Ford had to offer in that range was the Mercury, a vehicle that enjoyed only limited success. He envisaged 'a car for every purse and purpose', but saw the new model primarily as a smart car for the young executive or for a professional family on the way up. The design team were told to 'create a vehicle which would be unique in the sense that it would be readily recognizable in styling theme from the 19 other makes of cars on the road at that time'. If nothing else, the Ford Edsel was certainly unique . . .

The plans for the new car – still unnamed – were drawn up in May 1954. Its most striking feature was a horseshoe-shaped vertical front radiator grille, likened by some critics to an open mouth. The front of the car was low and wide and it had spreading horizontal wings at the rear to distinguish it from most of its contemporaries which featured sharp tailfins. Well, it definitely *looked* different. It contained the latest in modern technology with a gadget for every occasion. It had automatic transmission with push-buttons set in the steering wheel, self-adjusting brakes and a bonnet and boot that were also operated by push-buttons. Rounding it off was a big 345 hp engine. Richard Krafve called it the 'epitome of the push-button era without wild-blue-yonder Buck Rogers concepts' and when a clay model (with added tinfoil to represent chrome) was unveiled before Ford executives at a secret ceremony, they burst into a round of spontaneous applause.

The company was taking no chances with its new baby and, in a bid to ensure that its target area was spot-on, conducted market research tests with 800 car buyers in Peoria, Illinois, and a similar number in San Bernardino, California. Those questioned were asked about the sort of car they liked to drive or be seen in with a view to defining the ideal image for the new Ford. With so much competition, it was essential that the newcomer had a clearly stated image but, bearing in mind that it was aimed at the middle market, it was thought best to give it a sort of middling image – nothing too powerful and nothing too weak, something that was everything to everyman. In conclusion, the market research report forecast that the car would probably settle on a status position just below Buick and Oldsmobile.

The next move was to think of a name for the new car. Giving a car the right name is a vital stage of pre-launch strategy. Depending on the type of car under consideration, a name should suggest reliability, comfort, maybe even sexiness. Some names are a definite turn-off. Who would buy the Ford Rustbucket, Ford Herpes or Ford Hitler? Krafve favoured Edsel, named after Edsel Ford, Henry Ford's son who was company president from 1918 to 1943 and the father of Henry Ford II. However, the Ford family were less than enthusiastic and so a number of research teams were hired to conduct street tests with the American public. Some 2000 names were tested in this way, including Rover, Jupiter, Arrow, Ariel, Ovation, Dart, Mars and, of course, Edsel. The latter did not fare too well, being most readily associated in the public consciousness with 'hard sell'. Nevertheless, it remained on the list. With no outright winner, the poet Marianne Moore was asked to submit names that suggested elegance, sleekness and advanced technology. She came up with such gems as Utopian Turtletop, Bullet Cloisonné, Pastelogram, Andante con Moto, Intelligent Bullet and Mongoose Civique, but these too met with mixed reactions. The Ford Mongoose would have to wait its turn. In desperation, Ford approached Foote, Cone and Belding, a leading Manhattan advertising agency, to solve the dilemma. The agency produced a list of no fewer than 18,000 possible names, subsequently whittled down to a more manageable 6000. Ford executives gathered in a darkened room to see a slide-projector show of the nominations but were so numbed that they didn't even stir when 'Buick' flashed on to the screen. The list was eventually reduced to ten and finally to four: Racer, Ranger, Corsair and Citation. These were placed in front of the company's executive committee for consideration in early 1956, but chairman Ernie Breech didn't like any of them and sifted through the mountain of rejects again before finally deciding on Edsel. This time, Henry Ford II agreed to abide by the group decision but nobody else was particularly keen on the name. It was chosen for want of a better alternative, not because anyone thought it would be a good selling point. Indeed, the market testing had indicated precisely the opposite, that there were negative vibes attached to 'Edsel'. And therein lay the problem: what exactly did 'Edsel' mean? The great American public certainly weren't going to rush out and buy it simply because it was named after Henry Ford II's dad.

Having spent ten years on planning and research and a

record $250 million on development, Ford prepared to launch the Edsel in September 1957 for the following year. A separate division – the Edsel Division – was created within the Ford Motor Company solely to deal with the new car. The division boasted 1800 employees including its own distribution team. It was an expensive operation but it was thought that by making the salesmen part of a relatively small, individual unit rather than small cogs in a much bigger wheel, they would respond by displaying loyalty to the brand and a hunger for their work. Little did anyone realize at the time that the hunger for work would convert into a famine for sales.

The first Edsels rolled off the production line in July 1957. Publicly, Ford declared its ambition to capture between 3.3 and 3.5 per cent of the total US car market with the Edsel, which would translate into sales figures of a minimum of 200,000 cars a year. Privately, the company hoped for considerably better although it didn't expect to recover the $250 million development costs until the third year. But with trends still appearing to indicate an overwhelming desire for medium-priced cars and with a colossal $50 million being spent on advertising and promotion, the Edsel seemed a sure-fire certainty. The champagne glasses were already being raised in anticipation.

As the summer progressed, the advertising moved into top gear. However the actual look and shape of the Edsel were deliberately kept secret from trade and public alike in an effort to create an aura of mystique around the new vehicle. A typical advert in *Life* magazine showed a car covered in a white sheet beneath the heading: 'A man in your town recently made a decision that will change his life.' The man in question was supposed to be a dealer who had decided to stock the Edsel. And, as it turned out, stocking the Edsel *would* change the dealer's life – but not in the way Ford had hoped.

August saw a three-day press preview for the Edsel in front

of 250 journalists and the following month the prices were announced with models ranging from \$2800 to \$4100. On 4 September came the launch itself which by then had become the most expensive for any commercial product. But already there were worrying signs. In the 1950s, the motor car was the principal cause of death in the United States for the age group of five to thirty and in the population as a whole it was surpassed only by heart disease, cancer and pneumonia. Such was the concern throughout the land that in 1956 Congress held hearings to look into the situation. By then over 1,250,000 Americans had been killed in car accidents. Henry Ford II was all too conscious of the mounting fears and declared: 'We are frankly very fond of the people who buy our products. We would very much like to keep them all alive and thriving.' In the wake of the rising number of high-speed road accidents, the Automobile Manufacturing Association announced in 1957 that it had agreed in future not to advertise a car's power and performance. The Edsel, launched in 1957, was a powerful car, designed to be driven at high speeds. So not only was it bucking a nationwide trend towards less powerful vehicles, but its two – some would say, only – attributes could not be advertised.

Some 1200 dealers had been hand-picked to stock the Edsel and they displayed it with gusto as if it were the Second Coming – despite the fact that car sales in general were slowing down and many dealers had vast quantities of unsold cars dating back months. On the first day, orders were taken for 6500, but sales soon fell away sharply. They were not helped by adverse comments from the motoring journalists who had tested the car. 'The Edsel has no important basic advantages over other brands,' wrote one, while another described the Edsel as 'more uselessly overpowered . . . more gadget bedecked, more hung with expensive accessories than any car in its price class'. This scarcely amounted to an unqualified endorsement.

But Ford could hardly blame the Edsel's failure on negative press comments for there were many other factors which contributed to its demise. For a start, it was introduced too early in the year – at the start of September – and so it found itself competing with 1957 cars which were in the middle of clearance sales. Customers became confused – they didn't know whether the Edsel was a 1957 or a 1958 model. Similarly, the lavish advertising campaign peaked too early. There was a flood of publicity leading up to and during the launch but by October/November – when other companies were introducing their new models for 1958 – there was markedly less. At a time when the Edsel needed all the help it could get, it received none.

The advertising also led people to believe that the Edsel, wrapped in its shroud of secrecy, really was a major motoring innovation. Then it transpired that it was nothing out of the ordinary, with nothing more to offer than its rivals. It was a victim of its own hype. The more something is built up, the harder – and usually faster – it falls. Even the unique points the Edsel did have to offer were not exactly greeted with unrestrained enthusiasm. It offered yards of chrome when chrome was on the way out and a menacing-looking front grille which terrified children of a nervous disposition. A family car demands something that is gentle and reassuring, not a menacing machine that is likely to devour you the moment your back is turned.

Despite all the lengthy and costly market research, the Edsel finished up with a conflicting image. On the one hand, it was designed for speed; on the other, it was supposed to be aimed at upwardly mobile families. The two were simply not compatible. Young families were more interested in comfort and safety than speed. And there was another drawback to the market research. Most of it had been conducted some years before the launch with the result that it was hopelessly out of date.

But these points paled into insignificance compared to the biggest stumbling block that confronted the Ford Edsel – it was rapidly becoming a national joke. Rushed off the factory line at breakneck speed, the first Edsels produced more faults than the Horse of the Year Show. Virtually every car had something wrong with it. There were brakes that failed; oil leaks; dashboards that caught fire; doors that wouldn't close; irritating rattles; hooters that stuck; hubcaps that fell off; paint that peeled; push buttons that didn't work; batteries that went flat; bonnets and boots that refused to open; and transmissions that seized up, thereby earning the car a reputation for immobility. It was a classic case of the more that is put into a car, the more that can go wrong, although it could be argued that transmission, doors and brakes are hardly luxury items. Sometimes even the dealers couldn't get the Edsel to start – not exactly the ideal prelude to a sale.

As word spread about the Edsel's lack of reliability, it became the butt of countless jokes. And once such an image is established, it is extremely hard to reverse it . . . a bit like the Edsel, in fact.

The break-even targets needed between 600 and 700 Edsels to be sold each day but by the start of October 1957 sales were running at approximately 300 a day – less than half the minimum requirement. The next ten-day period (by which the US auto industry compiles its sales figures) made for even more disturbing reading. Sales had dropped to 2751 for those ten days and were in danger of going downhill faster than the Edsel itself.

Desperate to stem the tide, Ford spent $400,000 on a lavish, star-studded TV spectacular, broadcast on 13 October. Featuring Frank Sinatra and Bing Crosby, the show sang the praises of the Edsel but did nothing to improve sales figures. The rot had set in. The mood at Ford became increasingly gloomy although outwardly executives remained defiantly optimistic. 'Everyone who has seen it,' said one, 'knows – with us – that the Edsel is a success.' The captain of the *Titanic* was heard to offer similar reassurance.

The next plan to save the Edsel was a mass mailshot. Over 1,500,000 letters were sent to car owners, inviting them to test-drive the Edsel. By way of inducement, each was promised a toy model Edsel if they accepted. The offer was easy to refuse. Meanwhile, dealers were offered sales bonuses, enabling them to cut the price of the Edsels in their showrooms while at the same time retaining their level of profit margin on the car.

If 1957 was bad for the Edsel, 1958 was even worse. The United States found itself in the grip of a recession. The general slackening off of trade in the second half of 1957 continued until sales of anything other than economy vehicles almost ground to a halt. With money tight, those cars that did sell were in the low-price range. Few people had cash to spare for something as expensive – and over-priced – as the Edsel. To add to the woes of the US motor companies, the country was invaded by a swarm of small foreign cars which made sizeable inroads into the market. They were cheap and reliable – in other words, nothing like the Edsel.

Only 34,481 Edsels were sold in 1958, about one sixth of the hoped-for sales. The second-year model was introduced in November of that year and, being shorter, lighter and, more importantly, cheaper than the original, it created a mild flurry of activity. But the respite was short-lived and before long the Edsel Division merged with the Lincoln-Mercury Division where it became very much the poor relation. The introduction of the third-year Edsel in October 1959 aroused so little interest that the end was inevitable. Sure enough, on 19 November 1959, after a life of two years, two months and 15 days, production was discontinued. The Edsel was dead.

The only tears that were shed were those of Ford executives, particularly the finance department. In total, 109,466 Edsels had been sold, leaving the company with an additional $100 million loss on top of the $250 million spent on development and advertising. As one commentator noted: 'Ford would have found it cheaper to give 110,000 cars away in 1955 than to embark on the Edsel project.' The company stock also dropped 20 points as a result of the Edsel débâcle.

Henry Ford II made no attempt to disguise the Edsel's failings. Looking back, he said of the much-vaunted machine: 'Hell, we headed into 1958 and right into a recession, and everything went kaput . . . A lot of people didn't like the styling of the Edsel. We had a very weak dealer organization and the car's quality wasn't anything to write home about. We couldn't sell them, we were losing money, so we made a decision, "Let's quit", which was the right decision, I'm sure. I'd rather admit the mistake, chop it off and don't throw good money after bad.' When the company introduced the Mustang in 1964, Henry Ford II remarked caustically: 'We sold 50,000 more of them in their first three or four months of production than all the Edsels we sold in two and a bit years.'

Time magazine summed up the fate of the Edsel in one simple sentence: 'It was a classic case of the wrong car for the wrong market at the wrong time.' But for all its faults, the Edsel did have one redeeming feature for owners. In its entire history, there was apparently only one instance of an Edsel being stolen. It was either because it was so unpopular or because no thief could get the damned thing to start.

Chapter 2

Bankers' Errors

The Collapse of Barings: A Chain of Neglect

In simple terms, the 1995 collapse of Britain's oldest merchant bank, Barings, was the result of a plasterer's son from Watford running up debts of £869 million as a result of unsuccessful gambling on the Japanese stock market. But that rogue trader, Nick Leeson, was only able to operate undetected over a period of 32 months because of the general air of negligence and nonchalance that existed in and around the bank. As the then Chancellor of the Exchequer, Kenneth Clarke, remarked after the official inquiry into the Barings affair: 'Such a massive unauthorized position could not have been established if there had been effective management controls.' The finger was being pointed. So who was really to blame for the downfall of Barings?

The story of Barings dates back to 1762 when Francis Baring founded a merchant's business in the City of London. A disastrous speculation in soda ash in 1774 nearly put him out of business and when he endeavoured to corner the market in cochineal 13 years later, he fared little better. A more profitable line turned out to be lending money to governments, and the commission Barings earned on deals such as helping the United States to buy Louisiana (of which more later) set the firm up nicely. By the time Francis Baring died in 1810, his bank was renowned throughout Europe. There was a nasty scare in 1886 when the reckless Lord Revelstoke (the former Ned Baring) underwrote a £2 million share issue by the Buenos Aires Water Supply and Drainage Company. The deal meant that Barings sent the money to Argentina before it had sold the shares. However, the shares proved almost impossible to sell, plunging the future of the company into crisis. With total collapse imminent, Barings was bailed out by a Bank of England consortium. From then on, Barings acquired a reputation for conservatism, in keeping with a company which came to be known as 'the Queen's bank' – attributable to the role played by John Baring (the second Lord Revelstoke) as financial adviser to George V.

In 1982, Japanese companies raised money in the Eurobond market in London for the first time and, in order to help sell these bonds, warrants were attached that gave the holder the option to buy some of the company's shares. In a rising market, such as that of Japan in the 1980s, warrants represented a sound investment. One man who capitalized on Japanese warrants was Christopher Heath, a young broker with the firm of Henderson Crosthwaite. In 1983, warrants attracted the interest of Barings and they enlisted Heath to explain to them how the system worked. Barings were so impressed that they asked Heath to work for them and to bring his trading team with him. Thus in June 1984, Barings bought a highly efficient 15-man dealing and research team specializing in Far Eastern stocks for the sum of £6 million. The new team was called Baring Far East Securities. With Heath at the helm, Baring Securities prospered. Not even the Japanese stock market crash of January 1990 had an adverse effect on their fortunes since they had foreseen the crash. Forewarned was forearmed.

Nick Leeson joined Baring Securities as a clerk in 1989 at the age of twenty-two. He worked for Barings in Indonesia until early 1992 when he was transferred to Singapore. Baring Securities had been operating in Singapore since 1987 but didn't conduct their business on SIMEX, the Singapore International Monetary Exchange. By February 1992, the growth business was the convoluted world of futures and options, a veritable minefield to the unwary. A futures contract is an agreement to buy or sell a specified quantity of a particular commodity at a specified price, the details of the deal and the date of transaction being agreed between buyer and seller on the floor of an exchange or on a dealing screen. An option is the right to buy or sell futures contracts on a set date, the right being granted in exchange for an agreed payment. If the right is not exercised by the agreed date, the option expires. To operate the futures and options business, Barings formed a new subsidiary – Barings Futures (Singapore) Ltd – and applied for clearing membership of SIMEX. Most of the staff for BFS were recruited locally. Nick Leeson was an exception.

Leeson arrived in Singapore with two outstanding County Court judgments against him for unpaid debt. All traders were licensed by the Securities and Futures Authority who wouldn't have given permission for Leeson to trade had he admitted these offences on his application form. There is a distinct suggestion that Barings turned a blind eye to Leeson's past indiscretions, putting it down to the folly of youth. This, as it turned out, was the first of many gross miscalculations.

Barings thought Leeson had a bright future and put him in charge of heading the settlement operations – a settlement is the recording of a trade into the books of all parties involved in a transaction and prompts the payment of any outstanding balances. He was also made Barings Futures' floor manager on SIMEX – another colossal error. One of the basic rules of the securities business is that settlements and trading responsibilities should be kept entirely separate because they can have conflicting interests. The job of the settlements clerk is to make sure that the trader adheres to the rules and doesn't get into deep water; the job of the trader is to make as much money as possible. The two roles are not always comfortable bedfellows so to give one person control of both was to invite trouble. When in 1995 the inspectors appointed by Singapore's Minister for Finance reported on the collapse of Barings, they said that awarding Leeson a dual role was 'an ill-judged decision'. As an understatement, that was the equivalent of describing the Wall Street crash as a financial hiccup or saying that the Big Bad Wolf liked pork.

Baring Securities' top man in Singapore was Scotsman James Bax. His lieutenant was finance director Simon Jones. For both men, Leeson's new title seemed to create nothing but confusion. Right from the outset, there was a complete misunderstanding of his job. Bax believed at first that Leeson was in charge only of settlements. When he did discover the truth, he certainly appeared uneasy with the power and influence that the dual role accorded Leeson and, in a memo to Andrew Fraser, the head of equity-broking and trading at Barings' London head office, warned: 'My concern is that once again we are in danger of setting up a structure which will subsequently prove disastrous and with which we will succeed in losing either a lot of money or client goodwill or probably both.' Prophetic words indeed.

Simon Jones was said to be unhappy at not having total authority over Leeson who was told to report partly to Jones and partly to Gordon Bowser, the man responsible for futures and options settlements in London. If Jones had been given sole authority over Leeson, he might have monitored his activities more closely but because Bax and Jones were puzzled by, and dissatisfied with, the arrangement, it has been claimed that they were reluctant to supervise him. Basically, nobody seemed to have much idea as to Leeson's precise reporting lines. Everyone appeared to think it was somebody different. At one stage, Leeson claimed he was reporting partly to American Mike Killian who was based in Tokyo, but Killian denied this. Amid this widespread confusion, it was easy for Leeson to carry on unhindered. He also enjoyed the geographical benefits of isolation. For while Baring Securities' office was located on the 24th floor of Singapore's Ocean Tower, Leeson and Baring Futures were situated ten floors below, on the 14th. So it wasn't always easy for his bosses to keep an eye on him – even if they had wanted to.

Leeson's illicit activities began around July 1992. Disputed trades are placed in special accounts called 'error accounts' and on 3 July 1992, Baring Futures opened an error account on SIMEX: number 88888. Leeson soon began using the 88888 account for unauthorized trading and started gambling on futures and options. By the end of October, he had amassed losses of £4.5 million but that was small change compared with what was to follow. Leeson hid the truth from his superiors and was able to claim that, far from making a loss, he was returning sizeable profits. If anybody had taken the trouble to inspect the 88888 account, Leeson would have been unmasked.

That he remained undetected for so long was not helped by a panic reorganization of Baring Securities. After years of making huge profits under Christopher Heath, Baring Securities made a loss for the first time in 1992. The figure – £11 million – was not exactly ruinous by trading organization standards but it was sufficient to panic Baring Brothers into making wholesale changes in a bid to avert a repeat performance. Heath and most of his top men were removed and replaced by a corporate financier, Peter Norris, and by specialists from Barings in treasury, finance and settlements. Barings had this dream of a securities business with no risks attached, but the moves ended up causing far more headaches than they cured. The upheaval created widespread confusion at all levels of Baring Securities with some executives being asked to manage areas that they didn't fully understand.

This lack of understanding of the finer points of the futures and options business lulled the senior executives into a false sense of security. They didn't think they were taking any risks in Singapore and so they failed to impose an effective risk-management system. Risk-management is the means for countering dangers in derivatives markets, derivatives being the collective name for any financial instruments, such as a futures contract or an option. Under the old Heath regime, there was a degree of risk-management but under the new set-up there was nothing worthy of the name.

Those working in futures in Singapore had to make daily payments to SIMEX if their trades went against them. These cash payments are called 'variation margin payments'. Each day SIMEX makes a running calculation on the value of the futures bought or sold and if the price drops from the traded price, the trader has to pay up. If, however, the price rises, the trader receives cash via SIMEX. By cross-trading, Leeson managed to cover up his gambling and declare false profits for Barings. He cross-traded between the 88888 account and various Barings accounts in London and Tokyo at higher prices than those he had paid on the exchange. By pretending that he had sold contracts for more than the real sale price, Leeson was able to declare the difference as profit to Barings. The losses on these deals were put into the 88888 account, the very existence of which seemed a mystery to so many of Barings' senior staff. Through this deception, Leeson was able to declare profits of £8 million in 1993, making him one of the company's rising stars. He was promoted to general manager and by October 1993 had apparently proved so successful as to be allowed to decide when and at what price he would trade on behalf of Barings. In effect, he was given a free rein. To show their appreciation, Barings awarded him a bonus of £130,000 for 1993, compared to £35,746 for the previous 12 months.

If they had known the true situation, their appreciation would have been less effusive. After his initial losses in 1992, he managed to bring the 88888 account back into credit in the summer of 1993 by selling a number of option positions. Had he stopped there and then, probably nobody would have been any the wiser and Barings would not have suffered the losses of over £850 million Leeson incurred 18 months later. But, like any gambler, he couldn't bring himself to quit while he was ahead. Instead he continued to use the secret 88888 account with the result that by the end of 1993, his losses had risen to £24.39 million. So much for the declared profit . . .

As the profits continued to roll in (or so it seemed), nobody at Barings was keen to rock the boat. Any executives who did harbour suspicions that all was not well in Singapore didn't follow it through. In 1993, Leeson was in trouble with SIMEX after his trading records were found to contain a succession of minor violations. A formal letter listing these violations was sent to Simon Jones. One item referred to a trade ticket dated 18 February 1993 for the account numbered 88888. Even though the ticket was attached to the letter, Jones failed to launch a thorough investigation and Leeson was not required to explain precisely what the 88888 account was for. It was another example of the absence of the most basic internal supervision and control by Barings' management.

In that same year, a debit of £15 million mysteriously appeared in the accounts of Baring Securities. It was described in the balance sheet as 'loans to clients' but in fact there was only one client – Nick Leeson in Singapore. Moves were instigated to look into the mystery sum but were never followed through. As long as the profits were high – and 1993 appeared to be an exceptional year for Barings – everyone was happy. You don't change a winning team.

From the falsified reports that Leeson submitted to London, Barings understood that the profits from Barings Futures

(Singapore) mainly arose from inter-exchange arbitrage between the exchanges in Singapore and Japan . . . and at no real risk to Barings. To say the least, this was naïve.

If Barings had gone to the trouble of buying a system that enabled the settlements department in London to align trades made in any part of the world with clients' orders, instead of having to rely on branch offices like Singapore for the information, Leeson's fraudulent use of the 88888 account would soon have been uncovered. Such a system, known as BRAINS, would have cost in the region of £10 million – a pittance to such a huge company. But Barings didn't introduce it until January 1995, by which time it was too late to avert disaster.

If Leeson found it relatively simple to hoodwink the Barings hierarchy up to the end of 1993, it was to become even easier thereafter, thanks to a major reorganization of the Barings empire. In 1994, Baring Brothers and Baring Securities merged to create the Baring Investment Bank. The new expanded structure of the company made it more straightforward for Leeson to obtain large sums of money because more capital was available. And the greater the amount of money to which he had access, the more he was able to exploit the frailty of the situation. As with all mergers, a fair degree of chaos ensued. The new accounting system was more difficult to understand so that Leeson's losses became harder to detect on the balance sheet.

The chaotic system under which Barings operated enabled hundreds of millions of pounds to be sent to Leeson to finance his gambling without anyone querying it. Since nobody saw futures and options as a risk, any transfers made from one area of Barings to another – in this case from Baring Securities in London to Baring Futures (Singapore) – went ahead unchecked. Indeed, the transaction was considered to be so routine that it was assigned to humble clerks. Leeson always requested funds from London to finance margin calls on client accounts. A margin is the payment made to a clearing house by a member, or to a member by its customer, to act as security in the event of losses. However, London never reconciled those actual accounts with the money they were sending to finance them. These loans to clients appeared in the balance sheet as 'top-up'. But nobody could make head or tail of the balance sheet so no questions were asked.

Leeson was also unwittingly assisted by what was later described as 'an error of judgement' by Bank of England supervisor Christopher Thompson in granting Barings an 'informal concession' to exceed the 25 per cent limit on the Osaka Stock Exchange. Barings' exposure was not supposed to exceed 25 per cent of its capital base but in 1992 Barings were conducting so much business in Osaka that the Osaka Stock Exchange insisted on a large deposit for margin payments. The deposit was so big that it totalled more than the permissible limit of 25 per cent. So Thompson, apparently without referring the matter to senior management at the Bank of England (which was in itself a breach of internal guidelines), allowed Barings to exceed the limit with regard to the Osaka Exchange. Not surprisingly, Barings also took this generous concession to apply to their exposure in Singapore. To make matters worse, no limit was imposed on the concession. By February 1995, Barings' exposure had reached 73 per cent in Osaka and 40 per cent in Singapore. Thompson resigned as a result of the criticisms levelled at him in the wake of the Barings collapse.

In January 1994, Leeson's losses almost doubled. By the end of that year, his cumulative losses had risen to a staggering £200 million plus. Trying to recover the deficit, Leeson continued to gamble that the Japanese market would go up. He kept on buying contracts, exposing Barings to the most hideous risks, and all the time covering his losses by fraudulently seeking cash from head office. Then on 26 January 1995, his luck finally ran out. The Kobe earthquake sent the Japanese market into freefall. As the Nikkei Index kept on falling, Leeson wrote further derivatives contracts in a desperate last-ditch gamble to recoup his mounting losses. It was to no avail and in those few weeks after the earthquake, his losses quadrupled. With the net finally closing in, Leeson resigned by fax on 24 February 1995 and, as the scale of the collapse sent shock waves through the world's money markets, he fled first to Malaysia and then to Brunei. After five days on the run, he tried to return to Britain but was arrested on 3 March when his plane stopped at Frankfurt. Three days later, the Dutch bank ING bought Barings for a token £1.

The first report into the collapse to appear was that of the Bank of England, published in July 1995. It blamed Barings' downfall on the catastrophic activities of one man (Leeson) but also heavily criticized Barings' management for failing to exercise sufficient controls. The inquiry found that no fewer than nine warning signals had been missed by senior Barings management in the run-up to the crash. In August 1994, internal auditors had warned Barings executives of the 'significant risk' that Leeson could override controls. Had Leeson's superiors acted then, the ensuing crisis would not have been as crippling since most of the damage was done in the final two months leading up to Leeson's eventual exposure . . . after Barings' executives had been warned about his possible activities.

Peter Baring, the bank's former chairman, had described the failure of controls as absolute, a point seized on by the Bank of England report. 'It was this lack of effective controls,' said the report, 'which provided the opportunity for Leeson to undertake his unauthorized trading activities and reduce the likelihood of their detection. We consider that those with direct executive responsibility for establishing controls must bear much of the blame.'

Peter Norris, the chief executive officer of Barings' investment banking operations, was severely criticized in the report for failing to introduce tighter controls over the bank's Singapore office. Norris started to introduce additional controls into what was a relatively uncontrolled environment at Baring Securities in 1992, but even by 1995 these objectives had not been achieved.

Whilst the internal audit of August 1994 didn't unearth the existence of unauthorized activities as such, it did make specific recommendations about the separation of Leeson's dual roles. These recommendations were never implemented. That audit was circulated widely among management in London but most of those who received it said that it was the responsibility of others (especially the management at the Singapore office) to put the recommendations into effect. The report concluded: 'We consider that management in London was not justified in simply assuming that these recommendations would be acted upon. It is significant that when Tony Railton, a senior futures and options settlements clerk, was eventually sent to Singapore in February 1995, the discrepancies caused by Mr Leeson's unauthorized trading were uncovered within a relatively short space of time.'

The report added that there was no sufficiently informed assessment as to how Baring Futures (Singapore) could have generated such large reported profits from activities perceived to be essentially risk-free. Given the very high level of reported profitability, this was a serious failure. 'Neither Ron Baker, with responsibility for Mr Leeson's proprietary trading from the end of 1993, nor Mary Walz, as head of equity products and having responsibility for risk for equity products, had any real understanding of the nature or true profit potential of BFS's apparent trading.' Basically, everyone was just happy to take the money and not open the box . . . or in this case, the can of worms.

Barings' auditors Coopers and Lybrand also came in for criticism after coming to the conclusion, in November 1994, that the control environment within BFS was satisfactory. The report commented: 'We do not consider that Coopers and Lybrand London, auditors to Barings plc, performed sufficient tests to satisfy themselves that the controls over payments of margin and the associated accounting balances were operating effectively.' Yet another opportunity to uncover Leeson's fraud had been passed by.

The report issued by the Singapore government later in 1995 was even more damning. Laying the blame squarely at the feet of senior managers at Barings, it accused them of 'institutional incompetence'. It said that if Barings' management were unaware of error account 88888, it 'gives rise to a strong inference that key individuals of the Baring Group's management were grossly negligent, or wilfully blind and reckless to the truth'. Of Ron Baker, who had been recruited by Barings in April 1992 to set up the Debt Financial Products Group, the Singapore report found that he failed to check properly on the trading of BFS and did not take vigorous enough steps to curb Leeson's exposure to derivatives markets in both Japan and Singapore.

The Singapore authorities were particularly alarmed by the fact that no senior managers at Baring Securities in London had ever queried the funding lines being passed to Baring Futures (Singapore) nor asked for the incomings and outgoings to be reconciled. The report pilloried Leeson's superiors for the manner in which they accepted his profit claims without taking the trouble to ascertain precisely how he had achieved them. 'Mr Leeson's product managers,' it said, 'accepted the reports of his considerable profitability with admiration rather than scepticism.'

The report then turned to the internal audit of August 1994 which 'had identified as one key issue to be examined further in Singapore the fact that Mr Leeson occupied a very powerful position controlling both the front and back office of BFS. He was both chief trader and head of settlements and was thus in a position to record the trades that he himself had executed in any way he wished. The internal audit report, issued in the last quarter of 1994, specifically highlighted this fact as creating a significant risk that internal controls could be over-ridden. Nothing was done to remedy this. The internal audit report noted that insofar as Mr Leeson's trades were almost all executed for other Baring Group entities, these trades would be subject to reconciliation controls, which would mitigate the extent of any irregularities that might arise from this situation. *In fact, no such reconciliation controls existed.*'

At the same time that the internal audit was being prepared, Barings' Group Treasury proposed that someone be designated to the post of Asian regional treasurer and that this person be posted to Singapore or Hong Kong. One of the key areas of responsibility for the incumbent would, said the Singapore report, be 'the co-ordinating and resolving of all problems relating to funding in the region and supervising major cash flows in the regions, especially the funds remitted to BFS'. However, this suggestion was resisted by Peter Norris because it was deemed too expensive. Had it been implemented, it would have saved Barings hundreds of millions of pounds since Leeson's fraud would surely have been swiftly uncovered.

As photographs circulated of him in a back-to-front baseball cap, Nick Leeson became an unlikely celebrity in some quarters. Brazenly insisting that he was the true victim of the whole affair because he had been allowed to get away with it, Leeson fought a long extradition case in Germany in a bid to stand trial in England rather than Singapore. But in December

1995 he was tried in Singapore and, after pleading guilty to fraud, was sentenced to six and a half years in prison. The romantic dream evaporated and harsh reality kicked in.

So how did Leeson come to incur such massive losses? Whilst the climate of indifference and incompetence at Barings gave him the opportunity to run up huge debts, it must also be said that he wasn't terribly good at playing the markets – and certainly not anything like as clever as he thought he was. He gambled and lost and took a lot of people down with him.

Chaos in Lugano: The Mouse that Roared

Nick Leeson was by no means the first bank employee to embark on a solo gambling spree on foreign money markets that would culminate in his bank suffering enormous losses. Back in the 1970s, Marc Colombo, a lowly foreign-exchange dealer in Lugano, Switzerland, left Lloyds with a loss of £32 million after his attempts to capitalize on the system and outwit his bosses brought nothing but disaster. And, like Leeson, Colombo had been, according to the court president at his trial, 'encouraged in what he did by the veritable chaos that existed in the bank'.

Towards the end of 1972, Colombo, a twenty-six-year-old Swiss who had been working with the Midland Bank, took on a new job as a currency dealer in the small backwater branch of Lloyds Bank International, situated in the town of Lugano, near the border with Italy. Lugano was very much a tiny fish in the huge Lloyds pool. There were 59,000 names on the Lloyds payroll, but only 16 of them were employed at Lugano, the smallest of the bank's 170 overseas branches. It was a place where nothing much happened – until Colombo arrived, that is.

Colombo was hired for the equivalent of £9000 a year but

was told by his branch manager Egidio Mombelli, a man 12 years his senior, that he could expect to make five or ten times his salary by successful currency dealing. The prospect of such wealth appealed greatly to Colombo.

He threw himself into his new job with a vengeance and quickly proved adept at reading the volatile, fast-moving international markets where vast sums are transferred around the world by banks' dealers in a matter of seconds and currency values can rise or fall dramatically at the slightest whisper. He distinguished himself by making a good return for the bank and so impressed Mombelli that, within just a few months of his arrival in Lugano, Colombo was appointed head of the foreign exchange operation at the branch.

The Lugano branch had been in existence for five years and, like other Lloyds branches, its international currency dealing was regulated by a three-volume book of rules issued from head office in London. From time to time, staff from London would pop out for a flying visit of inspection and the Swiss authorities also required regular reports on how the bank was faring. Much as one might expect from Switzerland, everything seemed to be running with smooth efficiency.

But Colombo began to get ideas above his station. As he himself would later testify: 'A foreign-exchange dealer is by definition a speculator. Being one is always a hazardous operation. It is a gambler's profession.' While he studied the foreign exchange markets on a daily basis, watching the world's currencies changing value so rapidly, he knew that there were big profits to be made for someone brave enough and clever enough to buy and sell at the right price. It was all a matter of timing.

For Colombo, the catalyst for his daring gamble was the Middle East war of 1973. On 6 October, the Jewish holy day of Yom Kippur, Egyptian troops launched a sudden attack on Israel across the Suez Canal, catching Israeli soldiers, who were praying in their bunkers, completely unawares. While Egypt swiftly occupied most of the eastern bank, Syrian troops were invading the Israeli-occupied Golan Heights. As the war escalated, the United States declared its support for Israel, to the fury of the Arab oil states who raised prices by 70 per cent. At the same time, oil production was cut back in protest by 5 per cent and some Arab states imposed a total oil embargo on the US. The decisions caused panic not only in the States but also in Western Europe which relied on the Arabs for 80 per cent of its oil. The world exchange rates went mad. Prices rose and fell dramatically. It was a dangerously unstable period but Colombo reckoned one thing was certain – that with the United States under pressure and its economy in crisis, the price of the US dollar would fall. So in November he decided that the time was right to take the plunge and hopefully make a small fortune for Lloyds . . . and maybe boost his own career prospects into the bargain.

He sold $34 million in the 'forward' market, which meant that he contracted to deliver $34 million in three months' time, hoping that by then the rate of the dollar would be lower so that he could buy these dollars cheaply on the day-to-day market. All being well, he would be able to make a tidy profit when delivering them. However, things did not quite go according to plan. The US dollar obviously hadn't read the script and, instead of plunging, it went up. Colombo waited and waited in the hope that the dollar rate would drop but by January 1974 he couldn't hang on any longer. His position was so bleak that he knew that he would have to cut his losses and buy in the dollars he needed before the American currency rose any more. He ended up losing 7 million francs on the deal (about £1 million). It was a frighteningly large amount considering that the daily 'open' limit of the Lugano branch was not supposed to exceed 5 million Swiss francs. But then again Lloyds had just announced half-yearly profits of £78 million so maybe it wasn't that big a blow. The money would hardly be missed.

Nevertheless, Colombo decided that discretion was the better part of valour. He was only too aware that if he had reported the loss to Mombelli, he would, in all probability, have been sacked. So, disregarding the guidelines which stated that the management should be notified of all substantial losses, he opted to go for the gambler's favourite get-out manoeuvre – double or broke.

Raising the stakes didn't seem that much of a gamble to Colombo who was sure he was on to a good thing. Since the US dollar had, much to his chagrin, risen relentlessly over the past two months when it wasn't expected to, it was reasonable to assume that it would continue to do so. So, betting that the dollar would rise yet further, he decided to buy $100 million for forward delivery, paying for half in German marks and the rest in Swiss francs. Alas, Colombo got it wrong again. This time the dollar began to slide and by March he was sitting on overall losses of around 50 million Swiss francs.

Colombo found himself in something of a dilemma. As he saw it, he had three choices. The first was to own up and admit to his blunders, but by now he had gone too far for that to be a viable option; the second was to stay calm, do nothing and hope that the fortunes of the dollar would suddenly pick up; and the third was to reverse the position and pray that the dollar continued to fall. He didn't fancy a period of unemployment nor was he a man for inactivity so it didn't take him long to decide on the third course of action.

Risking everything – including Lloyds' name – he chose to sell $592 million forward, betting that the dollar would continue its decline and that the huge profits he would make on the deal would more than wipe out his losses. Once more, he got it horribly wrong as the dollar did another U-turn and rose steadily.

Colombo continued to deal in numerous positions on a day-to-day basis, vastly exceeding the £710,000 daily limit on debts or holdings as laid down by head office. In the course of these transactions, he made unauthorized deals with at least 15 Swiss and foreign banks with which the Lugano branch did not have any authority to operate. He was breaking every rule in the book . . . and a few more besides. To exacerbate the situation, he wasn't even covering his buying sprees with counter-balancing orders to sell. He was going downhill faster than Jean-Claude Killy.

He managed to finance his huge foreign-exchange positions by borrowing money from a variety of Swiss banking institutions in Lloyds' name and he covered up his losses by entering them as currency deals in the branch books instead of sending the appropriate documentation to head office and the Swiss authorities.

This deception would not have been possible in an efficiently run organization but Lloyds' Lugano branch was understaffed and overstretched. Branch manager Mombelli subsequently admitted that he hadn't noticed what was going on under his nose because he had been far too busy with other matters. He also confessed that he knew precious little about foreign exchange markets. 'It's a foreign-exchange Mafia,' he offered by way of explanation. 'For every dealer you need at least four administrators to check what he is doing. They do things that no ordinary banker understands.' Mombelli claimed to have told London that he didn't have the expertise to carry out checks on Colombo's operations and asked Lloyds on several occasions to appoint an inspector for the Lugano branch to ensure that the bank's rules on currency dealings were being adhered to. These requests were refused on the grounds that such an appointment would be too expensive. Even against a backdrop of corporate cost-cutting, you could hire a decent inspector for less than £32 million . . .

Oblivious to his worsening position Colombo continued to plough his lone furrow. Nobody at Lloyds suspected a thing until in early August 1974 a senior French banker casually remarked over the phone to a Lloyds man in London that Lugano 'has reached its limit with us' on account of some massive forward dealing. The call was overheard and sparked off a frenzy of activity within Lloyds' head office. A phone call to a German bank revealed that it too had been involved in huge unauthorized deals with Lugano. The alarm bells were ringing very loud indeed.

The next morning, a team of leading Lloyds executives left London on a secret mission to Lugano. They hadn't announced their arrival for fear of scaring off the culprit. In Switzerland, they confronted Colombo, Mombelli and Karl Senft, the head of Lloyds Bank International in Switzerland and the man with responsibility for all three of Lloyds' branches in that country. Seizing all the papers they could lay their hands on, the executives flew back to London along with the three Swiss employees.

The auditors moved in and spent the entire weekend sifting through the paperwork in an attempt to unravel Colombo's web of intrigue and deceit. They were appalled to discover that he had contracted forward deals worth £235 million which were still unpaid. Furthermore, he hadn't bothered to hedge his bets. This meant he had committed the bank to risking a sum described by the auditors as 'largely in excess of the combined capital and reserves of all three Lloyds branches in Switzerland'. Yet on the same day, 8 August, that the total open positions in foreign exchange exceeded £200 million, the official branch ledgers showed deals worth only £36,600. Something was not quite right.

Lloyds faced a race against time to try and minimize the damage caused by Colombo's recklessness. Obtaining special permission from the Governor of the Bank of England, they transferred vast sums of money to Lugano to cover the commitments that Colombo had made on their behalf. Operating under a cloak of secrecy – if news of the crisis had got out, it would have been much more difficult to effect a quick cure – the bank's international money market director, Robert Gras, spent three weeks working round the clock to put Lloyds' house in order. When all the debts were settled, Lloyds were left facing a loss of £31.98 million on Colombo's unauthorized deals.

The news of the Lugano débâcle was relayed to the financial world by Lloyds' chairman Sir Eric Faulkner. Colombo and Mombelli were suspended and Karl Senft resigned the following day. The biggest loss ever announced by a bank in Switzerland had the immediate effect of wiping £20 million from Lloyds' shares in London.

A year later, Colombo and Mombelli appeared in court in Switzerland, charged with a total of 26 offences committed between November 1973 and August 1974. The charges included criminal mismanagement, falsifying documents and assorted violations of the Swiss banking code. Mombelli was accused of helping Colombo to conceal the facts from Lloyds' senior management in Switzerland by falsifying accounts. Colombo admitted exceeding his authorized dealing limits and conducting transactions with unauthorized banks, but denied accepting illegal commissions and criminal intent.

The 16-page indictment compared Colombo's behaviour to a gambler trying to recoup his losses by betting ever-higher stakes. The prosecution said Colombo had acted as if he was out of control at a casino and described the lowly dealer as the mouse that made Lloyds tremble.

Nobody could comprehend why Colombo had backed so many losers and had allowed his losses to escalate so dramatically. He explained: 'There was the pride of the foreign-exchange dealer who will not admit failure. I was at all times convinced that I could recoup my losses, but it only takes a little unforeseen something to upset the market. I felt I was a prisoner of events.' Asked how he had managed to get away with his illicit operation for so long without any of Lloyds' senior staff suspecting a thing, he admitted: 'I have not known checking systems as lax as those at Lloyds at Lugano.'

Colombo also confessed that he had exploited Mombelli's ineptitude and that on at least one occasion he had made his branch manager sign a document unseen when he was particularly busy. Mombelli insisted that he hadn't a clue as to what was happening. The court president Gastone Luivini, hearing that Mombelli had initialled other papers without realizing their significance, agreed, labelling him hopelessly incompetent, 'as a bank manager a real disaster, a man without brains who did not know what happened in his own bank'. The president did not believe in mincing his words.

Kurt Roth, the credit manager at the Lugano branch, also savaged the carcass of the hapless Mombelli, telling the court that he had informed Mombelli that Colombo's transactions were reaching alarming proportions. Mombelli's only point of mitigation was that he had warned London that he wasn't really qualified to monitor Colombo's activities.

With everyone seemingly blaming somebody else, Karl Senft joined in the criticism of Lloyds' head office, claiming that staff at London had delayed giving instructions on accounting matters and had not been businesslike in their attitude to the Lugano branch. It certainly appeared that the laxity spread beyond the Lugano office with Lloyds' London staff admitting that they didn't see all the records relating to foreign transactions in Lugano. It was only after the loss was discovered that Lloyds introduced a unified system of recording – a classic instance of shutting the stable door after the horse has bolted.

Few emerged from the case unscathed but at the end of the

four-day trial, both defendants walked free from court. Colombo was given an 18-month suspended sentence for violating Swiss banking law and falsifying documents and Mombelli received a six-month suspended sentence after being found guilty of disloyal management and breaking bank law by negligence. Both were additionally fined £300, the lenient sentence reflecting the court's belief that neither man was interested in personal profit. Indeed Colombo seemed to have been driven purely by a desire to prove his worth to the bank. Bloodied but unbowed, he later had the temerity to suggest that if he had been allowed to continue gambling on the foreign exchange, his deals would, due to subsequent market fluctuations, have eventually brought Lloyds a nice £11 million profit. Lloyds were singularly unimpressed by this claim. By then, they had heard more than enough of Marc Colombo's speculations.

Chapter 3

The Sting

The Hitler Diaries: Distinguishing Reich from Wrong

A successful hoax can only thrive on the gullibility of others. And when that gullibility is laced with greed, as in the remarkable case of the faked Hitler diaries of the early 1980s, the outcome is even more spectacular. Rarely in the annals of mankind has embarrassment and humiliation been so acute as that experienced by executives of the mighty German magazine *Stern* who were duped out of some £5 million because they refused to contemplate the possibility that the diaries offered to them could have been forgeries. In fairness, they were not alone. Noted historians and handwriting experts were also taken in by a scam that left reputations in tatters and cost the jobs of at least four editors in three different countries. And what made the story of the Hitler diaries all the more incredible was that these luminaries of the worlds of publishing, art and history were brought down to earth not by some intricate far-reaching plot but by a simple one-man operation carried out by a petty criminal from East Germany.

That man was Konrad Kujau, known to his friends as 'Konni'. Born in the town of Loebau (which from 1946 to 1991 was part of East Germany), Kujau escaped to the West in 1957 to avoid arrest on minor charges of theft. He settled just outside Stuttgart and adopted the new identity of 'Peter Fischer', under which name he was jailed twice, again for minor violations. He teamed up with Edith Lieblang, who had also fled from the East, to open the Pelican Dance Bar in 1962 but the business proved a financial disaster and he was jailed again, this time for forging luncheon vouchers. The loyal Edith set up the Lieblang Cleaning Company and Kujau/ Fischer did his utmost to go straight but his luck ran out in 1968 when the police discovered that the two men were one and the same and that Herr Kujau was still wanted in East Germany. It was back to prison for Konni. Meanwhile, Edith's cleaning business was doing very nicely and on his release, Kujau could afford to visit his family in Loebau where he came up with the plan of advertising for old Nazi memorabilia. Then, as now, there was a thriving market in Nazi collectibles so Kujau knew there was money to be made. And for the right pieces, he reckoned the sky was the limit.

Over the next few years, he concentrated on smuggling as much as he could from the East to the West. He acquired so many items – Nazi helmets, uniforms, medals and flags – that by 1974 there was no more room in his apartment. Needing additional space to house his rapidly expanding treasure trove, he moved to a shop in Stuttgart's Aspergstrasse. But running a shop is a costly business and, in order to make ends meet, Kujau decided to raise his prices. To justify these increases, he took to forging documents of authentication, including a note from Rudolf Hess proclaiming that a rusty, nondescript First World War helmet was that worn by Hitler himself in 1917. Collectors willingly paid the extra money for something that they were sure was genuine. Kujau realized he was on to a winner and eagerly began to copy Hitler's handwriting and artistic style with a view to bringing further treasures on to the market.

One of his most ardent customers was Fritz Stiefel who owned a small engineering factory in the Stuttgart suburb of Waiblingen. After discovering Kujau's little shop in 1975,

Stiefel proceeded to hand over 250,000 marks (the equivalent of around £70,000) to Kujau in the course of the next six years for 160 drawings and paintings as well as poems, letters and speech notes, all supposedly in the hand of Hitler. Stiefel kept coming back for more, fuelling Kujau's greed to the point where he saw the demand for producing the ultimate item of Nazi memorabilia – Hitler's personal diary. By 1978, practice had enabled Kujau to perfect the Führer's handwriting and so, using pencil and ink and a 1935 Nazi Party yearbook, Kujau invented a chronicle of Hitler's daily life from January to June of that year and called it Hitler's diary. Stiefel snapped up the result and wanted to know if there were more.

But Stiefel was a novice compared to Gerd Heidemann. A photo-journalist with *Stern* magazine since 1955, Heidemann was so obsessed with the Nazis that his second wife had left him because she was tired of playing second fiddle to his collection of model soldiers. In 1973, he achieved one of his great ambitions by buying Goering's former motor yacht, *Carin II*. In doing so, he met Goering's daughter, Edda, and embarked on an affair with her. Some cynics suggested that he was thereby fulfilling another lifelong dream. Tiring of Edda, he married Gina, a former airline stewardess, in 1979 and took his new bride to South America for their honeymoon. Instead of lazing on sun-drenched beaches sipping exotic drinks, he set off in search of Nazi war criminals Martin Bormann and Josef Mengele, Auschwitz's infamous 'Doctor of Death'. Bormann and Mengele proved typically elusive but Heidemann found an acceptable substitute in Klaus Barbie, the 'Butcher of Lyons'.

Heidemann was highly regarded within *Stern*, whose management shared his interest in former Nazis. It was a subject that, however painful a reminder it appeared to those who wished to forget, still sold magazines. Heidemann earned 9000 marks a month from *Stern* but by 1979, with a new wife to support, his finances were looking distinctly unhealthy. The principal cause was *Carin II*, the upkeep of which devoured two-thirds of his salary. Realizing that it was a time for sacrifices, he tried to sell the beloved yacht for 1.1 million marks, but found no takers. In increasing desperation, he planned to sell some of his other Nazi memorabilia and was given the name of Fritz Stiefel as a likely buyer.

On meeting Stiefel, Heidemann set about selling him some of Goering's table silver from *Carin II*. Stiefel was suitably impressed and struck a deal for a sugar bowl, a water goblet and a match-holder. As the two men discussed their shared passion, Heidemann learned that Stiefel was also the proud possessor of a volume purporting to be Hitler's diary. Heidemann was immediately intrigued and begged to be allowed to see it. Accordingly, on 6 January 1980, the journalist visited Stiefel and was shown into a room guarded by a heavy steel door. There, Stiefel handed him a slim, A4-sized book with gothic initials in the bottom right-hand corner. Heidemann read these as 'A.H.'. Inside were over 100 lined pages, some half full; others blank. Some were written in pencil; others in ink. Many of the pages bore what appeared to be Hitler's signature. The text covered the period from January to June 1935.

Heidemann probed for further information but Stiefel was evasive, vaguely hinting that there were a further 26 volumes and, repeating what Kujau had told him, that the source of the diaries had influential relatives in East Germany. From his studies of the subject, Heidemann was all too aware that one of the last flights to leave the besieged city of Berlin on 20 April 1945 had been carrying Hitler's personal papers to his Alpine retreat until it crashed near Börnersdorf on the Czech border. Hearing Stiefel's story, Heidemann came to the conclusion that these personal papers must have contained Hitler's diaries which had obviously remained in East Germany ever since, undetected by the West.

Heidemann knew that his first duty was to relay details of his exciting discovery to his superiors at *Stern* but, instead of sharing his joy, editor-in-chief Peter Koch and his fellow executives were decidedly unimpressed. The only person to show a modicum of interest was Thomas Walde, editor of *Stern*'s historical section, and, on 15 November 1980, he accompanied Heidemann on a visit to the East German graves of the crew of the crashed plane. Walde was so enthralled by the story that, without telling Koch and the other editors, he commissioned Heidemann to search for the Hitler diaries. Heidemann's investigations brought him into contact with Jakob Tiefenthaeler, a former junior member of the SS, who said that he thought the diary had come from a dealer called Fischer. Tiefenthaeler agreed to pass on an offer of 2 million marks for the remaining volumes. Acting as an intermediary, Tiefenthaeler called Heidemann with Fischer's phone number. On 15 January 1981, an uncharacteristically nervous Heidemann made the call that was to change his life – and many others'. On the other end of the line was 'Fischer' (alias Kujau) who informed Heidemann that as well as the diaries he also had a number of other Hitler manuscripts such as a third volume of *Mein Kampf* and an opera that the Führer had composed in his youth, *Wieland der Schmied* ('Wieland the Blacksmith'). Heidemann could hardly contain himself.

Heidemann and Walde now made a momentous decision – to go over the head of Peter Koch to the senior executives of Grüner and Jahr, the owners of *Stern*. Heidemann was certain that Koch wouldn't be interested in the diaries: broaching the subject a few days earlier, he had been severely rebuked by Koch and told to drop his obsession with all things Nazi. Meanwhile, Walde thought that *Stern* were so desperate for a big story that they would have wasted the diaries for the sake of a quick scoop. So it was that

Heidemann and Walde found themselves in the offices of Grüner and Jahr on the ninth floor of the *Stern* building in Hamburg face to face with managing director Manfred Fischer, a man who loved making instant decisions; Fischer's deputy, Dr Jan Hensmann, the company's financial expert; and Wilfried Sorge, a third Grüner and Jahr executive who assumed the role of salesman. Fischer was fascinated by Heidemann's dossier on the Hitler diaries and listened patiently as Heidemann explained that many of the documents were in the hands of a highly placed officer in the East German army (Kujau's story) and that the books had to be smuggled into the West in secret. For this reason, no names could be revealed. There was too much at stake and careless talk could wreck everything and even put lives in danger. Heidemann added that neither Henri Nannen, the founder and publisher of *Stern*, nor Koch knew anything about the existence of the diaries. Nor should they be told. On the face of it, that was a huge confidence to expect the three men to keep but in fact Fischer shared Heidemann's dislike for the abrasive Koch and was perfectly happy not to tell him.

At forty-seven, Fischer was a man on the way up. His excitement at obtaining the Hitler diaries – and in the process orchestrating the publishing *coup* of the decade – was partly attributable to the boost it would give his future career prospects. For he was in line to take over the running of the vast Bertelsmann publishing empire which owned 75 per cent of Grüner and Jahr. Procuring the Hitler diaries would surely clinch his promotion.

And so Fischer wasted no time in giving Heidemann the go-ahead. Heidemann was immediately handed 200,000 marks as a deposit and caught a plane to Stuttgart that night. As a gesture of goodwill, he also took along Goering's dress uniform which had been a present from Edda. Heidemann's meeting with Kujau lasted for over seven hours. At first, Kujau seemed reluctant to agree to a deal, claiming that he had received an offer of $2 million from someone in the United States. But in the end it was the gift of the uniform that swung things. Kujau was already the proud owner of uniforms worn by Hitler, Himmler and Rommel so he needed Goering's for the set. The deal was struck and Kujau promised to set about obtaining the rest of the diaries which, unknown to Heidemann of course, meant getting to work with pen and paper.

On his return to Hamburg, Heidemann went to see Sorge and filled him in on details of the meeting. He told Sorge that the supplier of the diaries was a collector of Nazi memorabilia whose brother was a general in East Germany. Some of the diaries, he added, had been smuggled into the West inside pianos. Reiterating the need for secrecy, he warned Sorge that the general would stop supplying the diaries at once if he thought they were for publication in *Stern*. To avoid arousing suspicions, Heidemann was posing as a Swiss collector.

Over the next three weeks, Kujau rattled off the first three diaries. To make them look suitably aged, he bashed them around a bit and sprinkled tea over the pages. As a nice finishing touch, he attached a red wax seal of a German eagle on each cover together with a forged note from Hess declaring the diaries to be the property of A. Hitler. It was so amateurish, it was laughable.

But nobody at Grüner and Jahr was laughing. Quite the contrary. When Heidemann brought the first consignment of diaries to Fischer, Hensmann, Sorge and Walde on 18 February 1981, all present were overcome with awe as they tenderly handled the books. Fischer was particularly impressed by the slightly battered appearance of the books and described their arrival as 'a great moment' in his life. Once again, Heidemann and Walde emphasized the need for total secrecy, implying that lives were at risk. To preserve that secrecy, the two men argued against bringing in outside experts to examine the diaries until a full set was in the company's possession. Nodding sagely, the three Grüner and Jahr men agreed and anyway, even though none of the five present could actually read the old Germanic script of the diaries, each was utterly convinced that they were genuine.

And so, without consulting a handwriting expert, a forensic scientist or a historian, that day Fischer committed the company to the purchase of 27 volumes of the Hitler diaries at 85,000 marks apiece plus 200,000 marks for the third volume of *Mein Kampf* – a total outlay of some 2.5 million marks (about £700,000). To secure the diaries, Fischer signed a document authorizing the immediate transfer of 1 million marks from the company's main account. Nobody could accuse Fischer and his colleagues of letting the grass grow beneath their feet and on 23 February, just five days after producing the first diaries, Heidemann signed a secret contract with Grüner and Jahr for a series based on the diaries and for one, or perhaps several, *Stern* books. In return, Heidemann would receive an advance of 300,000 marks when eight volumes of the diaries had been received plus generous royalties. For Heidemann, it was a potential gold mine and one that was all the more tangible because he was dealing with such a trusting soul as Fischer. Indeed, knowing of Heidemann's financial plight, Fischer kindly agreed to have the advance paid into his account the next day (even though only three diaries had so far been delivered instead of the stipulated eight) as a gesture of good faith.

By now, a sixth person had been let in on the secret. The company's new finance director, Peter Kuehsel, had been understandably perplexed by having to find 200,000 marks after the banks had closed, drive to the airport, cram the money in a suitcase and hand it over to Heidemann without any questions. Not unreasonably, Kuehsel wanted to know what the money was for and why it had to be in cash. Fischer eventually told him, swearing him to secrecy. Now, a month later, Sorge asked him for authorization to draw out 480,000 marks for the latest shipment of diaries. A stunned Kuehsel had little option but to go along with it.

Kujau would have been similarly alarmed had he known that Heidemann was swindling him. Of the 85,000 marks designated for each diary, Heidemann was handing over only 50,000 to Kujau and keeping the other 35,000 for himself. In the meantime, Heidemann was so full of himself and so thrilled by the significance of his find that he contacted an old SS friend, Wilhelm Mohnke, and read out a few relevant extracts from the diaries. Mohnke instantly poured scorn on them, doubting their authenticity, but Heidemann remained unconcerned. Another opportunity to uncover the scam and save Grüner and Jahr an awful lot of money came and went in the spring of 1981 after Eberhard Jaeckel, Professor of History at the University of Stuttgart, revealed that some poems among his collection of Hitler's early writings were forged. He had obtained them from Stiefel and Kujau. A worried Walde considered whether the poems could have come from the same source as the diaries – the Börnersdorf plane crash – and sent Heidemann to check it out. But Heidemann didn't bother contacting Jaeckel. Instead he simply sent the poems to Kujau and asked him whether he had ever seen them before. Not surprisingly, Kujau said he hadn't. This was good enough for Heidemann who reported back to Walde that there was absolutely nothing to worry about – the diaries were genuine. There is no faith like blind faith.

In London, the *Sunday Times* were alerted to the Jaeckel story but, because of an economy drive, they refused to send a reporter to Stuttgart. Jaeckel would surely have led the newspaper to Stiefel and Kujau and the diaries would probably have been exposed as fakes. Once again, it was an opportunity missed. Kujau was leading a charmed life.

During this time, Peter Koch was becoming increasingly irritated by the fact that his star reporter, Heidemann, was continually unavailable for other assignments. In May 1981, Heidemann, under intense pressure, finally told Koch why he was always busy on other matters. Hearing about the deal for the diaries for the first time, Koch was understandably furious, as were his fellow editors-in-chief, Felix Schmidt and Rolf Gillhausen. But despite their anger at not being kept informed, they had no reason to suspect that the diaries were anything other than wholly authentic. Fischer duly achieved his promotion to be managing director of Bertelsmann and was replaced by Gerd Schulte-Hillen who, since his illustrious predecessor had approved everything, did not deem it necessary to question the arrangement with Heidemann. It was business as usual. Indeed Schulte-Hillen even ordered that Heidemann be given a pay rise. 'The man needs recognition,' Schulte-Hillen told Felix Schmidt, 'and he needs to be treated with special care.' Schmidt reluctantly agreed to the pay rise.

It seemed Heidemann could do no wrong. Everything was going according to plan. Between 1981 and 1983, whenever he received a call from Kujau informing him that a fresh consignment of diaries had arrived from East Germany, Heidemann would take a suitcase of money, fly to Stuttgart, collect and photocopy the diaries before placing them in Grüner and Jahr's safe. And nobody queried a thing. Even when Heidemann said the price per volume had more than doubled to 200,000 marks because the East German general who was supplying them had been obliged to pay out sizeable bribes, Schulte-Hillen willingly handed over the extra cash.

The enthusiasm with which Heidemann, Walde and the Grüner and Jahr top brass had greeted the existence of the Hitler diaries had tended to mask the fact that the contents of the diaries were desperately dull. There were precious few of the world-shattering revelations that would have been expected from the personal journals of a power-crazed dictator, just page after page of boring minutiae.

As the material was collated for early 1983 with a view to marketing syndication rights to the world's newspapers and magazines, *Stern* decided to prepare the story of precisely how the Hitler diaries had been unearthed. The magazine knew that, for extracts from the diaries to be sold overseas, thorough authentication would be needed. Three handwriting 'experts' had already stated that the writing was Hitler's but now the West German Federal Police conducted forensic tests on various items from the Hitler archive. The report came back on 28 March 1983 and declared that six of the nine documents tested were fake since they showed traces of a paper whitener not in use until after the Second World War. Heidemann rang Kujau who calmly shrugged it off. There was no cause for alarm, he insisted. Heidemann and Walde also took comfort from the fact that a statement by Rudolf Hess, the only page taken from the actual diaries, tested inconclusively. They still managed to convince themselves that the diaries were genuine – perhaps the other documents had become contaminated with whitener or there had been some kind of mix-up. They were in too deep to contemplate the awful possibility that the diaries were fakes. In the circumstances, they decided it was best not to pass the results of the tests on to *Stern*.

Rights to the story of the Hitler diaries had now been offered to Rupert Murdoch's Times Newspapers in London. The *Sunday Times* had suffered considerable embarrassment back in 1968 when it had spent £250,000 on Mussolini's diaries which turned out to be fake. Anxious to ensure that no fingers were burned this time, *The Times* despatched distinguished historian Lord Dacre (Hugh Trevor-Roper, author of *The*

Last Days of Hitler) to Zurich to authenticate the diaries. Prophetically, the date was 1 April.

Trevor-Roper was initially sceptical. He knew that Hitler hated writing and had virtually given up writing in his own hand after 1933. There had never been any historical evidence to suggest that Hitler had kept a diary, either from German archives or from the recollections of associates, and there was also considerable doubt as to whether Hitler would have had sufficient time to pen a diary. On the journey to Zurich, Trevor-Roper was handed a 20-page document (Plan 3) written by Heidemann and based on the so-called diaries. One extract purported to disclose how Rudolf Hess, Hitler's deputy, had undertaken his abortive peace mission to Britain in May 1941. According to the document, Hitler had known of Hess's plan in advance. This was indeed a sensational development – arguably the diaries' major selling point – but it flew in the face of all known findings. It also contradicted Trevor-Roper's own interview with Albert Speer, one of Hitler's henchmen, who had been waiting outside the Führer's study door at the very moment when Hitler heard about Hess's flight to Britain. Speer had told Trevor-Roper that Hitler had reacted to the news with 'an inarticulate, almost animal outcry' – hardly the reaction of someone who had known what Hess was planning all along.

Thus Trevor-Roper landed in Zurich ready to rubbish the diaries. At a bank in the city he met Peter Koch who showed him 58 volumes of Hitler's handiwork plus a bound volume of Hitler's original drawings and paintings and the trusty First World War helmet. Trevor-Roper was also invited to inspect the reports from the three handwriting experts. In no time at all, he was won over. He wrote in *The Times*: 'When I entered the back room in the Swiss bank and turned the pages of those volumes, my doubts gradually dissolved. I am now satisfied that the documents are authentic.'

This was a major *coup* for *Stern* and one that appeared to guarantee the financial success of the syndication. And Trevor-Roper was not the only authority to be persuaded of the diaries' authenticity. Another English historian, David Irving, also believed at first that they were genuine, if only because the handwriting in the diaries deteriorated as the years went by in a way that was compatible with someone who, like Hitler, was suffering from Parkinson's disease. Irving reasoned that no forger would be aware of Hitler's medical condition.

In the wake of Trevor-Roper's verification, Rupert Murdoch flew to Zurich in person and within 24 hours was leafing through the diaries in the bank vault. He offered *Stern* $3.25 million for the English language rights but then *Newsweek* offered $3 million for just the US rights. Believing themselves to be in a position of power, *Stern* tried to push the price up by playing the two publications off against one other. Jan Hensmann told Murdoch that the deal was off unless he paid $3.75 million. Determined to land the diaries, Murdoch eventually agreed to the new price, only for Gerd Schulte-Hillen and his colleagues to continue playing games. Their greed knew no bounds. Murdoch and *Newsweek* were summoned to Hamburg where Schulte-Hillen confidently expected them to bid against each other. But the two parties, fed up with *Stern*'s amateurism, decided to join forces. They would share the costs and split the diaries between them. *Stern* were horrified by this development and feared that they would no longer get the $3.75 million. But Murdoch and *Newsweek* played fair and said they were still prepared to pay $3.75 million. Wilfried Sorge breathed a sigh of relief and could scarcely believe his ears when Schulte-Hillen interrupted: 'We no longer think that is enough. We want $4.25 million.' At that, the British and American delegations walked out. *Stern* had blown it.

Over the next few days, *Stern* desperately tried to resurrect the deal. They had little choice because nobody else was willing to meet the asking price. *Time* magazine and the *New York Times* were not interested while Associated Newspapers (publishers of the *Daily Mail*) had only offered £50,000 for Plan 3 (the Heidemann document shown to Trevor-Roper) and even then demanded firm guarantees of authenticity. *Stern* were planning to run the story on 3 May but, realizing that *Newsweek* were already in possession of the story of the find as well as the first four instalments from the diaries (which had been sent out as a tempter), the Germans panicked in case *Newsweek* ran pirated extracts. With a worldwide circulation of more than 3 million, such a move by *Newsweek* would have wrecked *Stern*'s syndication plans. To counter this, the jittery *Stern* editors decided to bring the story forward to 25 April and went back to Murdoch who was now confident that he could buy the diaries on his own terms. And so he bought the British, Commonwealth and US rights for a knockdown $1.2 million and earmarked his scoop for the 24 April edition of the *Sunday Times*.

Despite Trevor-Roper's assertions (he stated that the world would have to revise its opinion of Hitler and view him as 'a compulsive diarist'), many of the staff at the *Sunday Times* held grave reservations about the diaries, not least because David Irving had told them about some fake Hitler documents just a few months earlier. And the fact remained that no German scholar had yet been allowed even to look at the diaries, let alone check them. It was an incredible oversight amidst a chapter of blunders by *Stern*.

Friday, 22 April 1983 was the day when the enormity of their folly began to dawn on the *Stern* executives. It began brightly enough with the magazine running its exclusive story announcing the discovery of the Hitler diaries to the world. But no sooner had the publication hit the news-stands than *Stern* received the results of a second batch of forensic tests which categorically stated that much of the Hitler archive was a fake. The documents included in these tests were letters, notes and meeting notices, plus paintings and drawings apparently signed by Hitler – in fact, the very items that had convinced Trevor-Roper that the entire archive (including the diaries) must be genuine. *Stern* started to panic again but decided that the only way to face the mounting flak was to persuade Heidemann to divulge his source – something he had hitherto steadfastly refused to do. Again, Heidemann remained tight-lipped and insisted that the diaries were genuine. Schulte-Hillen was impressed by Heidemann's determination and sincerity and told his doubting editors that they would simply have to trust the reporter.

But the fuss did not die down. On that same day, David Irving appeared on BBC television and denounced the Hitler diaries as fakes. Trevor-Roper now began to get cold feet . . . just as his article for *The Times* of 23 April, headlined 'SECRETS THAT SURVIVED THE BUNKER', was rolling off the presses. He rang *Sunday Times* editor Frank Giles to say that he had changed his mind about the diaries. He now thought they were forgeries. When details of the call were relayed to Murdoch, the latter snapped: 'Fuck Dacre! Publish!'

The *Sunday Times* duly carried its world exclusive on 24 April while its rivals, using material bought from Irving, laughed the whole thing off as a hoax. Under increasing pressure to disclose his sources, Heidemann began changing his story, thereby further fuelling Trevor-Roper's doubts. *Stern* finally published its first instalment of the diaries on 25 April and defended them at a press conference in Hamburg. However, Irving hijacked the conference and pointed out a glaring inconsistency. In his diary, Hitler was supposed to have written about the July 1944 bomb plot, yet a promotional film made by *Stern* and screened at the press conference quite clearly showed him greeting Mussolini a few hours after the explosion and having to shake hands with the Italian leader with his left hand. As *Stern* executives shuffled awkwardly in their seats, Trevor-Roper confirmed his change of heart and another academic, Gerhard Weinberg, expressed his incredulity that no Third Reich expert had been permitted to study the text.

Stung into action, *Stern,* somewhat belatedly, arranged for three of the diaries to be examined by experts at the Bundesarchiv, the West German Federal Archives, who passed them on to the Federal Institute for Forensic Investigation in Berlin. The preliminary findings drew attention to the presence of paper whitener, whereupon *Stern*, in their own bunker mentality, frantically set about trying to prove that such a substance had been in use before the war. *Stern* continued to issue defiant statements but received another blow when American handwriting expert Kenneth Rendell, who had been retained by *Newsweek* when they were bidding for the diaries, stated that the capital letters E, H and K appearing in the diaries were markedly different to the same letters in authentic samples of Hitler's handwriting. In short, Rendell was saying that the Hitler diaries were, as everyone outside *Stern* now suspected, complete fakes.

The full results of the forensic tests finally came through on 6 May and confirmed that the documents were forged. The chemical paper whitener present had not been used before 1955, while the labels stuck to the front of the books, and supposedly signed by Martin Bormann and Rudolf Hess, had all been typed on the same typewriter! Tests on the ink proved that the Hess volume had been written in the last two years and that writing from a 1943 diary was under a year old. The paper, the binding, the glue and the thread were all found to have been manufactured after the war. The archivists also discovered a number of factual errors within the diaries. For example, a law passed on 19 January 1933 was mistakenly entered in the diary under 19 January 1934. It transpired that Kujau's main source for his text had been the two-volume *Hitler's Speeches and Proclamations*. The archivists concluded that the documents weren't even the work of a decent forger. But these crude fakes had been sufficient to fool *Stern*.

Following the report, both *Stern* and the *Sunday Times* ceased publication of the diaries with *Stern* having to repay Murdoch the $1.2 million. In the event, the *Sunday Times* came out of it rather well, retaining 20,000 of the 60,000 new readers it had gained from the scoop. It is said that Murdoch didn't really care whether the diaries were genuine or not – it was just a great story. Editor Frank Giles was the unfortunate scapegoat. The story goes that he returned from holiday to learn that he was taking early retirement as editor of the paper but had been awarded the post of 'editor emeritus'. Asking Murdoch what the honorary title meant, he was allegedly told, 'It's Latin, Frank. The "e" means you're out, and the "meritus" means you deserve it.'

The blood-letting was greater in Hamburg. Heidemann was sacked while Koch and Schmidt were the unlucky pair chosen to carry the can. When they threatened to go to an industrial tribunal, they won compensation of 3.5 million marks on condition that they did not reveal the catalogue of errors that had typified the company's handling of the whole diaries business.

The trial of Heidemann and Kujau took place in 1984. Kujau was convicted of receiving over 1.5 million marks and was jailed for four and a half years; Heidemann was found guilty of stealing between 1.7 and 4.6 million marks and was sentenced to four years, eight months in prison. The judge said that *Stern* had been so reckless as to be almost an accomplice to the hoax. In the final reckoning, Grüner and Jahr ended up losing over 5 million marks while *Stern* were thought to have parted with more than 19 million marks. Their repeated failure to have the diaries properly authenticated before parting with large sums of cash had cost them dear. Given their slackness and failure to adhere to the most basic business principles, it is difficult to feel too much sympathy for them.

William Ralston: All that Glitters

There was only one thing that nineteenth-century American banker William Ralston loved more than food . . . and that was money. His great ambition in life had always been to become filthy, stinking rich. But he was never satisfied and no matter how much money he had, he always wanted more. In the end, greed, allied to a fair degree of stupidity, was to prove his downfall as he allowed himself to be outsmarted by a pair of harmless-looking old hicks.

Philip Arnold and John Slack could hardly have looked less like the people who were to bring the Bank of California to its knees when they sauntered into its San Francisco branch on a summer's day in 1872. Their wizened faces bore testimony to years of apparently fruitless prospecting for gold. To all intents and purposes, they were two of life's losers. They were carrying a drawstring pouch which they slowly handed to the teller, asking him to look after it while they went out and got drunk. Raised on the Ralston principle, the teller barely waited until they had left the building before taking a peek inside the pouch. What he saw sent him scurrying to his boss, the revered William Ralston. Although the teller was clearly excited, Ralston wasn't expecting to find more than a few pinches of gold dust but instead, on opening the pouch, he saw a fortune in uncut diamonds. Dollar signs lit up before his eyes.

All Ralston had to do now was track down the pair. After three days of searching the saloons of San Francisco, he found them toasting their success and new-found wealth in a seedy dive. Judging by their state, they seemed to have done a lot of celebrating and it took Ralston some time to sober them up sufficiently to be able to conduct a semi-coherent conversation. Unlike their diamonds, the men were totally cut. But even in a state of inebriation, Arnold and Slack proved no pushovers. Ralston wanted to know all about the source of the diamonds but the men were giving nothing away. It was only after lengthy and persistent probing that they confessed to having found a diamond field 'bigger than Kimberley'.

Ralston was beside himself which, given his ample girth, was an illusion he often created. However, the more questions he asked, the more withdrawn they became, just feeding him enough titbits to keep him interested. They explained that they didn't own the site of the field and flatly refused to tell him where it was. Realizing that, like him, the only language they talked was money, Ralston expressed an eagerness to invest in their discovery. Whilst they welcomed the prospect of his financial backing, they still wouldn't divulge the whereabouts of the site and insisted that anyone who wanted to inspect their find must make the journey blindfold. To Ralston's discomfort, Arnold and Slack seemed to be calling all the shots but he was sure that once he had found out where the diamond field was, they could be easily disposed of.

Ralston reluctantly agreed to their conditions and sent his mining engineer, David Colston, to accompany the pair to the secret site. Three weeks later, Colston returned, clutching a fistful of diamonds. The diamond field really did exist!

Seeing the chance for riches beyond even his wildest dreams, Ralston quickly put his dealings with Arnold and Slack on a firm financial footing. He paid them $50,000 a head upfront, put aside an additional $300,000 for their use and promised them a further $350,000 when the field started producing. Ralston also managed to interest other wealthy investors including Baron Anthony de Rothschild, General George B. McClellan and jeweller Charles Lewis Tiffany.

With a view to finding still more backers, Ralston sent another inspection party to the field, led by Arnold and Slack. The party travelled by rail to Rawlings, Wyoming, where the two prospectors blindfolded them and led them off into the wilderness. When the blindfolds were eventually lifted several hours later, the visitors could hardly believe their eyes. Ant hills along the valley floor were shimmering with diamond dust and glowing rubies were casually dotted around the landscape.

The party reported news of the amazing discovery back to Ralston who, his avarice now in overdrive, decided that it was time to dump the two old-timers. He told them they were out of their depth and when they protested he threatened them with complex lawsuits. If they didn't accept his generous offer of $700,000 for their share, he boomed, they could end up penniless. Bullied into submission, they took the money and ran, leaving Ralston to congratulate himself on hoodwinking the unsuspecting prospectors out of their rightful dues.

By now the discovery of the new field was the talk of the diamond world, but one person remained highly sceptical. Eminent geologist E. W. Emmonds had never seen the slightest sign of precious gems anywhere in Wyoming and set about tracking down the site. On finding it, he was immediately suspicious that it was only a few miles from the station at Rawlings. He couldn't help but conclude that the blindfolded party had been led around in circles by Arnold and Slack. Closer inspection revealed that the 'ant hills' were actually man-made and when he stooped down to pick up the first diamond, Emmonds noticed that it bore the marks of a lapidary tool, the favourite instrument of a diamond-cutter. Far from being in their natural state, all the diamonds and rubies had been carefully planted there.

Emmonds wired the bad news back to San Francisco where Ralston realized grimly that it was he who had been taken for a ride. He had been tricked out of $800,000. By the end of the day, Ralston's diamond syndicate had fallen apart. He was a laughing stock.

It emerged that Arnold and Slack – the two foolish old drunks – had planned the entire operation down to the last detail. To set up the scam, they had sailed to Europe and spent their life savings of $35,000 on the gems that they later deposited on Wyoming soil. To cover their tracks, they had left and entered the American continent via Halifax, Nova Scotia. The pair were never prosecuted. Slack disappeared without trace while Arnold, a shade ironically, founded a bank of his own in Kentucky. As for Ralston, he had lost all credibility within the banking world and his once-great institution collapsed in 1875.

The St Mary's Frescos: A Real Turkey

When the RAF dropped incendiary bombs on the West German town of Lübeck in 1942, they sparked off a war in the artistic world that was to end in bitter recrimination, acute embarrassment and the loss of $30,000 on worthless forgeries.

The RAF bombs scored a direct hit on the Marienkirche (St Mary's Church) in Lübeck. The flames from the bombs caused widespread damage to the building but also generated enormous excitement, for they burnt away the coating of whitewash from the pillars in the nave to reveal hitherto unknown scraps of thirteenth-century paintings. These became known as the St Mary's frescos.

Only the barest traces of the paintings were visible to the naked eye – little more than outlines of figures in sporadic patches – but they represented a major find. Although the church was gutted by the fire and remained without a roof for some time, thoughts were already turning to the restoration of the building as a whole and, more particularly, to the repair of the frescos. Drawings were made of the paintings and photographs taken so that whoever was given the job of restoration would have source material to work from. Clearly it was a specialized job that could only be undertaken by the most expert of restorers, and in July 1948 the West German Association for the Preservation of Ancient Monuments commissioned Dietrich Fey to do the work. Fey had something of a chequered past. That year he had been charged with handling forged paintings, but the charges were dropped. He was also a known associate of Lothar Malskat with whom he had worked before the Second World War, restoring sections of Schleswig Cathedral. Malskat specialized in faking paintings. He had copied around 600 paintings and drawings, by artists ranging from Rembrandt to Chagall, and in 1948 he had been caught trying to sell some of his forgeries. Usually he relied on Fey to do his selling.

It could be argued that it wasn't the wisest move to entrust the equivalent of $30,000 to two such shady characters but the anticipation surrounding the project was so great that common-sense seemed to fly out of the window. The work at St Mary's stimulated tremendous interest although Fey and Malskat insisted on visitors being kept away. Fey claimed that he was using a 'miracle fixative' that somehow peeled the murals from the mortar but nobody was actually allowed to see this take place.

Information continued to trickle out at a snail's pace but in the autumn of 1950 word filtered through that the frescos in the nave had been restored successfully and that Fey and Malskat were now working on other parts of the church, notably the walls of the choir where further fragments of old paintings had apparently been uncovered.

With excitement mounting by the day, the work was finally completed in 1951 and the church was reopened in time for its 700th anniversary. On 2 September, Fey proudly showed the frescos to West German Chancellor Konrad Adenauer. To commemorate the restoration, a special five pfennig stamp was issued.

The public flocked to see the magically restored paintings. They saw rows of saints, some 15 ft high, bible scenes, depictions of the parables and mythical beasts, all repaired to their former glory. Whilst the frescos in the nave were a joy to behold, even they were surpassed by the walls of the choir which featured a beautiful border frieze. Art historians went into raptures and praise was heaped upon the restorers to the point where Fey was awarded the Federal Cross of Merit.

And that was where the trouble started. Malskat became jealous that Fey was receiving all the attention and, in May 1952, he made the stunning announcement that the much-admired frescos were not faithful restorations at all but were entirely his (Malskat's) invention. In other words, they were fakes.

Nobody in authority really believed Malskat's claims, partly because they didn't think that he and Fey were talented enough to have created such beautiful works themselves and partly because they didn't want to believe that the frescos were fakes. A lot of money had spent on the restoration and there was also the considerable loss of prestige to be taken into account should the 700-year-old paintings be discovered to be twentieth-century forgeries. But Malskat was determined to be heard and took the unusual step of instructing his lawyer to file charges against Fey and himself.

Malskat insisted that he had been forced to fake the paintings in the choir because nothing of the originals had been found there. The stories about discovering outlines and fragments were just a tissue of lies. Instead he said that he had modelled the frescos in the choir from a book of medieval painting lent to him by Fey. The experts remained dubious until Malskat urged them to take a closer look at some of the highly praised choir figures . . . and there they discovered such biblical icons as Marlene Dietrich, Rasputin, Genghis Khan and Malskat's own sister!

Three months after his initial outburst, Malskat confessed to having faked the restored paintings at Schleswig Cathedral and he also asked for a number of other churches to be taken into consideration. In October, Fey's home was searched and a collection of modern forgeries was discovered. X-ray photographs of St Mary's showed that all the outlines of the choir frescos were modern – there was no trace of any medieval fragments. It was painfully clear that Malskat was telling the truth.

Clutching at straws, West German art experts and the Association for the Preservation of Ancient Monuments expressed the possibility that the nave paintings might be genuine, but Malskat quickly shattered their hopes. He said that they were his too and revealed how the original paint in the nave had been so decayed that it simply crumbled away at the touch of a brush, leaving nothing to restore. All that could be done, he said, was to scour the surface and start again from scratch. Once again, exhaustive tests proved that he was right.

Even though the West German authorities were still reluctant to admit that they had been tricked, Fey, Malskat and two others stood trial in August 1954. Both were found guilty, Fey being sentenced to 22 months in jail and Malskat to 20 months.

In the course of the trial, an equally amazing story emerged relating to Malskat and Fey's restoration of Schleswig Cathedral in the 1930s. Together with Fey's father Ernst, the pair had worked at restoring the cathedral's thirteenth-century murals, including a frieze in the cloisters that featured eight medallions, each decorated with a painting of a turkey. Fey Snr grandly pronounced that the paintings dated from the thirteenth century, overlooking the fact that turkeys were unknown outside the United States until the sixteenth century. Thinking on his feet, he came up with the explanation that the Vikings had discovered the United States before Columbus and had brought turkeys back home to Schleswig for food. A few of the birds must have survived and been painted. The story delighted the propaganda-hungry Nazis, who relished any opportunity to glorify Germany's role in world history, and articles were written in the German press in praise of the resourceful Vikings. But at the Fey/Malskat trial, it became apparent that nobody had listened to an elderly gentleman named August Olbers who had restored the Schleswig cloisters in 1888 and who was still alive in the 1930s. When the Feys and Malskat were carrying out their restoration at Schleswig, Olbers had maintained that, on being scored in readiness for repainting, the medallions had crumbled away to leave nothing. It had been Olbers' idea to add four turkeys and four foxes which the Feys and Malskat later amended to eight turkeys. But when Olbers made his claims, everyone dismissed him as a daft old man. If a little more attention had been paid to these allegations against Fey and Malskat, the German art world wouldn't have been left with the great fresco fiasco 20 years later.

The Rente Viagère: Bankers Drop a Brick

Thérèse Humbert was every inch a daddy's girl. Her father, a humble peasant, had managed to convince the people of Toulouse that he was really of noble lineage. On the pretext that the proof of his nobility lay in the family deeds kept in an old sealed chest, he succeeded in borrowing vast sums of money. It was only when he died in 1874 and his family opened the chest to discover nothing but a house brick that the truth emerged. But Thérèse was suitably impressed and resolved to try a similar ruse.

She found employment as a washerwoman in the house of the Mayor of Toulouse and, persuading the Mayor's son that she was about to come into a fortune, persuaded him to marry her. She proceeded to spend his money with great enthusiasm and when the deception was finally uncovered she came up with a new story. This time she said she had been left a legacy of $20 million by an American millionaire from Chicago, Robert Henry Crawford, whom she had temporarily nursed back to health after he had suffered a heart attack on a train. Under the terms of Crawford's will, the relevant securities and bonds were, she said, to be kept in her safe until her younger sister Marie, who was also a beneficiary, reached the age of twenty-one.

On the strength of the supposed Crawford inheritance, Thérèse borrowed vast sums of money to finance her exotic lifestyle. None of the banks ever questioned the legitimacy of her claims nor asked to see the contents of her safe. One Lille bank alone advanced her 7 million francs. Eventually a Lyons banker named Delatte, who had already handed her a small fortune, became suspicious and followed the trail of the mysterious Mr Crawford to Boston, Massachusetts, where Thérèse Humbert had said Crawford's nephews now lived. Nobody in Boston or Chicago had ever heard of the Crawford family, let alone the dead millionaire, but before Delatte could go public, he was murdered and his body found floating in New York's East River. Thérèse then invented an ongoing legal battle with the non-existent Crawford nephews which meant that the safe had to remain locked.

With Marie's twenty-first birthday rapidly approaching, Thérèse thought up a new money-making scheme: the Rente

Viagère, an insurance company that was to specialize in life annuities. She installed her brothers Emile and Romain at the helm and sat back while the money poured in. None of the cash was ever invested – it all went straight into the Humbert coffers apart from that which was set aside to pay annuities. The company prospered for 20 years during which time Thérèse spent some 64 million francs of other people's money. She became known as 'La Grande Thérèse', the darling of Parisian society, and bankers and financiers fell over themselves to invest in her company.

Finally Jules Bizat, a senior official at the Bank of France, became suspicious and inquired into the insurance company's investments. He was told gilt-edged securities but his investigations revealed that no such securities existed. Bizat decided to notify the Prime Minister, Pierre Waldeck-Rousseau, who, anxious to avoid a financial crash, chose not to expose Madame Humbert directly. Instead he encouraged the writing of a series of damning articles in the newspaper *Le Matin*.

Thérèse's lawyer, Maître du Buit, who believed in her implicitly, was outraged by the newspaper allegations and promised to end the speculation once and for all – by opening the safe in Madame Humbert's bedroom in full view of her many creditors. Her protests were in vain. On 8 May 1902, two days before the safe was due to be opened, a mysterious fire broke out in her apartment. The place was gutted but so was she when she saw that the safe was fireproof. The following night, in desperation, she and her family fled to Spain. The next morning du Buit and the principal creditors gathered in the charred remains of the bedroom and solemnly opened the safe. Inside they found nothing more than a house brick.

Furious at having parted with millions of francs on the strength of a simple brick, the bankers demanded that Madame Humbert be brought to justice. Seven months later, she and her family were traced to Madrid where they had been living under assumed names. Brought back to Paris, she was sentenced to five years in prison. Meanwhile, the safe, complete with brick, was displayed for a year in the window of a shop in the Rue Blanche and became one of the city's most unlikely tourist attractions. The financiers of France no doubt squirmed with embarrassment whenever they walked past.

The Great Arizona Land Swindle: Panic Payments

In the 1880s, hundreds of townsfolk, farmers and big businesses around Phoenix, Arizona, handed their hard-earned cash over to a complete stranger because they thought he owned the land on which they operated. In truth, he was a complete fraud but so frightened were they at the prospect of going out of business that the Southern Pacific Railway alone coughed up $50,000 and the Silver King Mining Company $25,000 . . . just to stay on 'his' land.

The stranger in question was James Addison Reavis who dreamed up the swindle while working in real estate in Santa Fe, New Mexico, in the late 1860s. There he learned about the 'Gadsden Purchase', a treaty signed in 1846 at the end of the United States' war with Mexico which stipulated that the USA recognize all the old Spanish titles to lands in parts of New Mexico and the whole of southern Arizona. Reavis landed a job as a clerk in the records room of the government office responsible for investigating Spanish land claims under the agreement and realized that, with careful planning, he could strike it very rich indeed. But the ancient documents he was intending to produce to establish his rights to the land had to look authentic and so first he had to acquire some knowledge of eighteenth-century legal Spanish, get hold of some old parchment and learn how to make quill pens and mix inks. He then had to invent some history and, after studying the most profitable land available, decided that in the mid-eighteenth century Ferdinand VI of Spain had granted some 11 million acres of Arizona to Don Miguel de Peralta, Gentleman of the King's Bedchamber, knight of several orders, son of Don José Gaston Gomez de Sylva y Montux de Oca de la Cerda y de Caullo de Peralta de los Falces de la Vega! Of course, the entire Peralta family were a figment of Reavis's imagination but their pedigree looked mightily impressive when set out on parchment.

Over the next 12 years, Reavis continued to prepare his scam. He journeyed extensively through Spain and Portugal, visiting churches, archives and government offices. With his impeccable manners and scholarly air, he found it easy to gain access to the records that he needed to steal, forge, copy or swap. By the time he had finished, the Peralta line was firmly in place. Reavis was certain that patience would have its reward.

Reavis needed one last link in the chain to connect Peralta to himself. He found it in the unhealthy shape of George Willing, a drunken ex-doctor, who gladly signed statements to the effect that he (Dr Willing) had bought the entire Peralta land grant for $1000 from an impoverished Mexican, Miguel Peralta, descendant of Don Miguel, and had resold the grant to Reavis for $30,000. It is not known whether Reavis paid Willing for his trouble but the latter was conveniently found dead in 1881.

Two years later, Reavis finally filed his claim to the lands which he insisted were legally guaranteed to him by the Gadsden Purchase. The area totalled some 17,000 square miles of Arizona, including the prize capture of the state capital, Phoenix. Submitting certified copies of all the appropriate documents to the US Surveyor-General, Reavis said that he didn't want to appear unreasonable and would be prepared to sell his claim to the government for, say, $50 million. Furthermore, he intimated that he would consider independent offers from individuals or companies who had unwittingly been trespassing on his land. He would allow them to buy quitclaims from him whereby he would formally renounce his claim to their land.

While waiting for his claim to be officially recognized, Reavis chose to exert a little pressure on the residents of Phoenix. Moving into the finest hotel in town, he posted notices on every available building, strongly advising those occupying the disputed land to contact him immediately or risk losing everything. Although the Surveyor-General had yet to pass judgement on Reavis's claim, local businessmen, big and small, were running scared. And with lawyers unable to find fault with the claim, there was a stampede to purchase quitclaims. Apart from the sizeable settlements by Southern Pacific and Silver King, Reavis collected $10 a head from local farmers desperate to retain their livelihood. If they had called his bluff, they could have kept their land and their money.

Some businessmen did hold out, encouraged by newspaperman Tom Weedon, who questioned the still unproved claim in a succession of articles, but the majority succumbed – enough to provide Reavis with an annual income of $300,000. Lawyers continued to study the claim at great length but were unable to find any holes in it. Meanwhile, Reavis was leaving nothing to chance. Realizing the necessity for a Peralta heiress to help substantiate his claim, he found a young half-breed orphan, Carmelita, and passed her off as the last known descendant of the Peraltas. To cement his position still further, he married her the moment she was sixteen and started calling himself Baron de Arizonac, Caballero de los Colorados.

Impressed by his new-found wealth, businessmen from all over the United States queued up to woo Reavis as a potential partner. He visited Washington and New York and launched a scheme to irrigate and develop the Salt Valley area of

Arizona with the assistance of a consortium of companies that had eminent lawyer Robert Ingersoll as its president and was funded by $50 million of equity capital. With a palace in Mexico City, a villa in Washington and a mansion in St Louis, as well as a luxury yacht or private train to travel in, Reavis now seemed the epitome of the successful businessman.

To underline his status, in 1890, he, his wife and two new sons embarked on a Grand Tour of Europe, en route being received by such dignitaries as Queen Victoria, the Pope, the King of Spain and Kaiser Wilhelm II of Germany. But that same year was to mark the beginning of the end of the good life for the self-styled baron. For Surveyor-General Royal Johnson finally got round to submitting his report. It had been widely rumoured that Johnson was in Reavis's pocket (hence the long delay) but his report made uncomfortable reading, not only for Reavis but also for his new business partners and those who had bought quitclaims from him. Examining the Peralta documents, the report pointed out a number of inconsistencies and errors, particularly some incorrect Spanish phrasing. As a result, Johnson refused to recommend the Peralta claim for government approval.

Reavis was stunned by this body-blow and immediately sued the United States government for $11 million. He called upon the support of powerful allies, such as California railroad millionaire Collis P. Huntington, who argued that Reavis ought to be backed to the hilt as a man of vision. A special Peralta Fund was even set up to help Reavis prepare his case. There was no shortage of contributors from the business world.

But worse was to follow and in 1891 Matthew G. Reynolds and Severo Mallet-Prevost, two lawyers from the newly established Court of Private Land Grant Claims, conducted a fresh investigation into Reavis's affairs. Concentrating on his pre-claim activities, they discovered that in his days with the

Confederate Army, he could forge his officer's signature well enough to obtain a leave pass. They also learned that he had spent a year in Brazil – long enough to acquire a smattering of grammatically incorrect Spanish. Testing the documents that Reavis had submitted, the lawyers found that while some of the top pages were genuine, others were written on parchment dating from a later period and with dogwood ink instead of the original iron ink. Prevost doggedly retraced Reavis's footsteps from Arizona to Mexico, Portugal and Spain. At the church in San Bernardino, California, where Carmelita had supposedly been born, Prevost noticed that Reavis had substituted an entire page in the births register to declare her birth. However the local priest's private index contained no mention of the birth. It mentioned only another child whose name was curiously absent from the forged page. Prevost had got his man.

In 1895, Reavis lost his case against the US government and was promptly arrested. He had to stand trial the following year and was found guilty of trying to defraud the government out of parts of its public lands. He served six years in jail, ample time for him to reflect upon his crucial slip-up and for his victims to ponder on how foolish they had been to part with their money so readily.

The Salad Oil Caper:
A Slick Operator Causes Financial Ruin

It is a sobering – perhaps even significant – thought that it was while searching for a substitute for leather upholstery in cars during the 1930s that Robert Boyer of the Ford Motor Company stumbled upon the process that makes soya meat. The soya bean is one of the oldest vegetables known to man, having been eaten in China around 2207 BC, but it was not until the twentieth century that its high protein content was discovered. Before then the plant had principally been used as an animal feed. With so many foodstuffs in short supply during the Second World War, the United States began growing soya beans on a commercial scale from the 1940s. Among its other uses, the soya bean, when crushed, yields a vegetable oil that goes into such diverse products as butter substitute, tinned fish and soap. The oil can also be processed to become salad oil and, in that form, any beans grown in excess of the nation's own requirements could be stored in readiness for export. With a flourishing overseas market, there was big money to be made out of salad oil.

Antonio de Angelis was quick to see the possibilities. Born in 1915, one of five children, Tino, as he was known, was a chubby little Italian raised in the Bronx. He started out in business in the meat trade but after the Second World War became embroiled in a row over the sale of sub-standard lard to Yugoslavia. His company, Gobel, won a prestigious contract to provide meat for school lunches but there was another whiff of scandal when the US Agriculture Department sued him, claiming that 19 lb of smoked meat that he had supplied for the Federal School Lunch Programme was off. De Angelis had to pay a $100,000 settlement and in 1953 his company went bankrupt. Further indiscretions followed – an investigation over income tax arrears plus another lard-for-Yugoslavia rumpus (only this time the lard didn't even exist) – until in 1955 de Angelis founded the grandly named Allied Crude Vegetable Oil Refining Corporation Inc. His goal was simple: he wanted to be America's number one in salad oil.

To reach that position, he knew that he needed to work with the major export companies in Manhattan who would buy from him at only a small mark-up price and also in huge quantities. These firms welcomed the fact that Allied would be challenging the big Midwestern crusher companies who shipped oil overseas via the Mississippi. Protective of their patch, the big boys of Manhattan saw export as their business, not that of the Midwest. The rivalry was intense.

But all was not smooth in those early years. Cans of oil sent by Allied to hot countries sprang leaks and the company was under-capitalized. De Angelis continued to think big, however. He visualized his Bayonne, New Jersey, warehouse site as becoming an international centre for salad oil with all the latest processing equipment. But in order to achieve that aim he needed more funds. Goods stored in a warehouse prior to sale represent excellent security for obtaining loans but, before agreeing to part with its precious cash, a lending bank would often require the commodity – in this case salad oil – to be stored in an independent warehouse that would then assume total responsibility for the goods. An alternative method is the field warehouse arrangement whereby a storage firm operates at its client's site, invariably within the client's own warehouse. In this instance, the field warehouse company is responsible for ensuring that the goods remain secure and undamaged and that the quantity stored tallies with what is recorded on the storage documents. This last point is essential since the storage documents serve as the receipts used in negotiations for a loan.

De Angelis's field warehouser was American Express, a firm whose international reputation would guarantee a loan against any warehouse receipt it might issue. The association between Allied and American Express began in 1957 when Donald K. Miller, head of Am Ex's warehousing subsidiary, was shown around the Bayonne site by De Angelis's cousin who worked at the warehouse. Miller, who knew nothing whatsoever about salad oil, saw five men in white coats, was told 'this is our laboratory' and naturally assumed that the quintet were chemists. It all appeared very efficient and prosperous. De Angelis desperately needed the kudos and credibility that went with being linked to American Express.

As a result of his earlier bankruptcy, no bank would lend to him but, as he explained to Miller, the export companies would accept his warehouse receipts if a reputable company such as Am Ex had issued them. Miller was impressed and, after getting the details of the business confirmed by Allied's bank, he recommended to his superiors that Am Ex should take on Allied as a client. In truth, Miller needed Allied's business and yearly payments as much as de Angelis needed American Express's good name. At the time the warehousing subsidiary was struggling; it was bringing in considerably less money than expected and there was the very real possibility that it might be sold off by the parent company or closed down altogether. So a business with the apparent potential of Allied was good news for Miller. It looked like a marriage made in heaven but was to prove so fragile as to be more like one made in Taiwan.

The first indication of a lack of harmony between the two partners occurred in 1960 when Am Ex conducted a surprise inspection of selected tanks at Bayonne. The tests were conducted by opening a hatch in the tanks, lowering a device to the bottom and then checking the contents. The warehousing firm's inspectors were horrified to find sizeable amounts of water in no fewer than ten tanks when the only water present should have been a tiny amount of condensation. The inspectors returned the following week and this time were directed by site manager Leo Bracconeri, de Angelis's brother-in-law, to the largest tank on the farm. Bracconeri insisted that only one hatch on that tank was available for use – the others were apparently shut for repairs – and invited the inspectors to carry out their testing. The sampling device was duly lowered into the tank through the one open hatch and, to everyone's satisfaction, a sample of pure salad oil was produced. Consequently, the inspectors passed the tanks as holding precisely what they were supposed to be and departed for their next port of call. However, de Angelis was still seething about the unannounced inspection and threatened to terminate his contract with American Express. It was almost certainly a bluff but Am Ex were taking no chances and cordial relations were swiftly restored.

In a four-year period, the weight of salad oil supposedly stored by Allied rose from 14.4 million pounds to 411.8 million pounds. And all the while American Express continued issuing receipts to that effect to help de Angelis secure further loans. For, just as de Angelis had predicted, no bank would quarrel with an American Express receipt. That would do nicely. By the end of 1962, Am Ex had issued receipts worth $45 million against 480 million pounds weight of stored oil.

With such solid backing, de Angelis continued to expand. Among the export companies with which he was dealing was Bunge of New York. Bunge saw de Angelis as the ideal person to keep its overseas market intact but one day in 1962 Bunge inspectors turned up unexpectedly at Bayonne and asked to check the oil in the tanks. Braconneri desperately tried to stall them until de Angelis himself suddenly appeared and immediately offered one of the inspectors a $25,000 bribe. But in his panic, de Angelis had miscalculated. The inspector was incorruptible and reported the attempted bribe to his bosses. Soon a delegation of leading Bunge officials arrived at the site. De Angelis had some quick thinking to do but, exercising every ounce of his Latin charm, he managed to explain it away as a simple misunderstanding. He apologized and everybody went away happy . . . for the time being at least.

Convinced that a Spanish deal worth $36.5 million was about to come off and that the price of salad oil would rise, de Angelis began buying salad oil futures in a big way. To obtain the loans he needed to keep the company expanding, he had to buy more oil and so he set about stockpiling supplies. Meanwhile, the news that American Express was about to dispose of its warehousing business failed to ruffle de Angelis's feathers. He was in possession of a pad of blank Am Ex receipts and had no qualms about simply writing them out himself. To sustain his orgy of buying, he also acquired another broker – the reputable, long-established firm of Ira Haupt. The Haupt empire was keen to branch out into the brokerage business and saw de Angelis as a big spender. Eager to please, Haupt happily accepted de Angelis's forged warehouse receipts whenever de Angelis was obliged to meet margin calls – the deposits which are payable as soon as there is a fall in the price of a commodity held as a futures buying contract. It seems that nobody at Haupt asked too many questions of the new client.

But by the end of 1963, Allied's salad days were over. The Spanish deal had fallen through – just as it had two years earlier – and Indonesia and India had also cancelled orders. And all this at a time when de Angelis was buying and buying. It was an unhappy combination of affairs. With Allied in trouble, de Angelis blamed his plight on erroneous government forecasts but confidently predicted that his 'friends all over the world' would rush to his rescue. It was never revealed exactly who these friends were.

De Angelis couldn't afford to let the price of salad oil drop. When the big Spanish deal failed to materialize, he knew that to sell his futures would incur crippling short-term losses. By October 1963, a mere 1 per cent drop in prices would have meant him having to find $13,560,000 in just 24 hours. Allied were then holding more than three-quarters of the cottonseed futures on the US Produce Exchange and in the period between 30 August and 27 September 1963, de Angelis's warehouse receipts amounted to 937 million pounds in weight of oil. Of that total, he managed to issue forged American Express receipts for 395 million pounds of oil.

Yet it was more than just the financial future of his company at risk; de Angelis's pride was at stake too. Over the years he had suffered his fair share of knocks – admittedly, mostly self-inflicted – and was determined to prove his doubters wrong. To sell the futures now would be an admission of defeat.

So de Angelis and Allied pressed on, hoping for divine intervention, until, on 15 November 1963, the company was unable to buy when trading opened. Haupt were not unduly perturbed by this turn of events since they thought they had a sturdy safety net in the form of de Angelis's warehouse receipts for over $13 million. Indeed they even accepted another receipt to meet his margin calls the following week.

But as Allied lurched into bankruptcy, Bunge were less confident and decided to check the oil supposedly held in their name. However, when Bunge's inspectors got there, the cupboard was bare. They were told that all of the oil had been pumped elsewhere but, much as they would have liked to believe de Angelis, realized that it would have been impossible to have pumped out 160 million pounds of oil in the four hours that had passed since a previous verification. It began to dawn on the business world that maybe Allied's stocks didn't match their receipts. Meanwhile, Haupt, borrowing in their own name to meet Allied's calls, were suspended from trading.

By the end of November, de Angelis was at last exposed and the true state of the Bayonne tank farm emerged in all its awfulness. The majority of the tanks held nothing more valuable than seawater. Of the rest, some contained an almost worthless vegetable oil residue, some were filled with petroleum and others were just a nasty, smelly mixture of water and sludge. So how had the inspectors been fooled for so long? The answer lay in the largest tank of all. Situated directly beneath the one useable hatch was a container tube filled with pure salad oil so that whenever the sampling device was lowered through the hatch, it dipped straight into the pure oil and produced a perfect sample. It turned out there was a network of tubing throughout the farm, enabling the contents of one tank to be siphoned into another. Thus although inspectors were checking different tanks, they were often checking the same supply of salad oil. The upshot was, of course, that de Angelis held nowhere as much salad oil as his documentation suggested – in fact, less than 10 per cent of the declared total. At the final reckoning, Allied were short of 1.8 million pounds in weight of salad oil, valued at \$175 million. Allied's chief financial officer, Alfredo Suarez, later admitted that he hadn't seen the company books for the past two years.

The repercussions of de Angelis's illicit activities were felt far and wide. The losses suffered by Haupt and the American Express Field Warehousing Company had a knock-on effect along a chain of export companies, banks and other commercial institutions and totalled over \$200 million. Haupt went into liquidation, American Express shares fell by 30 per cent and the US Produce Exchange was forced to close for a day. Recriminations were equally widespread but most of the criticism not directed at de Angelis himself was levelled at Donald Miller, the man who had been so easily hoodwinked by the ambitious and unscrupulous little Italian. Whilst not in any way guilty of any wrongdoing as such, Miller had been too trusting for his – and his company's – good.

De Angelis stood trial in January 1965. After pleading guilty to charges of fraud, he was sentenced to 20 years in prison. He remained defiant to the last, boasting: 'No one in the world ever did more for the economy of this country than I did.' In what respect, he didn't say.

The Sale of the Eiffel Tower: A Fool and his Money . . .

Victor Lustig was a prince among conmen. Born in 1890 at Hostoun, Czechoslovakia, near the border with Germany,

Lustig was a natural showman with a flair for languages. He could speak Czech, German, English, French and Italian but above all he liked to talk business. Sometimes he called himself Robert Miller; other times it was George Duvan. In all, he used 22 aliases with the result that he had more names than the local telephone directory.

His most celebrated scam came to him in March 1925 while he was idly flicking through the newspapers in a Paris café. His attention was caught by a story which said that the Eiffel Tower was in such a state of disrepair that the authorities were considering having it demolished and rebuilt. Lustig immediately saw possibilities for exploiting this situation and decided to pass himself off as Deputy Director of the Ministère des Postes et des Télégraphes, the government department responsible for maintaining the city's best-known landmark. Acquiring some headed notepaper from the Ministry, he then wrote to five leading scrap-metal dealers, inviting them to a clandestine meeting a week later at the city's Crillon Hotel.

On arrival, the five were escorted into a private suite by Lustig's 'private secretary', in reality a Canadian con artist by the name of 'Dapper' Dan Collins. Swearing them to secrecy, Lustig solemnly informed them that the Eiffel Tower was in such a dangerous condition that repairs were needed as a matter of urgency. However, he added, the French government couldn't afford to carry out such repairs and so it had been decided, with the utmost regret, that the Tower would have to be pulled down and sold for scrap. As a hush fell across the room, Lustig reiterated the need for secrecy, pointing out that the five had been chosen, not only for their standing within the business community but also because they were renowned for their discretion.

Having been suitably sweet-talked, the five were putty in Lustig's hands. Next he took them to the Tower in limousines, wined and dined them and invited them to submit their sealed bids for the contract to demolish and remove the Eiffel Tower, helpfully pointing out the considerable value of 7000 tons of scrap metal. The bids to were be sent to him at the Hotel Crillon within the next five days after which he would inform them of the government's decision.

All five submitted tenders, but Lustig had already chosen his victim – an up-and-coming provincial scrap-metal merchant named André Poisson whose clear desire for social acceptance within the Paris business world made him particularly susceptible to Lustig's flattery.

Sure enough, five days after the meeting, Lustig contacted Poisson and informed him that his bid had been successful. At first, Poisson sensed something fishy so Lustig got Collins to phone him and ask him to meet the 'Deputy Director' at the hotel. It was, said Collins, a matter so private that it couldn't possibly be discussed at the Ministry. Arriving at the hotel, Poisson overheard the 'Deputy Director' complaining about his 'inadequate salary' and strongly hinting that a bribe would be in order to ensure that the deal passed smoothly through official channels. On hearing this, Poisson's doubts vanished in an instant. He knew that if Lustig was asking for a bribe, he must be from the Ministry! After handing Lustig the cash bribe, Poisson gave him a banker's draft for the contract. In return, he received a worthless bill of sale. With that, Lustig shook Poisson warmly by the hand, showed him out and popped straight round to the nearest bank to cash the draft.

Within 24 hours, he and Collins were out of the country. Poor Poisson was so ashamed to admit that he had been conned that he didn't report the hoax to the police. Some say that as a result Lustig was able to sell the Eiffel Tower for a second time, to another unsuspecting businessman, but there is no firm proof of this. Still, it's an intriguing thought . . .

It was probably of little consolation to the hapless M. Poisson that he was by no means the last person to fall victim to Lustig's duplicity. Switching his attentions to Hollywood, Lustig posed as a successful Broadway producer to seduce Estelle Sweeny, an aspiring actress whose only previous claim to fame was as runner-up in a Miss Illinois contest. Taking her to Havana and promising her Broadway stardom, he did the rounds of the socialite parties where he let it drop that he was looking for a backer for his next big musical. Ronald Dredge, a New England businessman whose passion for the theatre was surpassed only by that for seeing his name in bright lights, was immediately hooked and said that he was more than willing to cough up the $70,000 that Lustig required. Ever the gentleman, Lustig replied that he wouldn't dream of taking Dredge's money until he had raised at least 51 per cent of the sum himself. If Dredge had needed convincing of Lustig's authenticity, this shrewd move did the trick.

Dredge returned to his home in Providence, Rhode Island, and waited for Lustig to call. Lustig deliberately let him stew for a few weeks before getting in touch. When he did, it was to announce that he had now raised the 51 per cent and was therefore ready to allow Dredge to invest his 49 per cent – a cool $34,000. Abandoning Ms Sweeny, Lustig lured Dredge to New York and arranged to meet him in a speakeasy. There, Lustig accepted Dredge's $34,000 and exited the room for a moment, on the pretence of counting the money. Dredge was left with Lustig's case, supposedly containing $36,000. After a while and with no sign of Lustig, Dredge became suspicious and opened the case. He found a few dollar bills covering a wad of old newspaper. He never saw his $34,000 or Lustig again. While the vengeful Dredge pursued Lustig across the States for months without ever quite catching up with him, Estelle Sweeny finished up as a stripper in a seedy club in Havana.

Another Lustig victim was Hermann Loller, a multi-millionaire whose business had sailed into choppy waters. This time posing as an Austrian count, Lustig met Loller in California and impressed him with a story about a money-making machine. Although Loller was keen to know more, Lustig maintained an air of indifference before reluctantly agreeing to show him the contraption. In his hotel room, Lustig showed Loller a box with a narrow slot at either end. He twiddled a few knobs and adjusted a couple of dials and then into one slot fed a genuine $100 bill and a blank piece of paper. Six hours later, he pulled a lever and out came two identical bank notes, apparently the result of some complicated photochemical reproduction process. Loller pleaded with Lustig to sell him the magic box and, after much persuasion, Lustig finally agreed to do so. As Lustig pocketed the agreed fee of $25,000, Loller headed back to his yacht to try out the device which he thought would solve all his financial problems. Opening the box, he found to his horror that it was empty but for two rubber rollers and several sheets of blank paper. Lustig was long gone and Loller himself was hardly in a position to go to the police. All he could do was mull over his stupidity.

Lustig even tried to swindle Al Capone out of $50,000 but thought better of it at the last minute and handed the mobster back his money. With Lustig pleading poverty, Capone actually took pity on him and gave him $5000. It was arguably Lustig's finest moment.

Just as Lustig managed to make a tidy sum from the sale of the Eiffel Tower, around the same time canny Scot Arthur Furguson succeeded in selling three of London's most prominent landmarks to gullible American tourists.

A former actor, Furguson had once appeared on stage as an American duped by a conman so perhaps this role came back to him one day in Trafalgar Square in 1925 when he spotted a wealthy visitor from Iowa staring in awe at Nelson's Column. Explaining the significance of the statue to the tourist,

Furguson went on to lament the fact that it and a number of other monuments were having to be sold and dismantled to help repay Britain's huge war loan to the United States. Furguson pointed out that he was the Ministry official in charge of the sale and was listening to offers . . . to the right buyer of course. Stressing the need for secrecy, Furguson inquired as to whether the gentleman might be interested.

The American was indeed interested. While Furguson disappeared, apparently to OK the sale with his government superiors, the tourist contemplated how wonderful Nelson's Column would look back home. Before long, Furguson was back with news that delighted both men – on behalf of Britain, he could accept a cheque for £6000 straight away. The American gleefully wrote out a cheque and Furguson handed him a receipt plus the name and address of a firm that would dismantle the column and ship it to the US. By the time the buyer had contacted the demolition firm who, needless to say, didn't have the faintest idea what he was talking about, Furguson had cashed the cheque. Even so, the awful truth didn't dawn on the poor tourist until Scotland Yard told him that he'd been tricked.

Over the next few weeks, the police heard from two other American visitors who had fallen prey to Furguson's schemes. One was complaining that he was being prevented from completing his purchase of Buckingham Palace even though he had already paid a deposit of £2000, while another insisted that he had bought Big Ben for £1000. Buoyed by his success, Furguson also 'rented out' the Palace of Westminster and the Tower of London for prices ranging between £1000 and £2000. Concluding that Americans offered rich pickings, Furguson sailed to the States where he managed to convince a Texan cattle rancher with more money than sense that the US administration was so strapped for funds that the President was having to lease the White House and move to smaller premises. The Texan was overjoyed at being able to lease the White House for 99 years at the knockdown rent of $100,000 a year . . . the first year's rent payable in advance.

By now, Furguson was seriously wealthy but he was so addicted to hoaxes that he found it impossible to retire. Thus it was that one day in New York he found himself explaining to an Australian from Sydney how the Statue of Liberty was having to be dismantled and sold because its presence was hampering a scheme to widen New York Harbour. Furguson mused that maybe the statue, available for a mere $100,000, would look good in Sydney Harbour.

The Australian wasted no time in trying to raise the money but his bankers were highly suspicious and advised him to contact the police. And for once Furguson had slipped up, having allowed himself to be photographed with his potential buyer in front of the Statue of Liberty. With Furguson beginning a five-year stretch in jail, the lucky Australian was the one that got away.

Herr Goering's Artistic Slip-Up: £160,000 for a Fake

Throughout the Second World War, Nazi chiefs plundered valuable works of art from lands overrun by the German army. The leading 'magpie' was Luftwaffe chief Hermann Goering who built up a priceless art collection at his Berchtesgaden mansion, most of it looted from the churches, art galleries and private homes of Europe. Just occasionally, however, Goering acquired a piece honestly – by actually paying for it. Indeed, one of his most treasured paintings was *Woman Taken in Adultery*, signed by Jan Vermeer, the seventeenth-century Dutch master. Goering had bought it for £160,000 from a dealer in Amsterdam, little knowing that the dealer in question was an accomplished forger by the name of Hans Van Meegeren.

Born in 1889 at Deventer, some 50 miles east of Amsterdam, Van Meegeren was a talented young artist but received no encouragement from his schoolteacher father who used to tear up his drawings. He went on to study architecture at the Institute of Technology in Delft where, despite failing his exams, one of his watercolours won a gold medal awarded every five years by the Institute for an outstanding painting by a student. The painting later sold for £100. Two years later, in 1914, he and his wife Anna moved to the small seaside town of Scheveningen, near The Hague, and Van Meegeren successfully copied his own watercolour that had won him the Delft gold medal. Anna refused to allow him to pass it off as the original and in 1917 they went their separate ways.

Van Meegeren staged his first exhibition in 1922 at The Hague but it received unfavourable reviews from the critics, foremost among whom was Dr Abraham Bredius. Dr Bredius was a devotee of Vermeer, an artist about whom precious little was known. There was a huge market for Vermeers at the time and Bredius was convinced that there were yet more works by Vermeer waiting to be discovered and that one would turn out to be a great religious painting. Vowing revenge on Bredius and the other art critics whom he despised as incompetent and corrupt (he claimed that one had even asked him to pay for a good review), Van Meegeren set about imitating Vermeer's style. He gained access to seventeenth-century canvases and perfected the recipes for Vermeer's brilliant colours. By baking the finished canvases in a cool oven, he was able to recreate the enamel-like surfaces favoured by Vermeer.

In 1937, Van Meegeren produced his first fake Vermeer, *Christ at Emmaus*. It was purely Van Meegeren's own creation since no similar painting by Vermeer existed but it fitted in perfectly with Bredius's prediction of a great religious work.

The critic was delighted to be proved right and eulogized: 'It is a wonderful moment in the life of a lover of art when he finds himself suddenly confronted with a hitherto unknown painting by a great master, untouched, on the original canvas and without any restoration, just as it left the painter's studio . . . We have here – I am inclined to say – *the* masterpiece of Johannes Vermeer of Delft.'

Bredius was completely fooled and at that point Van Meegeren had fully intended announcing that the painting was a fake. He had proved his point about the ignorance of critics and had shown that he himself could paint as well as any old master. But when Bredius encouraged Rotterdam's Boyman's Museum to buy the painting for £50,000, the offer was too good to resist.

Over the next six years, Van Meegeren sold another seven faked paintings for a combined total of £2 million (the equivalent of over £20 million today). Among them were five more signed Vermeers (including two versions of *The Last Supper*) and two de Hoochs. Apart from the one that caught the eye of Goering, three of the paintings were purchased by wealthy Dutch collectors and another was bought by the Netherlands state to prevent it from falling into Nazi hands. The buyers were all certain that they had bought great works of art and sound investments for the future.

The first inkling they got that they were instead the proud owners of clever forgeries came at the end of the war. By then, Van Meegeren was a rich man with a string of houses, hotels and nightclubs to his name. As the search began to weed out Nazi collaborators, Dutch police traced the 'Vermeer' bought by Goering back to the dealer, Van Meegeren. He was charged with treason for selling a national treasure to the enemy – a crime that carried the death penalty – and only managed to spare his neck by admitting that, far from helping the Nazis, he had tricked them by passing off his own forgery as the genuine article. Facing ridicule and professional ruin, Bredius and other art experts poured scorn on the story and labelled Van Meegeren a liar. They challenged him to paint *The Disciples of Emmaus* again but he preferred to come up with something new. And so, under guard in his Amsterdam studio, he created his final Vermeer, *Young Christ Teaching in the Temple*. The result was so impressive that the treason charges were dropped, only to be replaced by fresh charges of deception and forging signatures. Found guilty, he was sentenced to a year in prison but within six weeks he had died from a heart attack.

Another artist who led museums and experts a merry dance with his forgeries was Italian sculptor Alceo Dossena. He started out as a stonemason's apprentice where he learnt how to match repair work on the ornamental detail of old buildings to the original. Blessed with the ability to sculpt in wood, marble or terracotta, Dossena made a healthy living from his forgeries. In 1924, Helen Frick, daughter of the Fifth Avenue gallery owner, paid $225,000 to bring what turned out to be a Dossena fake to New York: two annunciation figures in the style of fourteenth-century painter Simone Martini. Much of Dossena's work was so immaculate that detection was nigh impossible but the Boston Museum blundered badly when buying what was described as the Savelli family tomb chest by fifteenth-century sculptor Mino da Fiesole. To persuade the museum that the chest was genuine, Dossena even forged Fiesole's receipt for payment. Yet there were elementary mistakes in the piece, the most obvious being that Caterina Savelli's sandal was minus its sole. But there were also basic historical inaccuracies. The Savelli family, for whom the tomb was supposedly made, had died out around the start of the fifteenth century and yet the date on the work was 1430. Most remarkable of all, Fiesole wasn't born until 1429, making him one year old when producing his masterpiece – the ultimate in child prodigies! Yet it appears that the Boston Museum never challenged any of these discrepancies.

It was only when Dossena fell out with his partner-in-crime, dealer Alfredo Fasoli, that the truth emerged. When his mistress died, Dossena wanted a big funeral for her. He claimed that Fasoli owed him $7500 (Dossena received a percentage of every sale) and when Fasoli refused to pay up, an angry Dossena not only sued him but told the world about all the fakes, including the Boston tomb chest. The news sent shock waves rippling through the museums of the world and the Cleveland Museum of Art reluctantly had to accept that what they had previously believed to be a thirteenth-century carved wood *Madonna and Child* was, in fact, a Dossena fake. To confirm the museum's worst fears, an X-ray examination revealed the presence of modern nails.

Alas, having made one mistake, the Cleveland Museum allegedly compounded the error. Dossena had produced a beautiful ancient Greek statue of Athena. On completing it, he had knocked a few of the fingers off to make it look suitably ancient and had shown it to Jacob Hirsch, an expert on Greek statues. Hirsch had no doubt that it was authentic. The Cleveland Museum was equally impressed and, unaware of its true origins, reportedly chose to replace the fake *Madonna and Child* with the statue of Athena at a cost of $120,000, only to discover subsequently that this too was a Dossena forgery . . .

The Authorized Biography of Howard Hughes: A Work of Fiction

There have been few more complex, more eccentric characters in the twentieth century than billionaire Hollywood movie producer Howard Hughes. The man who launched the career of sex bomb Jane Russell in *The Outlaw* and once dated some of the world's most famous film stars – including Ava Gardner, Elizabeth Taylor, Lana Turner and Ginger Rogers – spent the last 15 years of his life as a recluse. His descent into paranoia began in 1957 with marriage to his second wife, actress Jean Peters. He insisted that they had separate bedrooms, even separate refrigerators. He became obsessed with health and hygiene, and nobody else, not even his wife, was permitted to touch his food. Not surprisingly, the marriage was short-lived and after the divorce Hughes retreated to a bungalow in the desert near Las Vegas and hired his 'Mormon Mafia', a group of Mormons whose lot in life was to protect their master from outside contamination. So terrified was he of germs that any visitors were forced to stand for inspection in a chalk square drawn outside the house before being allowed near the front door. His own doctor was only permitted to 'examine' him from the other side of the room. As an added insurance against bugs, Hughes would touch nothing without first wrapping his hand in a paper tissue.

Before long, even the desert was too public a place for Hughes and he took to living in a series of anonymous hotels. Each move was made in total secrecy, his entire entourage departing via kitchen exits and fire escapes in the dead of night with Hughes strapped to a stretcher. The windows of the hotel were always darkened and taped and, apart from a bed and a chair, the only item of furniture was film equipment, complete with a screen. It is said that he watched *Ice Station Zebra*, starring Rock Hudson, no fewer than 150 times. During his self-imposed confinement, Hughes became a virtual skeleton. His diet was suitably bizarre. For days, he would eat nothing but ice-cream, staying with one flavour until every parlour in the district had run out. His beard hung down to his waist and his hair and nails remained uncut – only twice in ten years did he allow a barber to trim his hair or a manicurist to attend to his nails. From 1961 until his death 15 years later, he met just three people from the outside world.

By 1970, Howard Hughes was sixty-five. He hadn't given an interview for 15 years. Nobody knew what he looked like or even if he was still alive. He was rumoured to be the richest man in the world but his airline, TWA, was in financial trouble and its principal investors had sued him for mismanagement. Hughes had chosen to settle out of court, paying out $145 million in costs and damages before fleeing to his latest secret hideaway, somewhere in the Bahamas. The story of Hughes's bizarre lifestyle and the outcome of the TWA lawsuit were carried in a December 1970 article in *Newsweek* headlined 'THE CASE OF THE INVISIBLE BILLIONAIRE'.

The article made compulsive reading, not least for forty-year-old expatriate American author Clifford Irving. Born in New York, Irving was a moderately talented artist and an incurable adventurer. After graduating from Cornell University in 1951, he set off to see the world and lived with beatniks in California and drop-outs in Kashmir before ending up living with his wife Edith on the Mediterranean island of Ibiza, a favourite haunt of artists and writers. There, Irving made his living as an author and met with some success with his book *Fake!* about art forger Elmyr de Hory who also lived on Ibiza.

Irving's publishers were McGraw-Hill of New York, a company with whom he enjoyed a good relationship. They even advanced him money when he ran short and were generally supportive of his efforts. It was while he was sitting at home on Ibiza planning his next book for McGraw-Hill that he read the *Newsweek* article about Howard Hughes. Irving was immediately attracted by the possibility of writing a biography of Hughes and got in touch with friend and fellow writer Richard Suskind who lived on the neighbouring island of Majorca. But Irving didn't envisage writing any old biography of Hughes – this was to be a book with a difference, the publishing hoax of the century.

Meeting Suskind at Palma, Irving outlined his crazy plan. He suggested telling McGraw-Hill that Hughes had commissioned him to write an authorized biography but would not deal personally with the publishers. Hughes would only communicate with Irving. It seemed foolproof. Irving knew that any publisher would jump at – and, more to the point, pay big money for – an authorized biography of Howard Hughes but he also knew that there was no way that Hughes would ever speak to him. But if Irving were to make up his own 'authorized biography', using previously published material liberally sprinkled with invented quotes, who was to contradict him? Who would call him a liar? Certainly not Hughes. He was an ageing, sick hermit who shunned all contact with the outside world. If he wanted to challenge anything Irving wrote about him, he would have to appear in a courtroom and that would mean ending his years of self-imposed exile and isolation. And Irving was positive that Hughes would never consider going public.

It seems that at this stage Irving was intending nothing more than a practical joke, to which he would soon confess, but the whole thing began to spiral out of control. Suskind thought it was a wonderful idea and his enthusiasm encouraged Irving to proceed with the scheme. First, he wrote to his editor at McGraw-Hill, saying that he had sent a copy of *Fake!* to Hughes for his comments and, to his delight and surprise, Hughes had replied with a courteous note of thanks. Of course, no such communication had ever taken place – it was all a product of Irving's fertile imagination. Given that there was now, in Irving's mind at least, the basis of a relationship, he asked his editor whether there were any known plans for a biography of Hughes in the near future.

As luck would have it, *Life* magazine had recently carried a photograph of Hughes's handwriting from letters to two of his staff. Irving studied it at length and, obtaining a pad of legal paper as used by Hughes, wrote three letters purportedly from Hughes suggesting that the renowned recluse wanted Irving to write his biography. The letters said that Hughes, prompted by a small kindness from Irving (the sending of the book) and having once met his father, was interested in allowing Irving to assume the role of his official biographer. Each letter was more emphatic than the last, the third saying: 'It would not suit me to die without having certain misconceptions about my life cleared up and without having stated the truth about my life. I would be grateful if you would let me know when and how you would wish to undertake the writing of my biography you proposed.' The letters also stated that Hughes would let Irving record a series of interviews with him at locations to be arranged by Hughes himself.

Irving sent the three forged letters to McGraw-Hill, explaining that, encouraged by Hughes's reply to the copy of *Fake!,* he had written back to the billionaire offering to ghost-write his autobiography. Hughes, said Irving, had agreed and these were the letters from Hughes to Irving underlining his keenness to proceed with the project. All Irving needed to know now was, would McGraw-Hill be interested?

It has to be said that those first forgeries were poor. But, in fairness to Irving, the sample of Hughes's handwriting that he studied only featured five capital letters: A, I, M, H and R. He ingeniously worked around the shortage by making Hughes the supreme egotist, beginning almost every sentence with 'I' or 'My'. It was clever enough to fool the people who mattered. The problem confronting McGraw-Hill was that when Irving presented them with the first forgeries, they didn't have access to any genuine example of Hughes's handwriting to act as a comparison. This meant that Irving was able to take the letters away and re-forge them twice more before McGraw-Hill were able to compare them with the real thing. Ironically, it was a McGraw-Hill executive who eventually alerted Irving to a longer passage written in Hughes's own hand.

Having no reason to suspect that anything was amiss, McGraw-Hill did not take long to reach an editorial decision. In fact, they nearly bit Irving's hand off. Captivated by the letters and excited by Irving's account of telephone conversations with Hughes – something nobody else had been able to boast for over a decade – they could see 'world bestseller' written all over the book. The advance offered by the company's general books vice-president Al Leventhal reflected their enthusiasm: $100,000 to Hughes on signature, $100,000 on delivery of a transcript of taped interviews and $300,000 for the actual manuscript. A generous sum was also set aside for an advance and expenses for Irving.

With McGraw-Hill believing every word, all Irving had to do was string them along. But instead of using the money in his pocket for the purpose of courting Hughes, Irving spent much of it on courting his sometime lover Nina von Pallandt of the Danish singing duo Nina and Frederick, famous for such gems as 'Mary's Boy Child' and 'Little Donkey'. At one meeting in New York with his publishers, he proudly announced that he was off to a secret location in the Bahamas to meet Hughes. The McGraw-Hill executives hung on his every word. In reality he was flying to Mexico with von Pallandt. Changing planes at Mexico City, he had his photograph taken and when he got back to New York, he showed McGraw-Hill the photo, claiming that it had been taken by one of Hughes's aides. The publishers had no reason to doubt his word, particularly as it was backed up by the draft of a contract for the biography and a notebook recording details of two meetings with Hughes, or 'Señor Octavio' as he was referred to in order to preserve the air of secrecy.

However, a possible hitch appeared on the horizon when

McGraw-Hill's lawyer insisted that Hughes's signature be formally authorized. Irving could see no way around this and called Suskind to tell him that it looked as if the whole deal was going to fall through. But just as he was about to give up, Irving received a call from his editor, telling him that McGraw-Hill were now willing to accept the signature made in his presence by Hughes. Irving breathed a huge sigh of relief and flew to Puerto Rico on the pretence of meeting Hughes. He then flew on to New York and presented the publishers with two copies of a contract signed by Howard R. Hughes. The contract contained clauses supposedly inserted by Hughes stipulating that the entire project remain secret for the time being and a provision that: 'The money will be deposited as designated verbally or in writing by H. R. Hughes for deposit in any bank account of H. R. Hughes.'

Irving now set about making sure that all the money intended for Hughes ended up with him. He photographed his blonde Swiss wife Edith in a black wig and doctored her spare passport so that it appeared to be the property of H. R. Hughes. After opening an account with the Crédit Suisse Bank in Zurich as 'Helga Hughes', the resourceful Edith flew to Düsseldorf and, in the course of a family visit, stole the identity card belonging to her former husband's new wife, Hanne. Returning to Zurich, Edith opened another bank account, this time in the name of 'Hanne Rosencrantz'. Whenever McGraw-Hill handed Irving a cheque to pass on to Hughes, Irving instead gave it to Edith who paid it into the H. R. Hughes account before transferring it to the Rosencrantz account. Hughes never saw a cent – but then again, he didn't know he was entitled to one.

Now that everything was in place, Irving set to work on the manuscript. Throughout the summer of 1971, he and Suskind relaxed on Ibiza, taking turns to play Hughes in a series of long-winded taped interviews that would form the basis of the book. Irving was aided by two strokes of good fortune. *Life* magazine, having agreed to pay McGraw-Hill $250,000 for pre-publication serialization of extracts from the book, gave Irving access to all their files on Hughes. Left alone with the files, he furtively photocopied over 300 reports on Hughes's life, many of which had not been published. Also, while secretly working on his biography of Hughes, Irving was approached by literary agent Stanley Mayer and asked whether he would be interested in rewriting another biography of Hughes, written by a former Hughes employee, Noah Dietrich, in conjunction with freelance journalist Jim Phelan. Irving held on to the manuscript of the Dietrich book just long enough to have it photocopied before politely declining the invitation to rewrite it.

Thus he was able to include many more genuine insights into Hughes's troubled life than might otherwise have been possible. Although the quotes were entirely fictitious, there was a grain of truth in most of them. They were the sort of things which Hughes might have said if he had ever talked to anybody. Although the real Hughes story was compelling enough in itself, Irving could not resist embellishing it and adding a new angle to make the finished article all the more appealing to his publishers. So he came up with the notion that Hughes was a far more glamorous character than was generally perceived and that while everyone thought he was living the bleak life of a sheltered recluse in darkened rooms, he was frequently touring the world's hot spots incognito, enjoying the time of his life. This was indeed a hitherto unknown aspect to Hughes's life and just the sort of thing McGraw-Hill wanted to hear.

All the while, Irving kept McGraw-Hill at arm's length by inventing endless meetings with Hughes. Hardly a week would pass when he didn't claim to be off on some secret rendezvous with the billionaire. In total, Irving told his publishers that he had conducted nearly 100 secret meetings with Hughes in motels and parked cars between February and December 1971 – yet not one really took place. Among the supposed encounters was one with Hughes and the then US Vice-President Spiro Agnew in a car park at Palm Springs at five o'clock in the morning. As Irving himself wrote later: 'The wackier it is, the more they believe it. The wilder the story, the deeper their need to believe it. And, of course, it's less checkable.' If anyone at McGraw-Hill started asking too many questions, Irving concealed the truth by hiding behind Hughes's paranoia. The publishers couldn't be told too much, he said, because of Hughes's insistence on total secrecy. But Irving was shrewd enough to maintain their interest by advancing them short samples of the manuscript containing revelatory details of the great man's private life, along with further correspondence signed by Hughes. Everyone seemed happy – especially Irving who, with the aid of the Swiss bank accounts, was enjoying the proceeds of the cheques made out to Hughes. With paid-for trips to Europe, the Caribbean and Central America, staying at the finest hotels, dining at the most exclusive restaurants, life was indeed sweet for Clifford Irving that summer.

But his luck began to run out in August when it emerged that, by an unhappy coincidence, another publisher had been offered an authorized biography of Howard Hughes. This one had been written by Robert Easton, former husband of Lana Turner, one of Hughes's string of Hollywood lovers. McGraw-Hill rang Irving in a state of panic, since the appearance of a rival tome would jeopardize not only the prospects of their book in terms of sales but also the deal in which the serialization rights had been sold to *Life*. Irving was quick to nip the threat in the bud. He and Suskind flew to Palm Beach (near Nassau in the Bahamas where Hughes was actually hiding out) and from there they sent a telegram to McGraw-Hill to say that Hughes, after learning of the serialization deal, wanted his advance doubled from $500,000 to $1 million. They then despatched a second telegram from Hughes in which he denounced the Easton biography as a fake.

McGraw-Hill were greatly reassured by the telegrams and on 12 September Irving delivered the 999-page manuscript of just about the most eagerly awaited book in the publisher's history. It took company executives a week to read it. So delighted were they by the contents that, after Irving had just about managed to survive McGraw-Hill's lie-detector test, Al Leventhal agreed to raise Hughes's advance to $750,000 – 'but not a penny more'.

In November, McGraw-Hill were back on the phone with another tricky problem for Irving. That august periodical, the *Ladies' Home Journal*, was intending to publish extracts from the Robert Easton biography of Hughes in January, ahead of the *Life* serialization of Irving's book. McGraw-Hill saw a threat to their position and felt they could not afford to lie low any longer. They wanted Hughes to let them announce the book at last and to say that they were the sole publishers of his authorized biography. Irving responded with another forged letter from Hughes, this one accusing them of gross incompetence. They showed this latest item of correspondence to the same handwriting expert who had verified the genuine letter from Hughes which had appeared in *Life* a year earlier. He stated unequivocally: 'The chances that another person could copy this handwriting even in a similar way are less than one in a million.' He was not the only one to be taken in by Irving's forgeries. When Ralph Graves, editor of *Life*, saw Irving's very first effort, he didn't doubt for one moment that the letter was genuine and, comparing it to the sample that had appeared in his magazine, made a point of drawing attention to the way in which Hughes inked in his capital Is.

On 7 December, McGraw-Hill came out into the open and announced that they were publishing the authorized biography of Howard Hughes in 1972. The press release said that Hughes had chosen Clifford Irving as his ghost-writer 'because of his sympathy, discernment, discretion and . . . his integrity as a human being'. Even by the standard of most company press releases, this was something of an exaggeration. As soon as they got wind of the book, Hughes's lawyers dismissed it as a fake. Knowing Hughes's insistence on secrecy at all times, McGraw-Hill had anticipated such a reaction but neither they nor Irving were expecting Hughes's next move. Chester Davis, one of Hughes's lawyers, telephoned *Life* magazine to say that the world's most famous recluse would be prepared to talk to Frank McCulloch, a journalist who had interviewed him back in the 1950s. In a renewed state of panic, McGraw-Hill passed the three original 'Hughes' letters over to noted New York handwriting experts Osborn, Osborn and Osborn. All three Osborns had no hesitation in assuring McGraw-Hill that the documents were the work of Howard Hughes.

With doubt being cast on the authenticity of his manuscript, Irving decided that attack was the best form of defence. At a meeting at McGraw-Hill, he voiced the suspicion that maybe he was a fraud, adding: 'This possibility I intend to discard and I hope you do too.' To mutual relief, they did. Then at a sales luncheon for the book, Al Leventhal further eased troubled minds with a rallying speech. 'We who have had the privilege of reading the book,' he said, 'know that it would take a Shakespeare to invent such a work. And much as I admire our author, Clifford Irving, he is no Shakespeare.' All present laughed politely. They had either overestimated the skill needed to fake a biography or had underestimated the man with whom they were dealing.

But the Hughes camp had another trick up their sleeve and shortly after Christmas, they arranged a press conference – Hughes's first in more than 15 years – at which reporters in a

Los Angeles studio were invited to put questions to Hughes over a direct telephone link. Hughes took this opportunity to state categorically that he had never met Clifford Irving. Cornered, Irving appeared on CBS TV to claim that the voice on the phone was not that of Hughes, but that of an imposter. It was a desperate act by a desperate man, but the net was closing in.

In a bid to expose Irving, Chester Davis enlisted the services of Intertel, Hughes's own detective agency. The man who took charge of the case was Intertel president Robert Dolan Peloquin, an American lawyer who rejoiced in the sobriquet of the 'Sherlock Holmes of the jet age'. He was soon to live up to the title.

Meanwhile, McGraw-Hill continued to defend Irving and their book to the hilt, insisting that Irving had written the book with Hughes's co-operation. As proof, they cited the cheques made out to, and endorsed by, H. R. Hughes and deposited in a numbered Swiss bank account. They added that handwriting experts had declared the signatures on the cheques to be those of Howard Hughes. In a bold move, Harold McGraw went on America's early morning *Today* TV programme, brandishing three cheques worth a total of $650,000 and cashed by H. R. Hughes. Chester Davis saw McGraw's performance and got in touch with Peloquin who immediately obtained a video tape of the show. By freezing the relevant frames and getting the prints enlarged, he was able to decipher the name of the Zurich bank that had endorsed the payments. It was the Crédit Suisse Bank.

Peloquin caught the next available plane to Zurich where the bank revealed that H. R. Hughes was a woman. Acting on a hunch, he phoned his Washington headquarters and asked for a photograph of Edith Irving to be wired to him. He then showed it to the bank officials. The hair was different, of course, but the staff were fairly certain that Edith Irving was

H. R. Hughes. Peloquin alerted the Swiss police and they began investigating this 'Helga Hughes' who had drawn such large sums from the H. R. Hughes account in Zurich. When this news broke, Irving expected McGraw-Hill to be on the war-path but instead, in all their dealings with him, they remained warm, unfailingly polite and apparently not in the least suspicious. Maybe they were now trying to lull him into a false sense of security or maybe they were simply the most charming people to work for. One thing is for certain – they were too trusting for their own good.

No matter how convinced McGraw-Hill were of Irving's innocence, *Life* magazine were by now highly suspicious. The revelation that H. R. Hughes was a woman prompted a *Life* reporter to time Irving's movements on what he had claimed was a day full of meetings with Hughes. The reporter found the timings to be impossibly fast – there was no way that Irving could have travelled so quickly from one venue to the next. In the meantime, Frank McCulloch was certain that he knew the name of Irving's connection to Hughes – an ecologist named Meier who had worked for Hughes in the late 1960s and was now seeking election as Senator for New Mexico. He phoned Irving to confront him with the accusation but Irving was out, forcing McCulloch to leave a message, saying that he knew all about Meier. When Irving played the message back, he assumed McCulloch was referring to Stanley Mayer, the literary agent, who was indeed Irving's unwitting source. The other Meier had no connections with Irving whatsoever. But, confused by the message, Irving finally owned up to the deception when McCulloch and a colleague called again later the same day. It was, to say the least, ironic that the master hoaxer had been tricked into making a confession – albeit inadvertently.

Other nails were being driven into Irving's coffin. Nina von Pallandt admitted that at a time when Irving claimed he had been meeting Hughes, the author had really been in her company. And Jim Phelan, author of the unpublished Noah Dietrich memoir on Hughes, came forward when he saw Irving's manuscript and realized that some of its most fascinating stories had been lifted directly from his work. Phelan went to New York and placed the evidence before Harold McGraw who had to admit that it was all a bit too much of a coincidence. It was then that it finally dawned on him that McGraw-Hill had been conned by Irving.

Clifford and Edith Irving were arrested along with Richard Suskind. Between them, they owed over $1.5 million to McGraw-Hill, the taxman and their lawyers. They made a full confession. In June 1973, Clifford Irving was sentenced to 30 months' imprisonment, Edith Irving to two years and Suskind to six months.

But as well as the money which they were unlikely to recover, McGraw-Hill were left assessing the damage to their good name. Needless to say, 'The Autobiography of Howard Hughes' was never published. By 1976, Hughes was dead anyway. The opportunity to recount in personal detail the life story of one of the century's most bizarre celebrities had gone forever.

The Fleecing of Wetumka: The Day the Circus Didn't Come to Town

One day in early July 1950 was just like any other for the citizens in the sleepy backwater of Wetumka, Oklahoma. Nothing much ever happened there at the best of times and, with this day being excessively hot, the sense of lethargy that pervaded the town was greater than usual. In the cramped office of the local newspaper, the staff gazed idly up at the blue sky, hoping that a sensational story would somehow materialize before their very eyes. Their wish was about to come true.

Their peace was suddenly interrupted by the arrival of a stranger, J. Bam Morrison. Striding purposefully into the office, Morrison announced himself as the advance publicity man for Bohn's United Circus which, he said, was due to hit town in three weeks on 24 July. Now this was a story! Little did they know that Morrison was a liar and conman who delighted in preying on unsuspecting folk.

As news of the circus's impending arrival spread throughout Wetumka, there was widespread excitement. The town had never seen anything like it. Morrison whipped everyone into a frenzy, telling them how people would be travelling to Wetumka from miles around. The town would be a hive of activity, full of visitors with money to spend. It would, insisted Morrison, be great business for Wetumka, especially as the circus would happily buy everything it needed from the town's merchants. There would be advertising opportunities on the circus billboards or on the sides of the Big Top for enterprising local traders. The circus would put Wetumka on the map and would offer the chance for its businesses to make the sort of money in one day that they might normally expect to make in six months. Such was the sense of anticipation that the town council hurriedly called a special emergency meeting of the local chamber of commerce. Nobody wanted to miss out on the promised profits.

As the shops and hotels prepared for the invasion, the townsfolk fell over themselves to accommodate the friendly, smooth-talking Morrison. Many bought advertising space from him, including restaurateur Louis Charlton who, in return for buying so much advertising, was awarded the contract to feed all of the circus personnel. It seemed like a good deal. Meanwhile, the owner of the Meadows Hotel rushed out and purchased new mattresses so that the expected influx of guests could rest in comfort, the butcher stocked up with vast quantities of hot dogs, the baker got in extra flour for hamburger buns and the newspaper ran full-page ads announcing the date of the arrival of Bohn's United Circus. Even the proprietor of the town's feed shop ordered additional hay to cater for the circus animals. Between them, they spent a small fortune – and a fair amount went straight into Morrison's pocket.

After two weeks of this frantic activity and with his wallet bulging, Morrison decided that it was time to make his excuses and leave. On the pretext of returning to the circus to finalize publicity arrangements, he left town, informing all concerned that he would be back on the 24th. As Morrison disappeared into the distance, a legion of Boy Scouts began distributing leaflets to every household in the district. Roll up, roll up, for the biggest show in town.

Come the great day and Wetumka was heaving to capacity. The only thing that was missing was the circus. From early morning, children had been lining the streets eager to catch the first glimpse of the big parade but when noon came and went without any sign of a performing sea-lion, people began to get restless. As suspicions grew, the mayor received a parcel containing a handful of hay and a card that read: 'Regards, J. Bam Morrison'. It was then that it dawned on him that the only clowns around were the businessmen of Wetumka and himself.

Although Morrison had made off with their money, this particular sting had a happy ending for the innocents of Wetumka. The town council admitted that it had been conned but the people who had flocked there were determined to have a good time even without the circus and so takings for the day were well up on the norm. In fact it was so successful that from then on, the council chose to commemorate its blunder every 24 July with a special Sucker Day. And to show there were no hard feelings, the council even refused to press charges against Morrison when he was arrested in Missouri for another scam. Instead he was invited along to Wetumka's next Sucker Day. It is not known whether he had the nerve to show his face.

Chapter 4

Missed Opportunities

Dick Rowe: The Man Who Turned Down the Beatles

History is full of people who have passed up golden opportunities which, if taken, might have changed not only their own lives but also, in extreme circumstances, the course of the world. Take the companies that initially rejected the hovercraft because they weren't sure whether it was supposed to be a boat or an aircraft; the board game manufacturers who turned down Scrabble on the grounds that it was too dull to sell; or the executives of the Westinghouse Company, Pittsburgh, who allowed Formica to slip through their hands. In particular, the world of popular music is littered with cases of singers or groups who were dismissed out of hand by record companies before going on to eventual stardom. But none is more infamous than Decca's Dick Rowe, the executive who had to live for the rest of his life with the unwanted title of 'the man who turned down the Beatles'.

John Lennon and Paul McCartney first teamed up in 1956 in a Liverpool schoolboy skiffle group called the Quarrymen. In 1958, they added McCartney's friend George Harrison and the following year, with Stuart Sutcliffe on bass and employing various drummers, they changed their name to the Silver Beatles. In 1960, they found a regular drummer in Pete Best, shortened their name to the Beatles and started playing the clubs and ballrooms in and around Liverpool. They also made frequent visits to Germany. After one such trip, in June 1961,

Sutcliffe stayed behind in Hamburg and died ten months later from a brain tumour. During these formative years, the Beatles were loosely run by Liverpool coffee-bar owner Allan Williams who acted as their unofficial agent. Among the dates he booked for them was as backing to a stripper at a Merseyside cabaret club. Then in November 1961, they came to the attention of Liverpool record-store owner Brian Epstein who was anxious to find out more about the burgeoning Merseyside music scene. He went to see the much-talked-about Beatles at the Cavern club, one of their favourite venues, struck up a rapport with them and by 1 February 1962 was their official manager.

Even before he took over the reins officially, Epstein was working to secure the one thing that the Beatles needed above all others – a recording contract. Epstein's position in the music business – his family owned nine record shops in Liverpool and Epstein himself had founded the Liverpool branch of the Gramophone Record Retailers' Association – gave him a certain amount of clout and he began calling on his contacts to tell them about his new charges. Alas, Epstein's enthusiasm was not always mirrored by the record companies. One of his first ports of call was to EMI where he played marketing manager Ron White a disc of 'My Bonnie', recorded in Hamburg when the Beatles had been backing singer Tony Sheridan. Epstein showed White photographs of the Beatles and suggested that they might be a good group for EMI to sign. White replied that it was difficult to form much of an impression from a single where the boys were backing someone else but promised to take it round in person to all four of EMI's A&R (artistes and repertoire) managers and play it to them.

A few weeks passed and Epstein became anxious. He wrote to White expressing his disappointment at not having heard anything. In the letter, Epstein enthused: 'These boys who are superb instrumentalists also produce some exciting and pulsating vocals. They play mostly their own compositions and one of the boys has written a song which I really believe to be the hottest material since "Livin' Doll".'

White was as good as his word but received little encouragement from the A&R men. Norrie Paramor, whose artists included Cliff Richard and the Shadows and Frank Ifield, told White that he thought the Beatles sounded too much like the Shadows. And with the Shadows at their peak, he didn't need another group with a similar sound. Next, White took the disc to Walter Ridley, the man responsible for recording the likes of Frankie Vaughan and Alma Cogan. He didn't say they sounded too much like Alma Cogan but he wasn't interested anyway and rejected them outright. White then approached Norman Newall (who recorded pianist Russ Conway). Newall agreed that the Beatles sounded a little too similar to the Shadows and, because of that, he didn't want to sign them up and find himself competing with Norrie Paramor. The fourth EMI A&R man, George Martin, was away on holiday at the time . . .

On 18 December, White replied to Epstein with a formal rejection. He wrote: 'I am sorry that I have been so long in giving you a decision but I have now had an opportunity of playing the record to each of our Artistes Managers. Whilst we appreciate the talents of this group we feel that we have sufficient groups of this type at the present time under contract and that it would not be advisable for us to sign any further contracts of this nature at present.' White explained that because the fourth A&R man, George Martin, had been away, he hadn't approached him but pointed out that Martin's label, Parlophone, wasn't really a pop music label anyway but was concentrating on recording comedy artists such as Peter Sellers.

While waiting for a reply from EMI, Epstein was not sitting

around idly. The *Liverpool Echo* featured a Saturday disc review column called 'Off the Record' which was written by someone calling himself or herself 'Disker'. (Anonymous by-lines were very much *de rigueur* in journalism until the 1970s; witness the number of soccer reports penned in those days by 'Custodian', 'Scorer' or 'Whistler'.) In early December 1961, Epstein wrote to said Disker in the hope of getting a favour-able mention for the Beatles in the 'Off the Record' column. The reply came not from the *Echo* but from Decca Records since 'Disker' turned out to be the *nom de plume* of Tony Barrow, a London-based Liverpudlian whose work as a free-lance journalist included writing sleeve-notes for Decca. Ep-stein called on Barrow in London and played him a recording of the Beatles at the Cavern. The quality of the recording was poor, however, and Barrow was none too impressed. Further-more, he said he couldn't even give the Beatles a plug as it was policy only to write about recording acts. Since the Beatles didn't have a release, there was nothing he could do.

Yet there was something about the Beatles which niggled away at Barrow. He couldn't get them out of his mind and decided to make a few calls around Decca. He phoned the sales division who in turn contacted A&R, explaining that an important company client (the Epstein family stores stocked half a million records) was touting a group and that it would be diplomatic to follow it up. The head of A&R at Decca was Dick Rowe and on 13 December 1961, he sent his young assistant, Mike Smith, to Liverpool to see the Beatles play at the Cavern.

At the time, the British charts were dominated by American artists and what British acts there were seemed to be recording cover versions of American hits. So Decca were making a conscious effort to seek out some new British talent and Rowe had briefed his team accordingly. The American music trade publication *Cash Box* reported the exciting new developments at Decca: 'One of the most constructive moves to be made by Decca for many months is the formation of a new production team to handle the company's pop single output. Spearheaded by A&R manager, Dick Rowe, who will be directly responsible to the chairman, Sir Edward Lewis, the team is completed by Rowe's assistant and co-producer Mike Smith, Peter Attwood, recording engineer of three years' standing, and Tony Meehan, former drummer for the Shadows. Rowe, who will act in an advisory capacity, feels that this youthful team with their fingers on the teenage pulse, will be more than capable of producing the kind of sound that makes for chart success.'

The new set-up seemed to augur well for the Beatles' chances and at first everything looked hopeful. Smith liked what he saw and heard in Liverpool, an event remembered fondly by Epstein. 'What an occasion it was,' he later enthused. 'An A&R man at the Cavern!' Smith was sufficiently impressed to arrange immediately for the Beatles to travel to London for a record audition at Decca's West Hampstead studios on New Year's Day 1962. Stardom beckoned for the pre-Fab Four.

On the morning of 1 January, Lennon, McCartney, Harrison and Best sat in Decca reception, having arrived in the capital late the previous night at the end of a gruelling ten-hour journey through snow in a cramped van. Epstein had travelled down to London separately on New Year's Eve, staying overnight with his Aunt Frida in nearby Hampstead. Epstein and the Beatles had already discussed what they should play at the audition although band and manager weren't necessarily in agreement. Lennon favoured the raw rock 'n' roll numbers that had proved such a hit with audiences at the Cavern but Epstein advised them to play safe and stick to standards like 'Till There Was You' from the musical *The Music Man*. He also urged them to play as few of their own compositions as possible. Lennon and McCartney weren't too happy about this, but agreed to go along with it.

The day got off to a bad start when Mike Smith arrived late for the 11 a.m. audition. He had been recovering from an all-night New Year's party. Epstein was angry at having been kept waiting. Smith then proceeded to reject the group's amplifiers and told them to plug their guitars into the studio speakers instead. With nerves becoming distinctly fraught, they began their 15-song set, specially selected by Epstein to demonstrate every facet of their talent. It included just three Lennon and McCartney compositions – 'Like Dreamers Do', 'Hello Little Girl' and 'Love of the Loved'. The remainder were cover versions, taking in rock 'n' roll, rhythm and blues and even country and western. But the group seemed ill at ease initially. McCartney was so nervous that his voice started cracking up at one point, Harrison took a while to get going on the guitar and Lennon's singing was openly criticized by Epstein. In the ensuing argument, Epstein stormed out of the room and didn't return for half an hour.

Nevertheless when the session finished at 2 p.m. and the tapes were played back, everyone seemed delighted with the result. As Pete Best recalled later: 'Mike Smith said the tapes were terrific. We thought we were in.' Smith didn't have much time for pleasantries, however, and hurried the boys out of the studio because he had another audition to supervise – with Brian Poole and the Tremeloes.

In the aftermath of the audition, Tony 'Disker' Barrow asked Smith how it had gone. His *Liverpool Echo* column reflected the sense of optimism felt by the Beatles themselves. 'Latest episode in the success story of Liverpool's instrumental group the Beatles', he wrote. 'Commenting upon the outfit's recent recording test, Decca disc producer Mike Smith tell me that he thinks the Beatles are great. He has a tape of their audition which runs over 30 minutes and is convinced his label will be able to put the Beatles to good use.' However Smith did add a cautionary note – no firm decision could be made until Dick Rowe returned from America.

Epstein confidently expected a recording contract to be offered quickly but the weeks passed without any word from Decca. Epstein grew restless and tried to find out what was going on. Finally, in early February, Epstein heard from Rowe that Decca had decided against recording the Beatles. A stunned Epstein immediately fixed a meeting with Rowe and Sidney Arthur Beecher-Stevens, Decca's marketing manager, for 6 February at company headquarters on the Thames Embankment. There they reiterated Decca's disinterest. 'Not to mince words, Mr Epstein,' said Rowe, 'we don't like your boys' sound. Groups are out: four-piece groups with guitars particularly are finished.' Although Epstein protested, Rowe remained adamant. 'The Beatles won't go', he insisted. 'We know these things. You have a good record business in Liverpool – why not stick to that?' Epstein was furious. 'You must be out of your minds,' he told them. 'These boys are going to explode. I am completely confident that one day they will be bigger than Elvis Presley!' The Decca pair smiled knowingly – if only they'd had £1 for every time an agent or manager had told them that . . .

The story behind the Decca rejection is that, on his return from America, Rowe had been approached by an excited Smith telling him that, in his absence, he had discovered two hit groups – the Beatles and Brian Poole and the Tremeloes – and wanted to sign them both. Rowe asked him how long he had been with the company.

'Two years,' replied Smith.

'And how many hits have you had in that time?' pressed Rowe.

'None,' answered the young assistant, somewhat sheepishly.

Rowe went in for the kill. 'And now you've discovered two hit bands on the same day!'

Despite being the butt of Rowe's sarcasm, Smith remained convinced that both the Beatles and Brian Poole and the Tremeloes had tremendous potential. But Rowe would not be moved and told Smith that he could choose only one. To this day, nobody knows quite how that decision was reached but the most popular theory is that the arbitrating factor was something as simple as geography. Brian Poole and the Tremeloes came from Dagenham in Essex and were therefore much nearer to Decca's London base than the Beatles were in Liverpool, 200 miles away. On such a trifling matter as inconvenience, Decca passed up the chance of signing the group who were to become the most successful in the history of popular music. To be fair, Brian Poole and the Tremeloes were no slouches and, even though their lead singer ultimately returned to his trade as a butcher, notched up over 20 hits in the 1960s. But they were no Beatles.

Whilst Rowe may not have wanted Epstein's act, he was mindful of his position as one of the most prominent record retailers in the north-west and was therefore anxious not to upset him too much. So he came up with an idea, suggesting that his other assistant, Tony Meehan, hold a recording session for the Beatles for £100. Epstein felt insulted at being asked to pay £100 in advance for the hire of the studio and for Meehan's time but went along anyway the next day to see Rowe and Meehan. Once again, he was kept waiting – this time for an hour and a half – and was then told by Meehan: 'Mr Epstein, Mr Rowe and I are very busy men. We know roughly what you require so will you fix a date for the tapes to be made of these Beatles? Telephone my secretary to make sure I am available.'

Rightly or wrongly, Epstein came to the conclusion that Meehan wasn't really interested in the Beatles and, on 10 February, wrote to Rowe declining his offer. The letter began:

Dear Mr Rowe

    I am writing to thank you for your kind offer of co-operation in assisting me to put the Beatles on records. I am most grateful for your own and that of your colleagues' consideration of the Group and whilst I appreciate the offer of Mr Meehan's services I have decided not to accept.

    The principal reason for this change of mind is that since I saw you last the Group has received an offer of a recording contract from another company.

This last point was not true. While in London, Epstein had moved heaven and earth to land a record deal but had been turned down by Pye, Philips and a minor label, Oriole. However, three days later, a chance encounter brought him into contact with George Martin at Parlophone, the man who had been away on holiday when Epstein had originally approached EMI. Martin soon recognized what Rowe had missed – the Beatles' incredible potential. In June 1962, the Beatles signed a recording contract with Parlophone and within four months – by which time Pete Best had been sacked and replaced as drummer by Ringo Starr – had their first hit, 'Love Me Do'. The rest is history.

Although Decca wasn't the only record company to reject the group, it was Dick Rowe who was left to carry the stigma of being the man who turned down the Beatles. Although it is easy to say that record company executives have to listen to so many demo tapes that some good acts are bound to slip through the net, it seems inconceivable that Rowe could dismiss the Beatles out of hand after hearing their audition tape. No fewer than five of the 15 numbers the Beatles performed at the audition went on to be hits. The three Lennon/McCartney compositions – 'Love of the Loved', 'Hello Little Girl' and 'Like Dreamers Do' – achieved chart success for Cilla Black, the Fourmost and the Applejacks, respectively, while Chuck Berry's 'Memphis' became a hit for Dave Berry and Berry Gordy's 'Money' did the trick for Bern Elliott and the Fenmen. Intriguingly, another of the tracks from the Decca audition, 'Besame Mucho', was later recorded by Tony Meehan in partnership with ex-Shadows guitarist Jet Harris.

As for Rowe's assertion that four-piece groups with guitars were on the way out, that was as wide of the mark as the man who declared the *Titanic* unsinkable. For someone considered an expert in his field, he displayed a distinct lack of foresight on this occasion. As the Beatles continued to trot out number one hits and became a worldwide phenomenon, Paul McCartney said of Rowe: 'He must be kicking himself now.' To which John Lennon added: 'I hope he kicks himself to death!'

Ironically, it was George Harrison who subsequently helped to spare Dick Rowe's blushes. When the pair were judging a beat contest at Liverpool's Philharmonic Hall, Harrison told Rowe how impressed the Beatles had been by an unknown band they had seen in Richmond. They were called the Rolling Stones. Rowe was determined not to make the same mistake again and rushed straight down to London to sign up the Stones. With Beatlemania at its height, Rowe then tried to make amends for his lapse over the Fab Four by signing up the displaced Pete Best and his new group, the Pete Best All Stars. But when their début single bombed, Decca dropped them. Rowe had picked the wrong act again.

In the 1980s, Rowe started work on his autobiography appropriately titled *The Man Who Turned Down The Beatles*. But before it was finished, he died at the age of sixty-four.

One of the last words on the Decca débâcle was John Lennon's. 'I think Decca expected us to be all polished,' he said. 'We were just doing a demo. They should have seen our potential.'

George Harrison: A Fool's Gold

Unlike the Beatles' George Harrison, his South African name-sake had no business sense whatsoever. If he had done, he could have become one of the richest men in the world. As it was, he died much as he had lived – penniless. For Harrison had the dubious distinction of being the man who sold for just £10 the claim that subsequently formed the nucleus of the entire South African gold-mining industry.

Harrison was no stranger to gold prospecting. He was a veteran of the Australian gold rush of the 1850s but obviously hadn't succeeded in striking it rich, since by 1886 he was in the Transvaal district of South Africa and down on his luck. At the time, South Africa was rife with prospectors, all hoping to make that big find – the one that would change their lives forever. One day in July 1886, Harrison was wandering about the Witwatersrand when he spotted a lump of yellowish metal on the ground. He picked it up, studied it and was at once convinced that it was gold. He immediately pursued things through the official channels, taking the nugget to the owner of the land, Gert Oosthuizen, who in turn wrote to President Paul Kruger. Oosthuizen suggested that Harrison should relay details of the find to the President in person, but it is thought that no such meeting ever took place. Instead a government official contacted Harrison and advised him to set out his discovery in an affidavit. Harrison duly obliged, declaring that, from his experience, he thought the gold-field would prove payable.

Indeed it did. Harrison had unwittingly stumbled upon the one site where what later became South Africa's Main Reef – the greatest gold-field in the world – reached the surface. Over the past century, the crop of gold mines that sprung up on Harrison's reef have gone on to produce as much as a million kilograms of gold each year. A new city was born around the mines – Johannesburg. Today, over half of the world's gold is produced there.

Just two days after Harrison had signed his affidavit, a petition was drawn up requesting that Oosthuizen's land, and a sizeable area surrounding it, should be proclaimed a public gold-field. The petitioners were certain that vast quantities of gold would be found beneath the surface. The petition was granted by magistrates and Harrison was awarded claim number 19.

Curiously, Harrison did not follow up his find. While others embarked on a frenzy of digging, he seemed to lose interest in the whole affair. Maybe he didn't think there was much gold there after all or perhaps he was simply too much of a drifter. Whatever, in November 1886 he sold his claim for a mere £10 and left the area, never to return.

In his absence, the value of his claim rocketed out of all proportion. Three months after he had sold it, claim number 19 changed hands again, for £50. It was bought by one Alfred Hepple who subsequently sold it to the Little Treasure Gold Mining Company for the princely sum of £1500 plus shares worth £150. In September 1887, the Little Treasure Company also returned a nice profit by selling the claim to the Northey Gold Mining and Exploration Company for £2000 plus £8000 in shares. In less than a year, Harrison's claim had multiplied a thousand fold. Its worth continued to appreciate so that it became the most valuable claim in the whole field.

As for Harrison, nobody knows precisely what happened to him but the word was that he was eaten by a lion.

The Sale of Louisiana: Dreams of Napoleon Blown Apart

At the start of the nineteenth century, the boundaries of the United States were drawn in such a way that the nation had no direct access to either the Gulf of Mexico or the Pacific Ocean. The western extremity was marked by the Mississippi, beyond which was a vast, unexplored territory known as Spanish Louisiana. Meanwhile the south-western frontier of America did not extend as far south as the bustling port of New Orleans. Instead it turned eastwards at the 31st parallel, where nowadays the state of Mississippi joins the state of Louisiana, and ran across to the Atlantic coast at the southern edge of Georgia. The two territories that lay to the south of the 31st parallel were called West Florida and East Florida and belonged to Spain. Within these lands was situated New Orleans so that while American merchants and traders could ferry their wares along the Mississippi, the all-important access to the sea at New Orleans was under Spanish control.

Spain duly entered into a treaty with France whereby the latter acquired Louisiana. It was to be a key part of France's global expansion. Yet within three years, the Emperor Napoleon had foolishly sold the lands off to the United States for just $15 million. The Louisiana Purchase, as it was known, enabled the United States to double the size of its territories, to acquire lands rich in mineral deposits, to control the Mississippi and to find a gateway to both the Gulf of Mexico and the Pacific. It helped make America a world power. And it left Napoleon's dreams of world domination in tatters.

Back in 1800, the Mississippi was the major highway for the western United States, central to the region's economy. Barges and flatboats populated its waters as the early settlers fought off the combined dangers of deadly currents, appalling floods and murderous desperadoes to go about their everyday business. All manner of goods were transported along the mighty river and, with the number of settlers rising steadily, they began to seek more distant outlets for their trade. But as long as the Spanish held New Orleans, the American merchants who operated on the Mississippi would never be able to realize their full earning potential. The Spanish were not unreasonable, however. In 1794, Spain had recognized the Mississippi as the western boundary of the United States and had granted free navigation of the river to American citizens, along with the right to 'deposit their merchandise and effects in the port of New Orleans and to export them from thence without paying any other duty than a fair price for the hire of the stores'. But there was always the worry that Spain might suddenly change the terms and conditions, leaving the Americans high and dry.

To the west of the Mississippi, Spanish Louisiana stretched as far as the Rockies – an area of similar size to the United States itself in 1800. France had originally held the explorers' title to the region but had transferred it to Spain in 1769. However, it was not a popular move among the inhabitants of Louisiana and the colony remained essentially French. Not that there were too many inhabitants to take into account since less than 1 per cent of the area was occupied. The north was the undisputed home of Red Indians while some 40,000 Creoles had settled around the lower Mississippi. The principal crops were sugar cane and cotton, all the plantations being worked by slave labour. In addition, a handful of garrisons and trading posts were scattered along the Mississippi as far north as St Louis.

In 1763, France had been forced out of Canada by the terms of the Treaty of Paris at the end of the Seven Years' War (or the French and Indian War as it is known in America). This defeat at the hands of the British, who took control of Canada, came as a devastating blow and the French set about repairing one colonial loss by searching for a more profitable base in North America. As the new century dawned, the fiercely ambitious Napoleon Bonaparte had been swept to power. His plans for world domination relied on the consolidation of France's existing colonies and the acquisition of new ones and he saw the return of Louisiana to French rule as a major step towards his ultimate goal. Thus on 1 October 1800, he entered into a secret treaty with Spain to recover Louisiana.

Spain's decision was partly governed by fear. Spain was anxious to protect its colonial interests on the other side of the Rockies in California, where there was a sizeable Spanish settlement, and had always striven to keep the United States well away from the Pacific coast. As long as Spain held New Orleans, there was no chance of the Americans making headway to the west via that route, but Louisiana was altogether more vulnerable. Being so sparsely populated, Louisiana was particularly susceptible to invasion and Spain lived in fear that the US might one day seize California. So Spain reasoned that the presence of a strong French colony in Louisiana would actively deter American ambitions in that direction.

Spain's other interests in the Americas were of course in South America where the main enemy was Britain. Spain was in awe of Britain's naval power and decided that the best way to fight the British was to form an alliance with France. It goes without saying that the French had no qualms about entering into any arrangement that might damage Britain.

But there was another reason why Spain opted to hand Louisiana back to France. At that time, Spain was technically ruled by King Charles IV, but he was a weak monarch and left the running of the country to his queen, Maria Luisa of the Italian house of Parma, and her ambitious lover, Manuel Godoy, Duke of Alcudia. The Duchy of Parma had been conquered by the French Revolutionary armies in 1796 and now Napoleon was able to promise Maria Luisa that, in return for Louisiana, he would make her kinsman, the Duke of Parma, a king with enlarged territories. It was an offer she couldn't refuse. And with Godoy also under Napoleon's considerable influence, the deal was a formality.

And so France took control of the vast territories of

Spanish Louisiana, stretching from the Mississippi to the Rockies and from New Orleans to the border with Canada. Spain also agreed to support Napoleon's foreign policy. Apart from the favours to the Duke of Parma, Napoleon's only other concession was to promise not to dispose of Louisiana to a third power – a guarantee made to calm Spain's ongoing fears that the United States might push west towards California. However, as Spain soon discovered, Napoleon was not a man to be trusted.

Napoleon's long-term plan was to launch a major colonial offensive in America by setting up naval bases in the Gulf of Mexico and military posts on the Mississippi. He also intended to make inroads into the heartland of Spanish Louisiana, an area hitherto the domain of the Sioux and the Pawnee. But in 1800 Napoleon was too busy fighting the Austrians at home to pursue his global ambitions in the American continent. So he didn't take immediate possession of Louisiana and chose to keep the treaty with Spain a secret. Instead he sent a French expeditionary force to Hispaniola (modern-day Haiti) with orders to crush a rebellion of negro slaves led by Toussaint L'Ouverture. The idea was that once the upstarts had been put in their place, the French force would go on to take possession of New Orleans and Louisiana, but the slaves proved formidable adversaries and the French had insufficient numbers to quash the uprising. For Napoleon, it was an unwelcome irritant.

While Napoleon was contemplating his next move, an unexpected event occurred which threw his immediate plans into turmoil. Just as the United States had feared, Spain suddenly announced in the latter part of 1802 that it was closing New Orleans to American traders. It was a crippling blow to the American economy. At the time no reason was given for the drastic action although it subsequently became apparent that the Spanish governor of Louisiana was acting under direct orders from Madrid and that the measures were taken as a reprisal against American smuggling through New Orleans and also in response to accusations of unfair treatment of Spanish sailors in American ports.

As the tension between Spain and the United States increased, the American minister in London found out about the secret deal to hand Louisiana back to France. The news was duly relayed to Washington where it was received with great alarm. It was one thing having a relatively impotent nation such as Spain on one's doorstep but the prospect of the arrival of powerful French armies backed by a war-hungry Napoleon did not bear thinking about. With France in control of New Orleans and the west bank of the Mississippi, the United States considered that it would be only a matter of time before American traders were prevented from using the river at all.

Such a possibility had been anticipated by President Thomas Jefferson in April of that year. Watching helplessly while France had invaded Hispaniola, he had warned Robert R. Livingston, his minister in Paris: 'The day that France takes possession of New Orleans, we must marry ourselves to the British fleet and nation.' That the United States should even remotely consider an alliance with Britain less than 20 years after the end of the War of Independence was an indication of how seriously the nation took the threat of a French presence.

Predictably, the reaction to the Spanish closure of New Orleans was one of outrage. The mood of the populace was in favour of American troops being sent to occupy the port as a possible prelude to outright war but Jefferson favoured a more peaceful solution. He felt sure that some form of agreement could be reached with France who, after all, had sided with America during the War of Independence. In turn, there had been widespread sympathy within the United States for the goals of the French Revolution. Jefferson concluded that, recently at least, the two nations had much in common. So he ordered Livingston to do his utmost to prevent Louisiana from being returned to French control and, if that proved impossible, to try and buy East and West Florida and New Orleans so that US commerce would once again be able to operate in and out of the Mississippi. The acquisition of these territories would extend the boundaries of the United States right down to the coast of the Gulf of Mexico.

To smooth the passage, Jefferson managed to persuade Congress to approve the use of $2 million for 'expenses in relation to the intercourse between the United States and foreign nations'. To the annoyance of Livingston, Jefferson then despatched James Monroe to France as Envoy Extraordinary, making Monroe the senior negotiator. Monroe's instructions were to offer up to $10 million for New Orleans and the Floridas. If France refused or insisted on honouring the secret treaty with Spain, Monroe was ordered to offer $7.5 million for New Orleans alone. Should that be turned down, Monroe was to endeavour to negotiate a permanent agreement with France (more binding than the one that had existed with Spain) so that American merchants could use New Orleans for trade purposes and have the right of navigation and deposit. In the event of France not wishing to go down that avenue, Monroe could suggest the purchase of land on the east bank of the Mississippi to build a US port there. If all else failed, then as a last resort Monroe was to travel on to London and attempt to secure some form of alliance with Britain. At least he wasn't short of options.

Monroe sailed from New York on 8 March and arrived at Le Havre a month later. In the meantime, Livingston, anxious to steal Monroe's thunder, had already been trying to conclude a deal with the French and had been involved in lengthy discussions with French foreign minister Charles Maueice de Talleyrand-Périgord. In the midst of these discussions came news from London that, with war between Britain and France seemingly inevitable, the British were preparing to seize New Orleans. Employing these rumours to his advantage, Livingston chose to exploit a rare moment of French frailty and tried to press home a deal. He asked France to cede to the United States not only New Orleans and West Florida but also an area of Louisiana north of the Arkansas River. In fact, France was in no position to hand over either of the Floridas to the United States since they were not part of the 1800 treaty with Spain. But since the precise details of that treaty were still shrouded in secrecy, Livingston was none the wiser. His supreme gamble was in mentioning Louisiana since that was not part of his original brief. The move could have backfired on him but Livingston was to find that, on this occasion at least, fortune favoured the brave.

Against all the odds, Napoleon's expansionist plans in the New World had run aground in Hispaniola. The campaign to subdue the rebels was rapidly turning into a full-scale disaster. Although a total of 35,000 troops had been sent there, many of these had succumbed either to the enemy or to yellow fever. As a result of this setback, Napoleon cooled on the idea of taking over Louisiana, reckoning that colonies on the American mainland were worthless without having Hispaniola also under French control and that anyway Louisiana would probably be snatched by the British navy in the event of war. Rather than lose the territories to Britain, Napoleon thought it made more sense to sell them to the United States. Apart from anything else, the money he hoped to make on the deal would help finance his continuing round of European wars.

On 11 April, France broke off diplomatic relations with Britain. On the same day, with the newly landed Monroe making his way from Le Havre to Paris, Talleyrand suddenly asked Livingston what the United States would give France for the whole of Louisiana. Livingston was taken aback but came up with a figure of around $4 million. Talleyrand was not doing business at that price and told Livingston to go away and come back the following day with an improved offer.

By then, Monroe was in town and eager to take command of the negotiations. French financial circles were full of talk about Napoleon's plan to sell Louisiana to the United States and no sooner had he arrived in the French capital than Monroe was approached by the House of Hope and Baring with an offer to lend the money required for the purchase. A preliminary sum of $10 million at 6 per cent was agreed although at that stage Monroe had no intention of buying Louisiana in its entirety since he did not have the necessary authority. The new round of negotiations was conducted through François de Barbé-Marbois, the French Minister of Finance. The Americans reiterated their interest in New Orleans and the Floridas, only to learn that Napoleon had decided that he would sell the whole of Louisiana or nothing. He didn't want to know about the Floridas, mainly because, unknown to the Americans, they weren't his to sell. War with Britain was growing more likely by the day and so Napoleon wasn't prepared to wait long for an answer. He needed the money there and then.

With no time to get fresh instructions from Washington, the deal was closed on 30 April. Monroe and Livingston agreed to pay France $15 million (approximately £3 million) for the 828,000 square miles of Louisiana, an area roughly five times the size of France. The sum of $11.25 million was paid outright by the United States to France, the balance of $3.75 million being paid by the US to its citizens to satisfy their claims against France. Even with interest on the loan taken into account, the United States ended up paying just four cents an acre for an area so large that today it is divided up into no fewer than 13 states. In an additional clause, the existing inhabitants of Louisiana were granted American citizenship.

Both sides thought they had got a bargain but it soon became apparent that there was only one winner . . . and it wasn't France. As disbelief spread that a shrewd judge like Napoleon had given away so much land so cheaply, speculation grew as to why he had forced through the deal. Monroe thought that the need to raise money for the impending war with Britain was less of a deciding factor than Napoleon's fear of reprisals against the closure of New Orleans. It seems that Napoleon was worried that the anger felt by the American public at the loss of their exit to the Gulf of Mexico would lead to the United States troops taking New Orleans by force. 'Had the deposit not been suppressed,' wrote Monroe, 'and the affair turned on the relation between France and England only, we do not think that any proposition of cession to our government . . . would have occurred.'

Napoleon's own version of events was that he had ceded Louisiana to the United States in order to cement the friendship between the two republics of France and America. It all sounded very noble.

At first, the exact details of the Louisiana Purchase were a shade vague. Nobody was quite certain how far the territory stretched – initially it was thought to have included the Spanish colony of Texas although this later proved to be wishful thinking on the Americans' part. To ascertain precisely what his country had bought, Monroe went to Madrid and while he was there, he tried unsuccessfully to persuade the Spanish to part with East and West Florida. He also sought damages from Spain for the loss of revenue to American merchants as a result of the closure of New Orleans. But Spain remained evasive on all issues, still resentful of the fact that Napoleon had broken his promise about not selling Louisiana to a third power.

Not only had Napoleon broken the terms of his treaty with Spain but he had also violated the constitution of his own country which stipulated that no territory could be alienated without a vote of the legislature. To add to the complication, since France had never got round to actually occupying Louisiana it was still in Spanish hands, so Napoleon had disposed of lands that he did not possess. All this, coupled with the dispute over the extremities of Louisiana, and suddenly the deal negotiated by Monroe and Livingston began to look about as solid as a blancmange. There were even dissenting voices within the United States where critics denounced the Louisiana Purchase as being contrary to the American constitution, claiming that the President did not have the power to incorporate new territories into the United States by such methods nor could he award American citizenship to the occupants of said territories.

In view of these various moot points, there was a very real sense of trepidation among Jefferson and his supporters that the Louisiana Purchase might not be ratified by the Senate. Livingston, in particular, was worried in case Napoleon suddenly changed his mind and he urged senators to ratify the deal immediately. Realizing how much the United States had to gain, the Senate agreed. The transfer itself passed surprisingly smoothly. On 30 November 1803, the Spanish governor formally handed over Louisiana to a French prefect who then handed it over to the United States three weeks later. The southern part of the province was annexed at New Orleans on 20 December and the northern area at St Louis on 9 March 1804. In total, some 80,000 Louisiana residents were granted American citizenship.

If Napoleon had known exactly what he was giving away, he might not have been as hasty but then again he wasn't really interested in colonial development. He just wanted military glory and to be crowned Emperor of Europe. The irony is that the sale of Louisiana ultimately enabled the United States to achieve the greatness and power that Napoleon had coveted for France.

Of course, even the United States didn't know what it had bought at first. To obtain some idea of what lay beyond the Mississippi, President Jefferson appointed two army officers, Meriwether Lewis and William Clark, to lead an expedition across Louisiana. Their principal aim was to find a route from the headwaters of the Missouri to the Pacific coast. With a party of soldiers and frontiersmen, Lewis and Clark embarked on their great adventure in May 1804. From the head of the Missouri, they crossed the eastern slopes of the Rockies, over the Continental Divide, until they reached the Pacific at the mouth of the Columbia River in November 1805. *En route*, they catalogued plant and animal life and established good relations with the Indians. Two years and four months after setting out, Lewis and Clark returned to St Louis – a job well done.

But even Lewis and Clark could not have envisaged the wealth – mineral and agricultural – that this vast wilderness would yield. Louisiana as it was then has since been divided up into the following states: Arkansas, Colorado, Iowa, Kansas, Louisiana, Minnesota, Missouri, Montana, Nebraska, North Dakota, Oklahoma, South Dakota and Wyoming. Between them, these states boast some of the most fertile land and some of the most precious mineral deposits in the entire world. South Dakota became the biggest producer of gold in the United States; oil and natural gas were discovered in Montana, Nebraska, Kansas, Louisiana, Oklahoma and Arkansas; copper was found in Montana; Minnesota is home to 60 per cent of the United States' iron ore output; coal was mined in North Dakota, Wyoming, Colorado and Missouri; and the region has also thrown up supplies of tin, lead and uranium. The riches from these lands helped finance the expansion of the United States into the vast continent it is today. The Louisiana Purchase also gave the US vital control of the Mississippi River, such a central part of the American economy, and access to the Pacific coast, enabling it to become a two-ocean nation. Without these extra territories, the United States would never have developed into a superpower.

And France? The money from the sale was frittered away on further fruitless European wars that served only to ruin the nation's economy, destroy an entire generation of young Frenchmen and ultimately bring Napoleon himself to a wretched defeat. On the other hand, if he had chosen to keep Louisiana, France could have enjoyed tremendous colonial prosperity, a springboard for future glories. But for Napoleon personal glory was put before long-term economic strategy. For the man calling all the shots, it was a terrible deal – in every respect a wasted opportunity.

Chapter 5

Money Down the Drain

Gerald Ratner: A Word out of Place

It was the most famous four-letter word in business history: the day in 1991 when Gerald Ratner, chairman and managing director of the world's biggest chain of jewellers, described some of his store's products as 'crap'. It was meant as a joke – a light-hearted aside to liven up a business lunch – but the tabloid newspapers seized upon it and Ratners plunged into an alarming decline. Suddenly everybody's favourite High Street jewellers became a no-go area. Sales slumped, as did the share price of the Ratners Group. In October 1987, shares stood at 398p; by August 1992, they were down to just 12p. Shortly afterwards, Ratner himself left the company, having never recovered from that one off-the-cuff remark. On his own admission, he had made 'a terrible mistake'.

It wasn't the first time that a joke had got Gerald Ratner into trouble. He was expelled from Hendon Grammar School at the age of sixteen after telling the ageing headmaster at a teacher's funeral that he'd be better off staying in the cemetery. He left school with no qualifications but landed a job as a £6-a-week sales assistant at the family chain of jewellery shops that had been founded by his father Leslie in 1949. By the time of his expulsion he was working every Saturday morning in Ratners' Wood Green branch in North London so the transition to full-time employment was not too daunting. 'I liked selling and I was good at it,' he recalls.

By all accounts, he was something of a tearaway in his younger days – an inveterate gambler, both at poker and on the horses. He used to play poker with friends like Michael Green (now head of Carlton Communications) and Charles Saatchi who devised the advertisements that helped to sweep Margaret Thatcher to power in 1979. 'We were very competitive in our card games,' says Ratner, 'and that spilled over when we started running our businesses.'

Ratner had been unhappy with the way the family business was performing and decided to take matters into his own hands, reportedly while his father was away on a trip. In 1984, at the age of thirty-four, Gerald Ratner became managing director. At the time, the chain of 130 shops was losing around £350,000 a year. Ratner knew that big changes would have to be made . . . and quickly. In his first week at the helm, someone told him that a rival jeweller in Newcastle was taking £1 million a month and had queues stretching back across the Tyne bridge. Many of Ratners' shops weren't taking one tenth of that amount and so Ratner went straight up to Tyneside to spy on the opposition. It didn't take long for him to work out the secret of his rival's success: the shop window was plastered with posters offering bottom-of-the-range products at low, low prices. That was the new image that Ratner wanted for his shops. So out went the old-style Ratners – cold, aloof and unwelcoming with the general air of a funeral parlour – and in came the bright, brash modern retail outlet.

Business boomed. Customers flocked to the new-look stores and the pile 'em high, sell 'em cheap strategy worked a treat. Every day, there was some sort of special offer at Ratners and hardly a month went by without a heavily promoted sale. Comedians told anecdotes about the police suspect who could give precise details of his whereabouts for 11 July because he remembered it as being the only day that year Ratners didn't have a sale! The only sale that wasn't on the cards was a closing-down sale. 'It was fantastically exciting,' says Ratner. 'They were great times, watching the sales graph go up and up.' Within three years of becoming MD, Ratner had made his first million.

Ratner had the Midas touch and earned the nickname 'Lord of the Rings'. As profits continued to soar, Ratner set about expanding his empire. He bought the long-established and much-respected chain of H. Samuel with its 350 outlets. Valued at £90 million, Samuels was three times the size of Ratners and at the time of the takeover Ratner declared it to be 'the happiest day of my life'. But Ratner wasn't finished. In quick succession, he bought Zales (with 130 outlets) and Salisbury (with 235 shoe and bag shops). Then when the Monoplies Commission began hovering over Ratner, he looked abroad and entered America with the £125 million purchase of another jewellery chain, Sterling. Further acquisitions followed – the British group Ernest Jones and Kay Jewellers of America – so that by 1991, the Ratners empire employed 25,000 staff in 1300 shops in Britain and a further 1000 in the United States. There were 2400 Ratners shops worldwide, compared to 130 just seven years earlier. The group, valued at £11 million when he took over, was now worth £680 million. It was a remarkable success story, built on the charismatic Ratner's *coup* of making real jewellery accessible and affordable to the masses. That all this should be destroyed on the strength of a single, ill-judged quip amounts to just about the most remarkable commercial collapse of recent years.

It was on 23 April 1991 that it all went wrong. Twenty-four hours earlier, Ratner had been on top of the world, announcing record profits for the group of £120 million – the seventh successive year in which profits had doubled. It seemed that Ratner could do no wrong. On the 23rd, as one of Britain's highest-profile businessmen, he was addressing the annual convention of the Institute of Directors in London. An audience of 3000 company directors enjoyed a sumptuous seven-course lunch at the Albert Hall and listened to speeches from, among others, Chancellor of the Exchequer Norman Lamont, BP chairman Robert Horton, the Institute's Director-General Peter Morgan and President F. W. de Klerk of South Africa. Then it was Ratner's turn.

Confronted with a gathering that had reached the mellow stage, Ratner decided to grab their attention. Explaining Ratners' success, he said that in addition to jewellery 'we sell things like a teapot for two quid or an imitation open book to lay on your coffee table. The pages don't turn – but they have beautifully curled up corners and genuine antique dust. I know it is in the worst possible taste, but we sold a quarter of a million last year. We also do cut-glass sherry decanters complete with six glasses on a silver-plated tray – that your butler can serve you drinks on – all for £9.99. People say, how can you sell them for such a low price? I say, because they're total crap!'

Roused by Ratner's rhetoric, the company directors awarded him a round of applause. Suitably emboldened and realizing that he and his audience were on the same wavelength, he pressed on in search of more laughs. 'Some people,' he continued, 'say they cannot even see the jewellery for all the posters and banners smothering the shop windows. It is interesting, isn't it, that these shops, that everyone has a good laugh about, take more money per square foot than any other retailer in Europe. Why? Because we give the customers what they want. We even sell a pair of earrings for under £1, which is cheaper than a prawn sandwich from Marks and Spencer. But I have to say, the earrings probably won't last as long!'

The audience loved it. Ratner thought he was on safe ground because he had used the same lines before. Back in

January 1988, he had told the *Financial Times* that the sherry decanter, matching glasses and silver-plated tray – one of his bestselling Christmas gifts – was priced so low because 'it's crap'. And the prawn sandwich joke came about by default. When one of his companies first introduced a line of gold stud earrings for 99p (then the same price as an M&S prawn sandwich), Ratner had quipped, 'but the earrings last longer'. But then someone mischievously misquoted him as saying: 'But the earrings don't last as long as the sandwich.' It got a laugh so the showman in Ratner decided to include it in his repertoire and used it on a number of occasions in speeches to financial journalists and City advisers. It never failed.

As far as Ratner was concerned, his speech to the Institute of Directors was no different. He certainly hadn't expected a private joke at a business lunch to be widely reported, but this time his comments were picked up by the tabloid press. To his horror, they made the front pages of the following day's papers. 'ROTNERS' boomed the headline in the *Sun* while the *Daily Mirror* weighed in with 'YOU 22-CARAT MUGS'. It made uncomfortable reading. Ratner protested that his remarks had only been meant as a joke but the popular press had got the bit between their teeth. The *Sun* followed up with a feature on Ratner's lifestyle, namely his £1.6 million Victorian mansion on the banks of the Thames at Bray. It was labelled 'The House That Crap Built'. Next to this was another story, this time about a supposedly distraught newlywed whose husband had bought her £80 wedding ring from Ratners. Suddenly the whole world seemed to be up in arms as Ratner had committed the retailer's ultimate crime – he had insulted his customers.

Amazingly, the immediate effect of Ratner's gaffe was positive. Sales were 12 per cent up on the corresponding week for the previous year and shares in the Ratners Group rose by a healthy 10 per cent. Even the much-maligned 99p earrings proved attractive to customers. A total of 750,000 were sold in the month after Ratner's speech – more than double that in the previous month. 'It's the motorway accident syndrome,' Ratner told the *Sunday Times*. 'Everyone slows down to have a look – and then they see a bargain.'

Trying to turn the blunder to the company's advantage, a Ratners manager in Ayr came up with the idea of putting posters in the shop windows saying, 'What we mean by CRAP – Cheap, Reliable and Affordable Prices'. All of Ratners' shops carried the slogan. It was a valiant attempt. Ratner himself tried to present an accessible, almost matey, persona to the public, hoping that if he came across as a likeable chap who admitted to having dropped a bit of a clanger, the public would forgive him. He posed for photographs holding a replica gun to his own head in mock anguish. He was seen as the approachable face of big business, a man who liked a laugh but had just gone too far on one occasion. It might have worked, but mud has a nasty habit of sticking when you least want it to.

Ratner spent £500,000 on damage limitation advertising and continued to protest his innocence. 'The thing that has upset me most,' he said, 'is that everyone now thinks I'm a flash git who has no time for ordinary people. My approach has been to be honest with our customers and to make jewellery affordable for the man in the street. How else could we have sold £5 billion of jewellery in seven years? We couldn't have done that by tricking people.' In July he addressed the Ratners Group AGM and apologized to shareholders. 'My comment was made in a light-hearted manner . . . My mistake was in not realizing that a tongue-in-cheek joke would be so widely misquoted.' Instead of prawn sandwiches, Ratner was eating humble pie.

Despite the strenuous efforts of all concerned to repair the damage, the signs were not good. Ratner had made his monumental gaffe just as the country was starting to go into recession. Shops in high streets up and down the land found the going tough in the summer and autumn of 1991 and for Ratners, with its new image problem, it was tougher than most. Ratner still smarts at the memory. 'Suddenly we were regarded as a national joke. Staff morale fell. I used to stand up at management meetings and try to instil a sense of purpose, but the managers told me, "You don't inspire us any more", and I knew they were right.'

By October, sales had fallen alarmingly. The share price also tumbled 42 per cent in a five-week period, meaning that the Ratners Group was now worth just £237 million, compared to £680 million six months earlier. It was a company in crisis, one in urgent need of drastic measures. Nobody could do much about the recession, but it wasn't necessarily too late to salvage the group's reputation. The problem was perceived as being with the Ratners name. As Ratner himself acknowledged, ever since his little *faux pas*, Ratners had become something of a joke. It was no longer viewed as a shop where anyone would want to buy jewellery for someone special. And to receive a gift in a Ratners bag would have been considered an insult in some quarters. 'Nobody wanted to buy diamond rings from Ratners any more,' conceded Gerald Ratner. 'When you keep a box as a memento of a special occasion in your dressing table, you don't want it to be emblazoned with a name everyone associates with rubbish.'

In an attempt to distance the other chains in the group from the Ratners name, H. Samuel, Ernest Jones and Ratners were all repositioned in the market. Although H. Samuel and Ernest Jones had always been more upmarket than Ratners, the disparity among the three shops was not easily discernible to the customer. So now, in order for the public to be able to differentiate between its brands, the Ratners Group pushed Ratners further towards the bottom end of the market, stationed H. Samuel in the middle and elevated Ernest Jones to the top of the range. And in a general bid to rid Ratners of its joke tag, plans were introduced to increase the volume of classy gold and diamond products – all with guarantees. Other new measures included putting more items on display in the shops and reducing the number of bargain sales. Ratner explained the philosophy behind the changes: 'The pile-it-high, sell-it-cheap approach is not appropriate for the Nineties. From now on, we will focus on service, quality and exciting new products.'

But the recession was still biting hard and sales did not pick up. Where money is tight, jewellery is considered a luxury purchase. People will always have to buy essentials like food and, to a lesser extent, clothes, but items such as new carpets, suites, hi-fi systems and jewellery tend to become superfluous except at Christmas. In the six weeks leading up to the all-important Christmas period, group sales were down 15 per cent on 1990. Desperate to capitalize on the traditional festive spending spree, Ratners implemented yet more ideas designed to encourage customers to put their hands in their pockets. A whole range of discounts and incentives were drawn up for Christmas including giving full refunds on Rolex watches for up to a year after purchase, extending interest-free credit and issuing vouchers which offered massive discounts. As an added carrot, managers who met sales targets were to be invited to a party at Ratner's Thames-side home and given a bonus of £1000 on their way out.

'That Christmas I gave one last throw of the gambler's dice,' says Ratner. 'Because sales figures were suffering so badly we discounted everything, 25 per cent across the board. We were doing a Seiko chronograph watch for £64.50, a fiver below the cost price. It was ridiculous. When we rang up the manufacturers for more supplies, they said: "We suggest you buy them from yourself. We can't do it as cheaply." People who had sworn they'd never go to Ratners again came in droves. Then after the sale we went dead. Stock ran out. That year we made a loss which was a hell of a drop from a £120 million profit. For 18 months, I stayed on, firefighting. But as the fire stoked up, the fight in me diminished. We tried damage limitation exercises, we spent money on new fascias, on public relations, we had mission statements – but it was a complete waste of money.'

By offering 25 per cent discount vouchers in the final days before Christmas, Ratners had merely succeeded in depressing the group's margins without providing the anticipated boost in sales. True, sales did pick up a little but not sufficiently to compensate for the slump of the previous months. 'It was a panic measure that did not work,' admitted Ratner.

The arrival of 1992 brought no respite. In January, Ratner stepped down as chairman but stayed on as chief executive. As Ratners' sales and shares slumped in unison, the group announced in August that it was shedding over 2000 staff in Britain and the United States with the closure of 326 shops. The following month, Ratners suffered another blow to its fragile image when the company was fined £1000 after a pair of £3.50 earrings, described as opal, were found to be plastic and melted when tested. On 25 November, Ratner severed his links with the group when he resigned from the board as chief executive, saying that the continuing negative media attention that he had attracted since the fateful speech had led him to believe that it was best to quit. 'Those 18 months were a nightmare,' he confessed in 1997. 'There were some awful personal attacks on me in the newspapers. I used to get into a terrible state about them because I am very sensitive, not at all thick-skinned. In the end, I was relieved to get away.' At the time of his departure, Ratners was valued at just £49 million. Only the banks were keeping the group alive.

As media analysts picked over Ratner's fall, they all

concentrated on THAT speech. But there were other factors behind the decline. The rash of takeovers during the boom years had taken its toll, in particular the 1990 purchase of Kay Jewellers for an overpriced £234 million. Ratners had paid the price of buying into the US retail market on borrowed money and the group's problems had been exacerbated by the demise in the States of Zales. Even when there were clear warning signs that a recession was imminent, Ratners had continued its policy of expansion. At a time when caution should have been the order of the day, too many costly risks were taken.

And for good measure, there was the speech – the world's most expensive joke, which wiped out £500,000 of shareholders' money and cost Gerald Ratner a fortune, his £600,000-a-year salary, his luxurious home and his reputation as Britain's smartest high street trader. He was undoubtedly unlucky to see the joke reported so widely. After all, he had used it on countless occasions before. His error was to repeat it in front of the tabloid press.

'That remark was a terrible mistake,' said Ratner in 1997 at the launch of his latest venture, a health club. 'But I never applied it to our jewellery, which was actually very good value for money. I did not exploit our customers. Frankly, gold is gold and there was little difference between the jewellery in our cheaper shops and that sold by the more exclusive ones. There were some pretty diabolical, Del Boy-ish items like the phoney cut-glass decanter set and the open "antique" book which wasn't a book at all, but you do not achieve 50 per cent of the UK market by selling junk. You show me a major retailer who has been consistently successful selling second-rate goods. It can't be done.

'After I left, I felt angry: to have built up the business, acquired the opposition, beaten the competition, then to have it all snatched away. I try to think before I speak now. Because of one ill-judged joke, 25,000 people lost their jobs. I was one of them. I feel a dreadful responsibility for those lost jobs. Lads used to come up to me and say: "Gerald, you gave me a chance. Without you I'd never have been a manager." Then they lost their jobs because of my irresponsibility. I had become blasé. I thought I could get away with murder.'

Thinking back to the blunder and the subsequent press coverage, he added: 'I handed it to them on a platter really . . . a silver-plated one, actually.'

The Advanced Passenger Train: Full Tilt to Oblivion

One thing that the British rail network has never been accused of is being ahead of its time. Its trains have certainly never been – over the years they've been delayed by a variety of mishaps that would fill a book on their own. Among the most memorable were the wholly unexpected discovery of leaves on the track in autumn and the classic blizzard that contained the 'wrong kind of snow' for the trains to operate. Yet back in 1967, British Rail conceived the idea for an advanced passenger train that would carry the nation, if not into, then at least towards, the twenty-first century. This was exciting news for those who had waited what seemed like most of the century just to be carried into Waterloo. The project was loudly trumpeted with the promise that it would propel Britain to the forefront of the world's railways. But an all-too-familiar combination of management indifference and impractical cost-cutting, allied to over-ambitious technology, rapidly consigned it to the sidings for eternity. The Advanced Passenger Train finished up as a £50 million flop.

From drawing-board to scrapheap took nearly two decades. Rome was built in half the time. Throughout the 1960s, Britain's railways were struggling to compete with the new motorway network. Travellers found that they could get from city to city almost as quickly – and much more cheaply – by car than by rail. The Beeching report of 1963 had resulted in a decimation of the rail network. It was cut by a quarter with the closure of over 2000 stations, principally on branch lines. Whereas virtually every village had once had its own railway station, passengers now had to rely on cars or buses. The cost-cutting exercise had stripped British Railways (as it then was) to its bare bones but the aim was to make it leaner and hungrier, fully equipped to face the future. The only lame ducks would be those who had waddled onto a level crossing at the wrong time.

In the late 1960s, BR was looking at ways to improve its Inter-City services in both the medium and long term. Japan's sleek bullet trains had set the standard for high-speed rail travel while France was also planning to introduce 125 mph main-line trains. The best Britain could offer were the 100 mph electric trains that had been running from Euston to Scotland on the west coast line since 1966. Encouraged by the success of these and anxious to be seen to be moving with the times, BR commissioned a report to look into ways in which the network might accommodate trains capable of even higher speeds.

Meanwhile, in April 1967, BR's Derby research division proposed a technically advanced train powered by gas turbines. Tiny inside frame bogies and wheelsets whose flanges would not touch the rails when curving would incorporate suspension with powered body tilting. This combination, suggested Derby, would help the train run on existing track at speeds of up at 50 per cent faster than conventional trains – and at no extra cost. A great deal of the technology, notably the turbines and the planned lightweight body structures, had its roots in the aerospace industry, reflecting the background of many of the BR scientists at Derby who had previously worked in aircraft design.

When the BR study report appeared, it gave the Derby proposal the green light. With the inevitable shortage of funds preventing BR from even considering laying down new track all over the country, the idea of being able to run 150 mph trains on existing lines appealed enormously. If something could be done on the cheap, it was worth doing. Bends had long been the curse of the network – the whole system appeared riddled with them – and so any train that could corner faster than the present models had to be a bonus. Taking this into account, it was decided that the ideal route for the new high-speed tilting train would be the twisty west coast route. BR planned to have prototypes in passenger service by 1974. This date was to prove spot on . . . give or take seven years.

The research project was to be called the Advanced Passenger Train and in 1968 the government agreed to share the development costs. An APT development workshop was built at Derby, along with a 13-mile test track. Already the first changes were being made to the original specification, the tiny bogies being replaced by long articulation bogies. A pair of skeleton units were constructed to test the tilting concept.

After the skeletons came the APT-E, a four-carriage experimental train consisting of two power cars and two trailer cars, all able to tilt by up to nine degrees. The original aircraft turbines were substituted for a bank of four 400 hp Leyland turbines in each power car plus a fifth for on-board services. The claims that the APT could attain speeds of 150 mph on existing track ensured that the project aroused tremendous interest from other nations, notably the United States where the Department of Transportation was struggling with its own high-speed train trials and where track conditions were also less than satisfactory. Accordingly, on 27 October 1969, the Budd Company, wrestling with the ill-starred Metroliners, signed a licence deal for exclusive rights in the USA and

Canada to develop high-speed trains based on BR's new technology.

There was certainly no shortage of new technology being incorporated into the APT. Apart from the sophisticated tilting, there was a new form of hydro-kinetic brake that promised to halt the 150 mph train in the same distance as a conventional train travelling at 100 mph. Such was the confidence behind the venture that in 1971 Dr Sydney Jones, BR's board member for engineering and research, had talked openly of the 250 mph version of APT – and this was before the experimental train had even turned a wheel. He was a touch premature.

The APT-E made its début in July 1972, only to fall victim to the union strife that plagued Britain during the 1970s. The Associated Society of Locomotive Engineers & Firemen (known to long-suffering commuters as ASLEF) promptly boycotted it as part of a campaign to wring more pay out of BR for driving high-speed trains. The boycotting lasted for more than a year, severely hampering progress. In August 1975, APT-E touched 148 mph between Swindon and Reading and completed its trials the following year before rolling into its final terminus at York railway museum.

The next stage of the programme was to build a prototype train to carry fare-paying passengers. The plan was to construct four APT-Ps, as they were known, but the Labour government was squeezing BR spending and the number was cut back to three. These were authorized in the summer of 1974 and the first of the prototype power cars was completed at Derby three years later. BR wanted to run them on the electrified line between London and Manchester (the Leyland turbines had been found to consume too much fuel and were being replaced by electric power) but there was political pressure to run a service to Scotland so BR had to back down and agreed to extend the journey to Glasgow. The aim was to complete the journey in around four hours at an average speed of around 100 mph. In theory, this was a reasonable target. Railways in other countries had managed it, but then again they weren't running on a track network dating from the previous century.

Each APT prototype (to be built by British Rail Engineering Ltd at Derby) was to consist of two steel-bodied power cars positioned next to each other in the middle of the train, flanked on either side by six lightweight aluminium coaches, making 14 cars in total. It was a bizarre set-up, but a single power car would not have been able to cope with the stiff gradients at the Glasgow end of the line. The two power cars could not be stationed at one end of the train because such a move would generate unacceptably high buckling forces when they were pushing, nor could they be separated as they would then need their own pantographs and anyway the rear pantograph would not collect current satisfactorily at high speed from an overhead line of such simple design which had been disturbed by its counterpart at the front. If BR had not been obliged to cut costs on the Crewe to Glasgow electrification, more sophisticated apparatus might have been in place. So the only place left for the two power cars was in the middle where they could be fed from a single pantograph. However, since passengers were only allowed through the power cars in an emergency, this meant that there would have to be two buffet cars – one either side of the power cars. The additional catering costs alone thus negated some of the other savings being claimed for the new wonder-train.

BR continued to shout about the APT from the rooftops. 'Inter-City APT marks the biggest single advance in improved train performance achieved by any railway in the world,' crowed one glossy brochure, but already there were indications that the train might not be able to live up to its publicity. For a start, although the APT was designed for speeds of 150 mph, it was quickly decided to reduce this maximum speed to 125 mph when the train entered regular service. This was because the signalling was inadequate. A more advanced signalling system would have been needed for the higher speeds – a fact apparently overlooked until well into development – but nobody was prepared to pay for such modifications. Another reason for the reduction in speed was that BR was not convinced that the hydro-kinetic brakes were wholly effective in poor weather and that they would be able to bring a 150 mph train to a standstill within the required distance. So the high-speed passenger train of the future was reduced to 125 mph – exactly the same as a conventional diesel-powered Inter-City.

The years passed. There was much frenzied activity behind the scenes but precious little action on the track. The delays stemmed partly from the Derby workforce's unfamiliarity with aluminium-welding techniques and also from their propensity to go on strike at the drop of a hat. No fewer than 44 industrial disputes rocked production and testing between June 1978 and March 1979. Inevitably, the delays were causing unrest. Snipers were lining up to pour scorn on the entire project. It had even been vilified as a colossal waste of time and money by the more traditional members of BR management who despised and resented the innovative technology they were hearing so much about as it intruded on their own domain. Meanwhile as postponement followed postponement, the British public – ever cynical of PR-led operations – began to doubt whether the APT would ever see the light of day.

Against this backdrop of hostility, uncertainty and suspicion, APT advocates desperately needed some good news. They finally received some shortly before Christmas 1979 when an eight-car APT-P reached a British Rail record speed of 162 mph on a test run. But if they thought this indicated better times ahead, they were sadly mistaken. A few more delays, a few more teething problems and then suddenly BR announced the final, final date for the train's public début – May 1980. BR bosses wrote it into their timetables.

Anyone who has ever read a BR timetable will know how notoriously unreliable they are, and so it proved here. Just one month before the APT was due to carry its first passengers, disaster struck. On 18 April a prototype carrying assorted technicians and BR Vice-Chairman Ian Campbell was rattling along at 125 mph near Carnforth, Lancashire, when those on board became aware of a noise beneath one of the carriages. Moments later, the train was derailed. Luckily, nobody was injured and the train itself emerged remarkably unscathed, but the cause of the accident – a broken axle – resulted in all three prototypes being withdrawn immediately for inspection.

The trains returned to active testing in the summer of that year, only to be dogged by more mechanical problems. The friction brakes were dragging and the tilting mechanism was proving far from efficient. As a result, BR announced that it was postponing the introduction of the passenger service until 5 October. Two days before that auspicious occasion, a press trip was staged with reasonable success but further tilt and brake problems caused yet another delay. In the meantime, people were starting to ask awkward questions about the tilt. Was it safe? Was there a danger of collision on bends from two tilting trains travelling in opposite directions? And would standing passengers and catering staff be tossed around the coaches by the tilt? BR said there was absolutely nothing to worry about.

By now, even the sceptics among BR management had united behind the APT in a display of ostrich-like mentality. Having already spent £37 million without carrying a single fare-paying passenger, BR submitted a request to the Department of Transport to spend another £35 million on advance orders for a production version. In view of the difficulty even to get the thing to stay on the rails, this seemed a wildly optimistic request and, sure enough, BR soon had to ask the Department to sit on the application for the time being.

With no announcement of a new launch date (these were now regarded with the same suspicion as sightings of the Loch Ness Monster), testing began again in March 1981. Further stories appeared about the tilting mechanism, claiming that BR had discovered a fault on the APT which could lead to a crash. It was suggested that if the tilting mechanism failed and coaches of two approaching trains were locked in the leaning position, they could touch in places where the gap between the two tracks did not allow sufficient clearance. BR dismissed the claims as 'grossly exaggerated' but just to be sure installed a failsafe device which returned the cars to the upright position. Such a belated acknowledgement of a potential risk hardly inspired public confidence.

Breakdowns and system failures continued to occur virtually every day. The entire APT project was in danger of falling apart, particularly as the diesel-powered High Speed Trains with no fancy frills, no gimmicks and definitely no tilting, were proving so successful up and down the country. Desperate to rescue the APT before it was too late, BR management called in an outside consultant, Professor Sir Hugh Ford, to report on the engineering viability of the project. He was due to ride on a prototype on Friday, 23 October 1981 but the preceding week turned out to be one of constant mishap. On the Monday, the test run was cancelled due to a problem in the depot; on the Tuesday, the train struggled to Preston before returning to the depot with a leaking transfer gearbox, a dragging friction brake and a tilt system failure; on the Wednesday, with all the faults apparently rectified, the train left the depot, only to be forced to return almost immediately because of another dragging brake;

on the Thursday, another dragging brake brought the train to a halt outside Glasgow. Amazingly on the Friday, with Professor Ford and senior members of BR on board, the train ran without a hitch. Carefully ignoring the previous four days, BR confidently announced a final, final, final date for the first passenger service – 7 December.

The pressure to get APT up and running had been steadily mounting on BR that autumn. The French had leaped ahead and, in a blaze of publicity, launched its TGV service between Paris and Lyons. The TGV was capable of speeds of 162 mph, but this was because France had gone to the trouble of laying down new track. The French simply took away the bends and hurtled the TGV down a straight track. BR had preferred to muddle through. In the face of such stiff competition from across the Channel, BR could wait no longer and all eyes were turned towards December. One train was to make a round trip between Glasgow and London Euston three times a week. The second train would be kept in reserve in case of breakdowns while the third underwent further testing. At 7 a.m. on 7 December 1981, the APT pulled out of Glasgow on its first passenger run. It was seven years late. Even for BR, this was some kind of a record.

In testing, the prototype sets of 14 cars had experienced adhesion problems on the northern hills so on its first run the APT left Scotland with just ten cars – six crammed with passengers (including an array of journalists), two power cars and two carriages reserved for railway technicians. Against all the odds, the inaugural run was a success, arriving in Euston at the end of its 400-mile trip one minute ahead of its scheduled journey time of 4 hr 15 min. Fearful of any more adverse publicity, BR had taken the precaution of sending an empty train behind the APT in case it broke down but it wasn't needed. BR chairman Sir Peter Parker was waiting at Euston with a smile like a cat that had not only been at the cream but had found there was a free offer of a dead mouse with every carton. Several passengers had the effrontery to complain about nausea and motion sickness caused by the tilting (particularly when watching the horizon moving up and down) but these were swiftly brushed aside. Nothing was going to spoil BR's big day.

And nothing did . . . until the return journey. On the trip back to Glasgow the coaches refused to tilt as the train rounded bends north of Preston. The much-vaunted tilting mechanism which allowed the APT to take curves 40 per cent faster than a conventional train failed on six of the coaches. The failures (there were three in all) caused the coaches to revert abruptly to their upright position, jamming the electronically controlled doors, throwing food and drink off the tables, smashing large quantities of glassware and crockery and causing some passengers to be sick. A drinks' stewardess, asked how she coped with the tilting mechanism, said: 'I just stand with my legs open.' That may have made the journey more bearable for some of the male passengers but for most people it was a nightmare. APT limped into Glasgow 30 minutes late, having undone all of the good PR work on the outward journey.

Things got worse. During the second day of service – 9 December – the train broke down 20 miles out of Glasgow after developing a fault in the braking system caused by travelling at high speed in freezing conditions. Moisture had gathered in the air pressure system of the brakes and turned to ice. Passengers had to wait 20 minutes to catch a normal service to Euston. On the third day – 11 December – with northern England and Scotland in the grip of winter, heavy snowfalls caused further disruption and the APT got no further south than Crewe. The passenger trials were supposed to go on for two weeks but at the end of that first week – with a score of just one successful run out of six – BR gave up and withdrew the APT from service. After nigh on 15 years of research, the project had collapsed in just one week.

BR continued conducting trial runs, however, and on 16 December, APT managed to be four hours' late arriving in London. Fortunately there were no passengers on board. The regular daily passenger service had been due to start on 11 January but, to the surprise of no one, BR scrapped those plans and instead said that it was concentrating on further runs without passengers. It was an interesting new policy for a public transport system.

Over the next few months, BR maintained its programme of trials and tests in the hope of finding solutions to the various problems that were plaguing the APT. If proof were needed that salvation was not at hand, it broke down twice more on a test run in March. BR's dreams of a fleet of 60 APTs to take over the Inter-City services on the west coast main line seemed light years away. In any case, the on–off (mainly off) saga of the APT had destroyed any reputation it might have had and BR had already lost practically all of the London–Glasgow business traffic to the British Airways shuttle launched in the mid-1970s. The outlook for the APT appeared bleak, especially as the Department of Transport was insisting on a year's trouble-free public service before authorizing the money for more APTs.

BR had no desire to admit defeat but, with new express trains urgently needed for the second half of the 1980s, it began to look at ways of developing the High Speed Train (HST) rather than the APT. Cyril Bleasdale, BR's passenger director, said of the APT: 'The prototype is obviously not the train we want. Perhaps we failed to recognize it was a prototype as with Concorde, where the first one built was destroyed. But we have learnt enough to know the concept is right.'

Carrying a passenger load consisting solely of BR employees and their families, the APT underwent further trials and modifications. The tilting mechanism was altered as was the suspension to offer a smooth ride instead of being whipped from side to side whenever the train took a bend. Nevertheless, in autumn 1982, BR finally admitted what everyone had long suspected – namely that the APT prototypes would never see active service but would remain in use for 'engineering development'. Director of engineering Ian Gardiner insisted that APT was not being abandoned, adding that 'APT continues to be central to British Rail's Inter-City strategy and is expected to provide 60 to 70 per cent of passenger services on the planned electrified network we are all so anxiously awaiting.' He went on to describe something called APT-U which was nothing like its predecessors. The hydro-kinetic brakes would be replaced by high-power discs similar to those on the French TGV which had been ridiculed in the past by BR engineers. Tilting would remain for the time being but already tests were being conducted to determine how fast conventional non-tilting Inter-City trains could take curves without upsetting passengers or carriages.

By 1986, the end was nigh. It was clear that the APT was never going to be commercially viable in anything resembling its prototype form. More standard electric trains were introduced instead and the APT name was so inextricably linked to failure that BR decided to drop it in favour of Inter-City 225. The project was finally abandoned and the coaches dismantled. The train that was supposed to revolutionize rail travel ended up in a Rotherham scrapyard. Of all its innovative features, the only one anybody seemed to miss was the toilets that could be flushed while in a station. Was that added convenience really worth £50 million plus?

Otherwise, most of the innovations were a curse. There were simply too many new concepts in one machine: the sensor-operated tilting mechanism, the self-steering bogies and the hydro-kinetic brakes. The brake design was basically inefficient while in the latter stages BR made so many major alterations to the tilt system in an effort to fine-tune it that there was insufficient time in which to improve the system's reliability.

On top of that, the APT suffered from bad engineering, poor public relations, awful industrial relations, a fair amount of bad luck and injudicious management. Right at the start, the project was adopted too hastily without all of the implications being considered properly. France and Japan built special high-speed rail networks for their high-speed trains, but Britain tried to scrape by half-heartedly, hoping that the existing track and signalling would be good enough. In its infinite wisdom, BR dreamed that the APT would run like clockwork. With hindsight, perhaps it would have been easier and cheaper to have simply wound it up . . .

Tulipmania: A Blooming Disaster

At various times in history, nations are gripped by crazes. It is usually something as innocuous as the humble yo-yo which took off in the United States in 1929 or the hula-hoop which swept through the same country in 1958, selling a staggering 30 million in six months, but just occasionally a craze comes along that has more sinister consequences. Thus it was that in the 1630s the eminently sensible people of the Netherlands dived headlong into an orgy of investment which brought financial ruin to thousands and even threatened the fabric of the national economy. What is more remarkable is that the object of their desire was the tulip.

That the Dutch should choose to worship a bulb as opposed to, say, an emerald, may seem peculiar to us nowadays but back in the seventeeth century it was considered to be exotic, alluring and even dangerous. It certainly wasn't something that you would sacrifice to the area of the garden that formed the cat's litter tray. On the contrary, it was a much-prized commodity, one that was extremely valuable and inaccessible to all but the wealthiest in the land. To own a tulip was to be in possession of a status symbol the equivalent of today's yacht or Rolls-Royce. If the tulip had remained the preserve of the upper classes, the mania that almost destroyed Dutch society would not have taken place. But when the bulb suddenly came within the reach of small buyers and people realized that there was big money to be made on the tulip market, everyone wanted a piece of the action, regardless of the consequences.

Tulips came from Turkey originally (the name deriving from the Turkish word for 'turban') and the first tulips reached Europe from Constantinople in the 1560s. They became particularly popular in Germany and Holland and were much admired for their urn-like shape and vivid colours. But for the connoisseur, the real fascination with tulips lay in their 'breaks'. Most tulips produce the same flower year after year – as do all the smaller bulbs or offsets which grow from the parent – but some varieties change their colouring after a few years and 'break' into an eye-catching striped pattern. These freaks of nature, believed to be caused by some form of virus, may seem imperfect to the purist but are beautiful specimens in their own right. It was these unusual blooms that caught the imagination of the Dutch who saw them as hugely collectible. And the beauty of tulips is that they multiply. Whereas a collector of Ming vases would have to spend a fortune to expand his stock, a tulip collector simply has to let nature take its course each year . . . and at no extra charge. So Dutch enthusiasts quickly realized that, by growing the coveted 'freak' tulips, they could make a fortune from selling the offsets. It was like breeding rare cats or dogs and selling the kittens or puppies.

These irregularly striped varieties were divided into three

groups: the roses (red and pink on a white background), the violets (lilac and purple on a white background) and 'bizarden' (red or violet on a yellow background). They were named after heroic figures of the day which, in the Netherlands at that time, meant admirals and generals rather than royalty.

Not everyone was besotted – Calvinist preachers saw the tulip as yet another dangerous vanity to be added to the catalogue of sins that were afflicting the nation – but by the early seventeenth century, it was a mark of poor breeding for a wealthy Dutchman *not* to own a collection of tulip bulbs. And just as people climbing the social ladder often aspire to larger houses or bigger cars, so the upwardly mobile Dutch saw the acquisition of a cluster of tulips as a sign that they had finally 'arrived'. In the Netherlands, you were nobody without a tulip.

To meet the demand, growers strove to produce new, more handsome varieties. New shades appeared, new shapes and new sizes. In 1612, Emmanuel Sweerts published his *Florilegium* which contained over 100 plates showing the varieties that he was selling in Amsterdam. The royal families of Europe began to take an interest and soon there was a huge range of varieties available, designed to attract not just the wealthy collector but thousands of smaller buyers. One of the most sought-after varieties was 'Semper Augustus' which boasted a red and white striped flower with a blue-tinted base. The tulip expert Wassenauer summed up the importance of the bulb in 1623: 'No tulip has been held in higher esteem,' he wrote, 'and one has been sold for thousands of florins; yet the seller was himself sold (so he said), for when the bulb was lifted he noticed two lumps on it which the year following would have become two offsets, and so he was cheated of two thousand florins.' Wassenauer knew full well the value of tulips and described the offsets as the 'interest, while the capital remains'.

Money Down the Drain

Up until the middle of the 1620s, the tulip trade was monopolized by gentlemen horticulturalists and their estate gardeners, sales invariably being on a large scale. But as the market expanded rapidly over the next ten years, it became possible to buy tulips in smaller quantities, by the pound or by the basket. This had the effect of making them affordable to the middle classes and even to the lower orders. Small shop-keepers would endeavour to gain a modicum of respectability by acquiring a handful of tulips and it became commonplace for the humblest of peasants to part with half of everything they owned in the world just to acquire a single bulb. Children began to go without food and clothing for the sake of their parents owning a tulip.

The timing of tulipmania – between 1634 and 1636 – coincided with the lower classes having more money than was customary. This was the unexpected benefit of a great plague that had swept through the land from 1633 to 1635. The resultant labour shortages had improved wages to the point where, in some cases, a little extra disposable income was available for luxury purchases. The trouble was that once people started to get addicted to gambling on the tulip market, they didn't know when to stop.

Although dealers liked to concentrate on the more expensive tulips, they also stocked the cheaper, single-coloured varieties in order to appeal to a wider clientele. Buyers could purchase tulips almost anywhere. Whereas previously the bulbs had been the domain of nurseries and specialist shops around the major cities, growers now employed itinerant salesmen to take their wares to village fairs and markets in rural areas.

What made the tulip unique was that, unlike other decorative goods, there was a chain linking the prized striped blooms at the top end of the market (which were still only affordable to the gentry) with the more modest single-coloured reds and yellows which could be bought by those who were less well off. Therefore the tulip was able to remain a precious jewel while being within reach of the masses. And for a moderate outlay, the common man could enter into the complicated and hazardous world of buying and speculating on the tulip market. Fortunes could be won . . . and lost.

Another aspect which made the tulip a suitable case for speculation was its growing season. For true amateurs, the buying season was confined to the period between June (when the bulbs were lifted) and October (when they were planted out in readiness for blooming the following spring). Nobody would have considered buying for delivery some months away. However, as the increasing demand from the public made it necessary for growers to sell tiny offshoots, the situation changed. These could only be supplied after a wait of at least a few months with the result that buying in the winter became acceptable practice and soon extended to the 'future' sale of whole bulbs. With such a long period leading up to delivery, buyers were inevitably tempted into some form of interim deal, either selling again to a new buyer (making a tidy profit in the process) or else upgrading their own stock. Of course, all of this was done without ever seeing either the blooms or the bulbs. It became increasingly risky and reached the point where buyers would approach potential sellers whom they knew full well were not actually in possession of the stock. They in turn offered a 'paper' price dependent on delivery so that the 'paper' sale could be passed on to yet another third party. As prices based on expectation rose with the approaching spring, so the turnover of what amounted to a trade in tulip futures escalated. By early 1637, at which time the speculation in tulips was at its height, the point of the purchase had long since ceased to be the actual bulb but had instead become nothing more than a negotiable piece of paper bearing a notional delivery date. As a bill of exchange, it was open to all manner of abuse. And the closer to delivery that the deal was struck, the greater the risk of the buyer having to settle with the grower or, more enticingly, the greater the prospect of making a sizeable profit from tulip prices which continued to rise and rise.

A contemporary writer described a typical scenario. 'Oft did a nobleman purchase of a chimney sweep tulips to the amount of 2000 florins and sell them at the same time to a farmer; and neither the nobleman, chimney sweep or farmer had roots in their possession or wished to possess them. Before the tulip season was over, more roots were sold and purchased, bespoke and promised to be delivered than in all probability were to be found in the gardens of Holland; and when "Semper Augustus" was not to be had, which happened twice, no species was oftener purchased and sold.'

The extension of tulip production to include the cheaper varieties produced a surge of demand during the course of 1634 and 1635. As growers bought more and more bulbs in the hope of coming up with a valuable 'freak', so many new varieties were introduced that prices began to drop. This brought tulips within the reach of the ordinary man in the street. But then suddenly prices went through the roof as demand outstripped production. By lifting time in 1636, many varieties – even the more common ones – had at least trebled in price. An 'Admiral de Maan' tulip that had sold for 15 florins in 1634 fetched more than 175 florins two years later while a 40-florin 'Centen' saw its price soar to 350 florins. The top of the range tulips, such as an 'Admiral Liefkin', were valued at around 4400 florins while one bulb of 'Semper Augustus' sold for 4600 florins plus a new carriage and two dapple grey horses. At the height of the mania, a few bulbs of 'Semper Augustus' fetched as much as 6000 florins. To put these sums into context, farmers could buy a pig for 30 florins or an ox for 100 florins.

Although it started out as a harmless obsession, tulipmania was becoming a serious threat to the Dutch social and economic system. As mass hysteria swept the land, families made and lost fortunes in a single day. Any spare money was invested in bulbs. Normal economic and industrial activity went by the wayside as thousands embarked on a career in tulips. One man paid an incredible 100,000 florins to buy just 40 roots. Prices were getting out of control.

To accommodate the lower classes, sellers began to accept part payment in kind so that if a poor farmer had exhausted his cash supply, he could make up the difference with worldly goods – maybe his land, his farmhouse or his livestock. For one 'Viceroy' bulb, the following payment in kind was made: two loads of wheat, four loads of rye, four fat oxen, eight fat pigs, 12 fat sheep, two hogsheads of wine, four barrels of beer, two barrels of butter, 1000 lb of cheese, a bed, a suit of clothes and a silver beaker – total value 2500 florins. A quarter of a pound of 'White Crown' tulips was bought for 525 florins plus four cows; a one-pound 'Centen' went for 1800 florins and immediate transfer of 'best shot coat, one old rose noble and one coin with a silver chain to hang round a child's neck'. A 'Viceroy' that had been bought for 900 florins was resold while still planted out for 1000 florins on delivery and the immediate exchange of a suit and coat. People would sell just about anything to acquire a tulip. In 1637, the artist Jan van Goyen paid a Hague burgomaster 1900 florins for ten bulbs, promising additional payment of a picture by Salomon van Ruysdael and another painting of Judas by van Goyen himself. Four years later, he had still not delivered the painting nor discharged his debts and died insolvent.

Some extraordinary stories came to light. In one incident, a rich merchant – and leading collector of tulips – heard from a sailor that his eagerly awaited cargo had arrived at the docks. To express his gratitude for the information, the merchant invited the sailor to his counting-house and gave him a large herring to eat for his breakfast. All manner of goods were laid out on the counter, including what the sailor took to be a discarded onion. Thinking it would go nicely with the herring, he picked it up and took it away with him. Shortly afterwards, the merchant noticed to his horror that the 'Semper Augustus' tulip bulb, valued at 3000 florins, which he had left on the counter, had vanished. He searched everywhere to no avail until he suddenly remembered the sailor and assumed that he must have stolen it. A hue and cry was set up and eventually the sailor was found sitting on a pile of ropes by the quayside, resting after a hearty breakfast of herring and 'onion'. Aghast that his prize bulb had been eaten, the merchant had the sailor charged with theft and thrown in jail.

Elsewhere a syndicate of Haarlem florists heard that a shoemaker from The Hague had grown a black tulip. They arranged to call on him and make him an offer for the bulb. The amateur grower was delighted to strike a deal at 1500 florins but after the men had paid up, one of them proceeded to hurl the bulb to the ground and crush it underfoot. They told the stunned cobbler that they had a black tulip of their own and were hell-bent on eliminating all competition. They added that they would have been prepared to go up to 10,000 florins just to get him to take his tulip off the market. It is said that the poor man immediately retired to his bed where he died of shock. This shows what a cut-throat business it had become. All was fair in love and tulips.

Theft became rife. Whereas robbers had traditionally concentrated on cash, they now turned their attentions to tulips. Suddenly the *Monty Python* sketch where highwayman Dennis Moore demands 'your lupins or your life' doesn't seem so unlikely any more. Small growers went to considerable lengths to protect their investment day and night. One man in north

Holland rigged up a trip wire in his garden to which he attached an alarm bell to warn him of intruders.

By 1636, tulips were big business. Apart from the Calvinists, the only dissenting voice was Evrard Forstius, professor of botany at Leyden University, to whom the tulip was about as welcome in Holland as a high tide. The professor hated the things to such an extent that apparently he couldn't see a tulip without attacking it furiously with his stick. Regular tulip sales were held at the Stock Exchange in Amsterdam as well as at centres in towns like Rotterdam, Haarlem, Alkmaar, Hoorn and Leyden where special clubs, or Colleges as they became known, would meet in taverns at specific times. As greed overcame the snobbery that had previously been associated with tulips, speculators gambled everything in the hope of making a quick killing. The result was that those with the skill to manipulate the market grew rich at the expense of the naïve amateur investors who foolishly believed that there would always be a demand for tulips in Holland. It didn't occur to them that prices might suddenly fall again, that the market might crash.

The first alarm bells began to ring at the end of 1636 when city magistrates and growers alike became concerned at the fact that the mass speculation had been reduced to a paper gamble. The more gamblers that became involved, the more prices started to fluctuate. It reached the stage where the price for any one bulb was likely to treble in a day so the aim became to snap up paper delivery obligations and then off-load them again for a high mark-up. The speed of turnover depended on whether the punter thought his contract would continue to appreciate or whether he would be better advised to cash in quickly. It was not always easy to implement the latter course of action since many buyers made offers that were conditional on payment being delayed. This meant that sellers were, in effect, dealing with stock they did not yet possess for prices they could not realize. It really was a market for experts.

The rules of the Colleges were as complicated as those on the Stock Exchange. There were three methods of buying. The most straightforward was through Dutch auction whereby the seller started out at a high price and reduced it until a bid was made. However the commonest method of dealing was either 'through the plates' or 'through the nought'. The former involved the use of wooden discs inscribed with value units. These were circulated among the gathering and anybody receiving one was obliged to make a bid. Sellers were not permitted to offer their own goods directly but had to intimate vaguely that they would sell for a price that had been offered. When the two parties appeared to be nearing agreement, they got together and haggled in private, marking their final price in chalk on the discs. If the deal went ahead, the marks remained but if it didn't, they were removed. Whichever of the two parties backed out of the deal had to pay a small fee to the other as compensation. For the 'in the nought' method, the seller drew a design on a slate and placed a sum of money on it to act as a premium incentive to whoever happened to bid highest at the auction. These College sessions were accompanied by copious amounts of drinking. In the event of a successful sale, the buyer splashed out on drinks all round. A good time was had by all, unless it happened to lead to your losing the roof over your head.

Genuine tulip fanciers tended to steer clear of the rough-and-ready College gatherings, and as the pace of dealings intensified there and on the Stock Exchange, the major growers and professional speculators became increasingly worried that a sudden crash might leave them vulnerable. They knew that tulip prices could not go on rising indefinitely and feared being saddled with worthless stock. In early February 1837, they decided to sell in a big way. Suddenly everyone was advised to stop buying. On 4 February, tulip prices dropped like a stone. Widespread panic set in. Prices continued to fall by the hour until, by the end of the week, you could hardly give tulips away. As for tulip futures, these had become worthless as soon as the prices had started to tumble. Thousands of people – rich and poor – were facing financial ruin.

The main dealers tried to restore confidence by conducting mock auctions but these did nothing to stem the tide of discontent. Buyers began reneging on contracts they had entered into for delivery of bulbs that summer and, with the situation worsening by the day, representatives of all the major growing centres met in Amsterdam on 24 February in an effort to thrash out a solution to the crisis. The conference decided that all sales prior to November 1636 should be honoured but thereafter, any buyer who had paid 10 per cent of the asking price was given the option of withdrawing from the contract. This move was designed to protect the growers and to provide them with a certain amount of security for goods that they had already sold on paper but were waiting to deliver. However it merely served to create widespread resentment and resulted in a flood of litigation. Furthermore, the resolution could not be enforced without the agreement of the High Court of Holland and that body was far less inclined to let the growers off lightly since it considered that they were the ones responsible for starting the whole tulip craze in the first place. Accordingly in April 1637, the court elected to ignore the Amsterdam resolution and rendered null and void all deals made since the planting of 1636. The 10 per cent rule was also overruled but any grower who could not make his buyer pay up was to be allowed to sell any languishing stock to a third party for what he could get and then to recover the difference from the original purchaser. This left the growers still bearing much of the financial burden for the crash since they would not only find it difficult to attract new buyers but they had little hope of recovering sums owed to them by customers from 1636.

The growers protested their innocence, maintaining that the crash had been caused not by them but by the recklessness of the masses. With it becoming clear that tulip prices would never return to anything like their 1636 levels, those speculators who had lost heavily urged the government to take action. The government realized that no individual group was to blame for the disaster and that if the horticultural industry was to be rescued, the growers would at least have to gain some partial recompense. So from 1638 a series of commissions was set up across the country to arbitrate in contract disputes. Most sellers settled for a sale at around 5 per cent of the original contract price, not because they thought that represented a fair deal but simply because they could not afford to wait any longer.

The effects of tulipmania were far reaching. Countless professional growers had seen their livelihoods destroyed while the amateur gamblers had gone from rags to riches and back to rags again. But it wasn't always a case of returning to the status quo since the maelstrom of hysteria and greed in which they had allowed themselves to be caught up had, in many cases, swept away their savings and even their homes. The poverty that followed the crash was far worse than anything that had gone before. To the people of the Netherlands, the tulip boom had offered a get-rich-quick scheme beyond their wildest dreams. It gave them a chance to dabble in the stock market. It seemed wildly exciting and a sure-fire winner. But these amateurs were way out of their depth and made the gambler's biggest mistake of betting more than they could afford to lose. Those who had over-extended themselves were left with nothing.

Individuals were not the only ones to suffer. For the two

years when the mania was in full flow, Dutch trade had fallen away badly. Farming and industry had declined, allowing other countries (particularly the English) to snatch foreign markets . . . and all because the Dutch were busy with their tulips. It took the nation many years to recover these losses. No wonder the government was anxious to make sure that nothing like tulipmania ever happened again.

The Commonwealth Sentinel: A Short Story

Billed as 'Britain's most fearless newspaper', the *Commonwealth Sentinel* rolled off the presses in London for the first and last time on 6 February 1965. The paper was the brainchild of one Lionel Burleigh who boldly predicted that it would appeal to citizens throughout the Commonwealth. He was convinced that, at 1s a copy, the capital's Australian, New Zealand and Canadian residents would snap it up, along with the British themselves. So after carefully selling advertisements and compiling suitable stories, Burleigh sat back and waited for the money to come pouring in.

Alas, his hopes were dashed by a telephone call from the police wanting to know what 50,000 copies of the *Commonwealth Sentinel* were doing blocking the Albemarle Street entrance to Brown's Hotel.

'We had forgotten to arrange any distribution,' lamented Burleigh, 'and they were just dumped outside the hotel where I was staying.' The entire experience proved so traumatic and expensive that he instantly scrapped plans for any further editions. Only one copy of the *Commonwealth Sentinel* was ever sold – by Burleigh's daughter to an unsuspecting passerby. A true collector's item!

The Osborne Computer Corporation:
A Rapid Fall from Grace

Adam Osborne was one of the new breed of dynamic computer buffs of the 1980s. Plugging into the growth market of portable computers, he launched his business in 1981 amid a fanfare of publicity. At first, it seemed he could do no wrong. Profits were reported to be phenomenally high; everyone wanted to jump on the gravy train. Then just as quickly as his star had risen, so it fell. Rumours suddenly started to circulate that the company was in trouble and in September 1983, Osborne Computers crashed. Rather like the Dutch tulip buyers of the 1630s, Adam Osborne's fortunes had swung full circle in just over two years.

Born in Thailand, the son of a British professor, Osborne was educated at Catholic schools in India. His later schooling took place in Britain and in 1961, at the age of twenty-two, he moved to the United States. After obtaining a Ph.D in chemical engineering at the University of Delaware, he joined the Shell Development Company in California but soon tired of the endless bureaucracy so readily associated with big business. He saw himself as more of a free spirit and, growing ever more interested in computers, set up his own computer consulting company in 1970. At that time the computer industry was dominated by IBM who boasted 70 per cent of the market, leaving the smaller firms to scrap for the leftovers. Like IBM itself most of the computers on the market tended to be large and expensive. But new technology was being developed all the time and as micro-electronics became more advanced, computer parts became smaller. In 1974, the first mini-computer appeared and proved an instant hit, both with small businesses and enthusiastic amateurs.

The following year saw the birth of the personal computer.

Among the pioneers was Apple, co-founded by former college dropout Steven Jobs in 1976 in a family garage with capital of $1300. By 1982, sales were running at $583 million and Jobs was one of the richest men in America. Adam Osborne embraced the personal computer philosophy with tremendous zeal but angered many in the industry with his outspoken comments about overpricing. In particular, he denounced the companies for increasing prices with every new feature – no matter how small. To firms raised on the profit ethos, this was a red rag to a bull. Osborne's mouthpiece was initially his computer column in the magazine *Interface Age* but then he put his thoughts into a book, *Introduction to Microcomputers*. When it was turned down by mainstream publishers, Osborne went ahead and published the book himself, selling 300,000 copies into the bargain. By 1975, his company had produced around 40 books on microcomputers, over a quarter of which had been written by Osborne himself. Business was so good that in 1979 he sold out to the publishing house of McGraw-Hill who had happily recovered from the fiasco of the fake Howard Hughes autobiography. Thus Osborne found himself in a position to put his money where his mouth was.

The industry still viewed him as a brash upstart and so when, in early 1981, he announced plans to manufacture and market a new low-priced personal computer, a lot of people scoffed at him. They thought he was all talk.

Osborne spotted a gap in the portable computer market and hired an expert to design a powerful model that weighed just 24 lb and was sufficiently compact to be placed into a briefcase capable of fitting under an airline seat. It was ideal for businessmen who travelled a lot – it was, in effect, the first portable business computer. With characteristic reticence, Osborne declared: 'I saw a truck-size hole in the industry, and I plugged it.'

Not only was the Osborne I, as it was known, more

sophisticated than its portable predecessors but, at $1795, it was also considerably cheaper – about half the price of an Apple. Osborne was able to fulfil his promise of low prices by keeping overheads to a minimum. He didn't believe in plush offices for his senior management, preferring to install them in spartan warehouses. He managed to reduce his software costs by not employing any programmers. Whereas other personal computer manufacturers operated with in-house programmers, Osborne chose to rely on independent software companies to provide programs for him. As a further cutback, he offered some of his software suppliers shares in the company. As a result of these savings, he was able to provide nearly $1500 worth of software packages as part of the overall price of the Osborne I.

Although Osborne himself subsequently stated that this first product had 'no technology of consequence', it took the computer world by storm. By the end of 1981, sales had reached the $10 million figure – a remarkable achievement bearing in mind that the Osborne I hadn't even been ready for distribution until July of that year. Sales were helped by Osborne's natural flair for showmanship. He was a born entrepreneur in the Richard Branson mould, someone who could spot a publicity opportunity a mile off. He certainly stole the show at the 1981 West Coast Computer Fair in San Francisco. Whereas the other computer companies opted for traditional, staid stands, Osborne splashed out on a giant see-through tower topped with his company logo, the Flying O. It dwarfed the competition.

Osborne believed in saturation distribution – he wanted to see his product in as many retail outlets as possible. Unlike most other computer company chiefs, he didn't want to restrict sales to specialist shops but looked towards department stores like Macy's and basically any retailer who was interested. By 1982 he had signed a deal with Computerland

Corporation, America's largest computer retailer, which had the immediate effect of doubling the number of outlets stocking the Osborne computer. The policy worked and by the end of that year, after just 18 months of operation, sales had topped $100 million. For 1983, almost 1000 retail outlets were selling Osborne portables which had now captured some 85 per cent of the market share. He had every business covered – large and small. He had brought computers to the mass market. Everyone wanted to know the secret of his success and Osborne was only too happy to tell them – just as he had always been. Analysts predicted that the majority of his management team would be millionaires by the time they were forty or even thirty and the company was able to dispense with the penny-pinching approach that had marked its arrival on the scene. Money was no problem – it just kept rolling in. All at the Osborne Computer Corporation were swept along on this tidal wave of euphoria.

There is an old adage that pride comes before a fall and so it was to prove here. But as 1983 began, with Osborne computers at the head of the market, everything seemed rosy. And Osborne himself continued to make all the right moves. The company now had in the region of 800 employees. The little acorn had grown into a mighty oak and was in danger of becoming the sort of big business with which Osborne had felt so uncomfortable. He conceded that his strength was as an entrepreneur, rather than as a businessman and, at the urging of investors who were keen to ensure that the company was run on a professional footing, he agreed to move upstairs to chairman and bring in an outsider to control the day-to-day running of the firm. The man brought in as president and chief executive officer was Robert Jaunich II, formerly president of Consolidated Foods. Over the coming weeks, Jaunich elevated a number of the Osborne 'old guard', allowing himself room to introduce his own team into key roles. Jaunich had no intention of making any great changes to the distribution network – a key element in the company's soaraway success – but merely sought to improve it. Additional avenues were explored such as the news service United Press International (UPI) which boasted 1000 subscriber newspapers. The Osborne Corporation planned to sell portables to each and every newspaper on the list as personal workstations. And with the new sales team also looking at hotel chains and airlines, the sky seemed the limit for the fledgling firm.

The trouble with success – particularly overnight success – is that it makes the competition all the more determined to retake the high ground. It also captures the imagination of companies operating in other branches of the same industry. Other firms could hardly help but note the rise of the Osborne Corporation and set about playing it at its own game. The outcome was that Osborne faced fresh challenges on two fronts – from existing competition hell-bent on undercutting Osborne's prices and from computer firms new to the seemingly lucrative market of portable machines. It was a challenge not to be underestimated.

Computer technology was moving at a frightening pace in the early 1980s. Almost every year brought some startling innovation with the result that last year's model quickly proved obsolete. Companies had to move quickly to stay ahead of the game, something which, as we have seen, even an experienced outfit such as IBM found difficult on occasions. With a stream of competitors beginning to make their mark in the field of portables by virtue of producing cheaper and more advanced machines than the Osborne I, the Osborne Corporation set about updating its merchandise. A new, even cheaper version of the Osborne I – the Vixen – was mooted, along with an Executive series. The Executive I was unveiled in the spring of 1983 with the Executive 2 scheduled for late summer. Both offered greater storage capacity and bigger screens than the Osborne I. The Executive I was to be priced at $2495 (with some $2000 worth of software) while the IBM-compatible Executive 2 ran out at $3195.

Both seemed sure-fire winners and the company confidently predicted that sales of their various computers would top $300 million for 1983. To keep pace with this ambitious projection, the sales force was expanded and advertising was stepped up. The eight-strong sales force was augmented by another 30 or 40 specialist staff, allowing them to target specific areas such as point-of-sale displays and direct mail campaigns. A total of $3.5 million had been spent on TV, newspaper and magazine advertising in 1982 and this figure was to be increased for 1983 with campaigns concentrating on differentiating between the various Osborne products. If a company wanted to stay up amongst the big boys, it had to spend in a big way.

But although nobody at Osborne realized it at the time, the company didn't have that kind of money to spend. The first hint of trouble occurred towards the end of March 1983 when the previous month's results came through. With a record number of shipments, all supposedly with high profit margins, February had been expected to be another bumper month for America's fastest-growing computer company. Projections had indicated profits of around $750,000 for the month with plenty more to come, so it came as a nasty shock to Osborne executives when the figures revealed that, instead of making another nice fat profit, the company had lost over $600,000 in February. The loss was attributed to heavy promotional spending and the cost of new facilities. Hopes that it was merely a temporary blip were shattered with figures that revealed a loss of $1.5 million for the fiscal year – despite sales of over $100 million.

The news couldn't have come at a worse time. On 29 April, the Osborne Corporation was planning to go public. The world's statesmen had been badgering Adam Osborne for stock in his company and this was to be their opportunity. It was estimated that the flotation would raise in the region of $50 million and would make Osborne and his top brass extremely wealthy. So the last thing the company needed on the run-up to the flotation was a set of disastrous figures which would raise serious doubts as to the company's potential.

As gloom and despondency engulfed the company, the news grew progressively worse. On 21 April, Robert Jaunich learned that the previous figures were an underestimate. The $1.5 million loss related to February alone while the deficit for the full year came to a frightening $4 million. The principal cause appeared to be massive inventories of old stock which the company did not even realize it had. While questions were being asked about internal efficiency – or rather, its absence – Jaunich pondered what course of action to take regarding the stock flotation. He decided to sit tight and hope that the company could ride the storm. If confidence could be retained, perhaps the flotation could still be a success.

Those slender hopes were finally dashed three days later when Jaunich was informed that the losses would be greater still – $5 million for the quarter and $8 million for the year. Again the inventory was at the root of the problems, allied to a number of unrecorded liabilities and some bad debts. That day – 24 April – Jaunich decided to scrap the flotation. Who would want to buy into a young company that had predicted massive profits but was suddenly announcing huge losses? The Osborne Corporation was no longer an attractive proposition.

When the final report was published, the year's losses amounted to over $12 million. Osborne himself was shocked almost beyond words at his company's plight. As the heavy losses continued through the spring and summer, Osborne tried to steady the ship. All the investors who had previously been so keen to have a piece of the Osborne cake were suddenly on a diet, but Osborne was able to use his personal magnetism to wring out $11 million of vital funding in June. But the financial state was so perilous that $11 million was just the tip of the iceberg. The company calculated that it needed an additional $20 million to launch a competitive new product on to the market and that was not forthcoming. The outlook was bleak.

On 13 September the Osborne Corporation filed for protection from creditor lawsuits under Chapter 11 of the Federal Bankruptcy Code after three creditors had filed lawsuits claiming that Osborne owed them $4.7 million. Osborne's petition stated that it owed secured and unsecured creditors around $45 million but had assets of just $40 million. The news of the filing shocked the industry and three days later, there was another shock – this time for the company's workforce. From the moment in the spring of 1983 when it first became apparent that problems lay ahead, staff cuts were instigated. In the course of the summer numbers were reduced by over a half until by September there were only around 400 on the payroll. On Friday, 16 September, 300 of those employees were made redundant with immediate effect. Handed their final wages, they were given just two hours to empty their desks. The company had all but closed down.

Chapter 11 of the Federal Bankruptcy Code protects a company from creditors while it is trying to work out ways of paying off its debts. It also allows a company to continue operating, and by the end of 1984 the company was rising from the ashes. However it did so without Adam Osborne who had left the company and had turned his attentions to marketing software. He also wrote and published a book, *Hypergrowth: The Rise and Fall of the Osborne Computer Corporation*, in which he attacked Robert Jaunich.

But who was really to blame for the fall from grace of the Osborne Corporation? Much of the fault would appear to lie with the original composition of the company. It started out as a small firm with big ideas. Right down to the cold, grubby offices, it was almost an amateurish concern. And it didn't have the authoritative, experienced leadership that was needed from the top. On his own admission, Adam Osborne was not a businessman. 'I had no professional training whatsoever in finance or business management,' he said. He didn't care much for big business and had never managed more than 50 people in his life yet as the company blossomed overnight, he found himself in charge of nigh on 1000. It is said that he didn't believe in forward planning and preferred to deal with problems as and when they cropped up. The day-to-day affairs of running a business – monitoring staff, dealing with paperwork – simply didn't interest him that much. He was far happier in his role as an entrepreneur, a showman, someone who made things happen. He liked to leave the boring stuff to somebody else. But the problem in those formative years of the company was that there was nobody else. And by the time Osborne was persuaded to relinquish the reins and hand over to a professional manager – Robert Jaunich – it was too late. The damage had already been done.

To be brutally frank, in its early years the Osborne Corporation was poorly run. There was an appalling lack of controls with no efficient method established to oversee inventories of finished products. The result was that managers had no idea how much stock they had or how much they were spending, or needed to spend. And for a company specializing in information communication, this was a commodity sorely lacking. A total lack of financial expertise in key areas led to predicted profits turning out to be vast losses. With so much misinformation coming out of the company, confidence in its ability to continue its success story plummeted rapidly. To add to the catalogue of ineptitude, liabilities went unrecorded and bills had a habit of going astray before reaching the accounts department. The system bordered on the shambolic. And when plans were made to open an expensive new European HQ on Lake Geneva in Switzerland, insufficient capital was set aside for the project.

Another factor that contributed to the crash was the sheer speed at which the company was transformed from a small-time operator into one of the leaders in its field. At such a rate of expansion, even the most experienced managers can have difficulty keeping track of events so some of the big-business novices at Osborne naturally found it difficult to cope with the transition. And as money appeared to be flooding in from all angles, the lack of controls allowed expenses to soar. The frugal attitude of Osborne's early days was replaced by a policy of spend, spend, spend. All of a sudden the company acquired the trappings of success, complete with plush offices. When Jaunich took control, he tried to curb some of the excesses but by then the die was cast.

Osborne himself blundered by announcing the new model, the Executive, too soon. The Executive was not intended to be in competition with the Osborne I but when Osborne unveiled the newcomer in April 1983, a number of dealers immediately cancelled their orders for the Osborne I. Since there was no plan to phase out the Osborne I at that stage, this resulted in further inventory write-offs. To make matters worse, the Executive was delayed and was not ready for distribution until May. With orders for the Osborne I being cancelled left, right and centre and the Executive failing to meet its deadline, sales ground to a standstill in April – at a time when company cash flow had already been reduced to a trickle.

The company was also too slow in reacting to market changes. With other firms such as Compaq introducing even cheaper portables with just as much software, the Osborne I suddenly faced stiff competition. And when IBM introduced its trail-blazing personal computer towards the end of 1981,

Osborne was too slow in producing a compatible model. Other companies rushed out computers that were IBM-compatible but Osborne dragged its heels. The result was that the technologically inferior Osborne I was soon out of date, a situation reflected in falling sales. And the planned successor to the Osborne I, the Vixen, proved a disaster. A poorly designed circuit board caused production delays and in the end the Vixen was scrapped in favour of the Executive line.

Osborne was not the only computer company in crisis during that period. With over 150 firms producing microcomputers, the market was severely overloaded. Only the strongest would survive. But Osborne's internal failings meant that it faced an uphill struggle. Those early dreams had been replaced by harsh reality.

The Groundnut Scheme: An African Adventure

For centuries the British had taken it upon themselves to colonize uncivilized foreign lands and teach the locals the rudiments of industry and social etiquette. But they met their match in Africa in the late 1940s when a scheme to convert barren soil into fertile fields capable of producing a mighty groundnut harvest fell flat on its face. From start to finish, the episode was an unmitigated disaster – one that left the British government with egg on its face, a bill for over £50 million and a few sackloads of groundnuts.

The idea was born out of the wholesale rationing that afflicted Britain in the immediate post-war years. Although bananas reappeared in Britain in February 1946 for the first time in seven years, a world food shortage – mainly caused by the need to feed 30 million Germans for whom famine was looming in the wake of the destruction of their agricultural industry – brought about the return of war-time rationing.

The wheat content in bread was reduced to 1942 levels and the butter, margarine and cooking fat ration was cut from 8 oz a week to 7. To alleviate shortages in all areas, the ever-helpful Ministry of Food issued a recipe for squirrel pie and women were implored to wear shorter skirts to save cloth.

These were desperate days for the British housewife. Not only did the order for shorter skirts follow hard on the heels of the coldest winter in living memory but among items imported to pep up the family diet was an unsavoury South African fish called snoek. Edible fish are rarely noted for their beauty but the blue snoek was so hideous that its picture on the can completely put people off either buying it or eating it. The British weren't that desperate.

But amidst all the doom and gloom came a ray of hope in the unlikely shape of the groundnut, also known as the monkey nut or, more commonly, the peanut. The groundnut is a versatile chap. When crushed, it provides oil for margarine as well as a basis for cattle feed and therefore a source of butter. At a time when there was such a chronic shortage of fat, the groundnut seemed the answer to everyone's prayers.

The people at Unilever certainly thought so. The company dealt with millions of tons of fats and oils each year and produced two of the leading corner-shop margarines – Stork and Blue Band. Unilever was always looking for new areas in which to grow groundnuts and when Frank Samuel, head of the United Africa company – a Unilever subsidiary – reported back that he had found the perfect spot in Tanganyika, excitement was running high. Samuel's idea was to develop a whole area of arid scrubland into a major groundnut plantation. There appeared to be no obstacles to success.

Britain's Labour government adopted the plan with equal enthusiasm. It appealed to them on two fronts: it would provide a much-needed source of additional oil and fat for the beleaguered British public and it would earn the government Brownie points by bringing employment and therefore wealth to an underprivileged corner of East Africa. It fitted in nicely with the government's socialist principles. Thus in April 1946, the government sent a special mission to investigate the feasibility of the Tanganyika site. It was led by John Wakefield whose report on his findings could scarcely have been more positive. For an outlay of a mere £24 million, three and a quarter million acres of Tanganyika wilderness were to be tamed and the land cleared in readiness for the great harvest which was expected to yield 600,000 tons of groundnuts, enough to keep everybody happy. It didn't take long for the groundnut scheme to win the approval of the new Minister of Food, John Strachey.

The Wakefield Report was a noble document, but one almost totally devoid of realism. It spoke with tremendous fervour about how the scheme would provide jobs for the poor and food for the hungry but it completely overlooked any associated problems. The theory was fine but the practical side had barely been considered. It was all very well to announce that thousands of acres of African scrubland would be cleared – he hoped to clear the first 150,000 acres by the end of 1947 – but little thought appeared to have been given to precisely how this was to be achieved. Tanganyika was a backward nation with only 3 per cent of the country under cultivation. Its people were not versed in modern agricultural methods – most had probably never seen a tractor in their lives – yet Wakefield was expecting them to be able to repair and drive expensive machinery. Even assuming that the people could be trained, where were the facilities for undertaking such tasks? Of course, there was no suitable machinery in Tanganyika but importing tractors and bulldozers was similarly fraught with problems. The main port of Dar es Salaam was hopelessly ill-equipped to handle giant freighters while the road and rail network linking the capital with the site was all but non-existent. Wakefield had made the mistake of confusing Africa with Britain. Such a scheme might have been practical in this country but in an undeveloped land it was quite impossible. And for everything to be up and running within the anticipated time scale would have required some kind of overnight industrial revolution. It had taken Africa centuries to reach even that level of technical sophistication. To expect its people to be able to embrace new ideas at the drop of a hat just because a few Brits had turned up on their doorstep represented the height of folly. Perhaps if Wakefield's mission had been granted the services of an engineer, some of the impracticalities could have been pointed out before it was too late. But in their haste to be seen to be doing some good, Wakefield and the British government ignored any potential pitfalls and rushed headlong into an economic abyss. The groundnut scheme may have been soundly conceived but it was ill prepared.

Yet there was no shortage of willing disciples. Over 100,000 men – many of them British soldiers struggling to adapt to civvy street – volunteered their services to the so-called Groundnut Army, although only 2000 were actually needed. After the drudgery of life at home, this seemed the ultimate African adventure. They descended on Tanganyika in their droves and headed for the first clearing site at Kongwa. If they had known that Kongwa was native for 'to be deceived', they might have turned round and gone home but, as with so much of the groundnut affair, ignorance was bliss.

Meanwhile, the British government had finally been giving some consideration as to what sort of equipment might be needed to clear the African bush. There were bound to be plenty of heavy-duty tractors knocking around at home, they thought. But British farmers no longer needed machinery to cut swathes through the countryside. The cupboard was bare. So the government turned to the United States in the hope that they would have tractors to spare. They didn't. Just as things were beginning to look a touch ominous, Canada came up trumps. And then, joy of joys, a squadron of abandoned US Army tractors was found in the Philippines. There were 200 of these monsters and, because they were about to be converted into scrap, they were available on the cheap. If there was one thing the British government liked in such times of austerity, it was a bargain.

Having located the necessary equipment, there remained the small problem of transporting it to the site. Wakefield's recce had singularly failed to draw attention to the abysmal lack of transport in the Central province of Tanganyika where Kongwa was situated. Roads were no more than bumpy tracks with a tendency to disappear into marshland, while the only railway transport came courtesy of a wood-burning engine that chugged along on a single track. Things were no better at Dar es Salaam where, because there were no deep-water berths to cater for the machinery-laden freighters arriving at the docks, the heavy equipment had to be brought ashore in stages using lighters. The planning, such as there was, quickly fell behind schedule. And all the while the machinery and goods that were unloaded from the ships were left piling up on the quayside, in no particular order. There was everything from generators to tinned food, light bulbs to second-hand army surplus trousers. The scene resembled the world's biggest car boot sale. Chaos reigned supreme. But when the British upper lip was at its stiffest, it took more than a few minor inconveniences to cause heads to drop.

It was just as well that the British were so indomitable because when they were finally ready to ferry the equipment inland, the solitary railway line was washed away by the Kinyasungwe River bursting its banks. With the railway out of action, they had no option but to take the tractors and bulldozers along the rickety road. It was an arduous journey, made more interesting by the fact that the route took them across the crocodile-infested Ruvu River. The only way to cross the river was by ferry but that promptly sank. Gamely they fought off the attentions of elephants, lions and baboons while pondering their next move. While the tractors were driven by road to Kongwa, a makeshift railway was built to transport the mighty bulldozers. But the blades were too wide for the railway cuttings, making progress painfully slow. Whenever the bulldozer blades got stuck, the African workers had to race ahead and widen the cuttings. The entire transportation operation was a nightmare.

In the meantime, the rest of the army arrived at Sagara, some 14 miles from Kongwa. Theirs too was an eventful journey. Their African workers had gone on strike for more pay, leaving them with just one cook, and their bodies were feeding the entire mosquito population of Africa. At Sagara, they were greeted by George Nestlé, a great white hunter resplendent in a python-skin belt and with a leopard-skin band around his hat. His belly hung out over his shorts to such an extent that he appeared likely to topple over at any minute and his moustache was almost as bushy as the Tanganyika jungle. But no beauty queen ever looked better to these weary pioneers since he was able to feed them with eggs, ham, sausages and copious amounts of Bristol Cream sherry – a luxurious feast for people in the grips of rationing. One of the party bore the grand title of soil-tester although his equipment consisted of nothing more technically advanced than some sort of tea-strainer contraption and a few pieces of litmus paper. It came straight from the world of Heath Robinson. Bearing in mind that so much time, money and manpower had already been invested in the project, it might have been prudent to have tested whether the soil around Kongwa was suitable for growing groundnuts at a considerably earlier stage. But regardless of such trifling considerations, the tester plunged his apparatus into the ground and declared that the soil was perfectly adequate. Quite how he reached this conclusion remains a mystery since the soil at Kongwa was in fact heavy clay. So in hot, dry weather – of which there was an abundance – it became rock-hard, breaking rakes and ploughs that were applied to it. The result was to render the harvesting of groundnuts almost impossible.

The original idea had been to establish permanent base camp at Sagara, which had the advantage of a nearby waterfall to provide running water. However, it was a place used by the locals to water their livestock and Nestlé feared that the Africans would be none too happy about sharing the facilities. So it was decided to move to a new site, still seven miles from Kongwa but with no running water. This was not a clever move.

The procession of jeeps left Sagara and headed off towards Kongwa. A couple of vehicles finished up in a marsh but somehow everyone made it safely to the site. Most of the 2000 or so British thought they had done the hard part just by getting that far. After all, many of them had survived the North Africa campaign so peacetime Tanganyika was thought to hold few terrors. If they could cope with enemy fire, they could certainly cope with planting a few groundnuts.

Farming in Britain may have looked a straightforward matter but farming in Tanganyika was altogether different. The scrubland was described as so dense as to be impenetrable to anything other than a rhinoceros or a snake. With the arrival of the bulldozers delayed, all hope rested on the tractors. The consignment of 200 from the Philippines was scheduled to arrive in February 1947 but none of them materialized. The bitterly cold British winter had meant that the ships due to ferry the tractors out to Africa had been frozen in harbour. It was not until April that the first batch arrived – and even then there were only 16. The rest limped along to Kongwa in August, two-thirds of them breaking down on arrival or immediately afterwards. Nobody possessed the foresight to consider that the tractors might have needed overhauling. By the end of the year, every one had broken down. Another organizational masterstroke!

The few tractors that were operational were fitted with bulldozer blades in a bid to clear the land. This ploy was reasonably successful until the machine encountered a baobab tree. Some of these were over 20 ft in diameter but, more significantly, the hollow trunks were used by the Africans as a burial place – especially for those who had died from infectious diseases. One tractor attacked a baobab, only to discover that it was housing two natives. That particular tree apparently served as the local jail. On another occasion, a tractor dislodged a human skull from a baobab and the army manager was forced to calm a threatened uprising by the natives who were furious that the spirits of their ancestors had been insulted.

On top of that, there were countless natural hazards which the boffins in London had failed to recognize. There were swarms of killer bees, many of which inhabited the baobabs and exacted revenge for the loss of their home by attacking the tractor drivers. There were six-inch scorpions, tsetse flies and rhinoceroses that delighted in charging the tractors. Smallpox was rife and much of the drinking water was of poor quality – more conducive to diarrhoea than thirst-quenching. For good measure, work was often brought to a halt by herds of drinking elephants who would lumber to their water-hole just when the groundnut army wanted to press on. Up to 13 hours at a time was lost to this ritual. But nobody in London had thought about elephants and rhinoceroses. You don't get too many of those in Godalming.

Supplementing the British workers were in the region of 30,000 Africans, some of whom were given the tasks of driving or repairing the tractors. With no experience in either field, they ended up wrecking the tractors quickly and repairing them slowly. Determined to adhere to its socialist principles at all costs, the British government decided that the African workers should be organized into trade unions. Two trade unionists were sent over from Britain to ensure that the correct procedural channels were followed. Their impact was immediate. Within days of their arrival, the workers at Kongwa had come out on strike, demanding more pay and better food!

The workers were duly given a pay rise but this also caused prices to go up. Suddenly villagers were no longer able to afford essentials such as milk and eggs with the result that malnutrition became widespread and the death of children commonplace. It is symbolic of the failure of the groundnut scheme that many of the African workers themselves began to starve. The majority had left their farms to join the British, but the promise of riches had quickly turned sour. Due to the incompetence of Whitehall, the scheme did not even produce enough groundnuts to feed its own workers, never mind the world's hungry millions.

It was clear by the summer of 1947 that Wakefield's targets were ridiculously optimistic. Of the 150,000 acres that were supposed to be cleared by the end of the year, a mere 1000 had been tackled by June. And the dearth of effective machinery plus the concrete-like soil, baked by the relentless sun, ensured that progress would remain desperately slow. But nobody connected with the project was prepared to admit failure just yet and, in a move that somehow typified the crazy planning behind the entire operation, Wakefield came up with the idea of converting tanks into tractors. There was a precedent of sorts – tanks had undertaken clearance work in Normandy in 1944 – and so the order went out for the Vickers Armstrong company to convert Sherman tanks into giant tractors. The result was a half-tank, half-tractor known as a 'Shervick'. Repeating the headless chicken act that had characterized its involvement from day one, the British government immediately ordered 580 'Shervicks' without for one moment thinking about sending a couple out to Africa for advance trials. Rarely was the proverb 'fools rush in' more appropriate. On arrival in Tanganyika, the 'Shervicks' were found to be unsuitable for handling the African terrain and had to be modified before they could set to work. Even then, they didn't last long. One by one they broke down and were eventually left to rust.

The African climate continued to play havoc. If it wasn't the heat, it was torrential downpours of rain. It was during one such cloudburst that it was discovered that the stores and workshops at Kongwa had been built on the bed of an old lake. As the heavens opened, the tents and shanty buildings were simply washed away.

By the end of 1947, just 7500 acres had been cleared – one twentieth of the target figure. So the goal for the following year was lowered dramatically, to 60,000 acres. It was still hopelessly out of reach.

In February 1948, the newly formed Overseas Food Corporation despatched a new man to the front line – Major-General Desmond Harrison. He immediately set about putting the operation on more of a military footing but he was fighting a losing battle. There was a brief flurry of activity when a new method of chain-clearing made it possible to shift 40 acres a day. Two tractors pulling the ends of a 160 ft-long chain were able to rip up trees and bushes at will but that didn't solve the problem of how to dig the unyielding soil in readiness for sowing seed. And even on the rare occasions that conditions combined favourably to produce a groundnut harvest, the yield per acre was well short of Wakefield's original prediction.

Endeavouring to combat the problems with the soil, General Harrison decreed that operations should be restricted to the period immediately before or during the rainy season. This, of course, served to halve production which was the last thing Britain's housewives wanted to hear. After all, from the outset they had been promised 'more margarine, cooking-fats and soap in the reasonably near future'. Two years on and there was precious little to show for these words of optimism.

With Harrison sinking in a sea of paperwork – the burden of administration grew to the point where he had to reply to 104 items of correspondence from Britain during one two-week period – he was ordered home on sick leave towards the end of 1948. Civil unrest had already been stirred up around Kongwa as crime, drunkenness and prostitution became serious social problems. The European settlement had disrupted the fabric of African life. Then in 1949 came the drought. Hardly any groundnuts could be harvested and the villagers began to starve. Back in London, Food Minister Strachey was keeping his head buried firmly in the sand. He boasted to Parliament about his 'hard-headed' business approach and, while admitting that costs had escalated, still referred vaguely to 'a really large acreage running into millions'. When the Conservative opposition ridiculed his comments, government ministers rounded on them and accused them of trying to turn a worthy cause into a music-hall joke. Whatever could have given them that idea?

Strachey was deluding himself and the British public. The bleak truth was the rising cost of the project, which had more than doubled to over £50 million. But the total harvest was a mere 2000 tons of groundnuts – one three-hundredth of the target. The groundnut army had consumed more food than it ever produced. The government finally put the groundnut scheme out of its misery in January 1951 by which time it had done more harm than good. Britain's fat shortage had not been solved nor the African economy improved. Indeed, because so many Africans had abandoned their farms to work on such a fruitless project, local food supplies were actually reduced, causing considerable hardship. Among the scheme's expensive white elephants were a sawmill at Noli, 20 miles west of Kongwa, built at a cost of £1 million and a 100-mile oil line constructed to link the clearing site to the coast. The oil line did its job by filling fuel tanks to keep the machinery going but, with the project cancelled, it lay idle. One reason why it could not be used was that to transport fuel by that method would take away vital business from the equally expensive railway. Not for the first time, the government had succeeded in cutting its own throat.

There was general relief at the termination of the East African operation. *The Times* referred to 'the unhappy business of winding up the results of past mismanagement and folly'. As an exercise in foreign aid, the groundnut scheme is best forgotten; as an exercise in incompetence, it will long be remembered. Quite simply, it was in a league of its own.

Laker Airways: Freddie Takes a Pounding

Freddie Laker was the people's champion, the most popular businessman in Britain in the 1970s. Although his success brought him considerable wealth, the head of Laker Airways liked to see himself as the ordinary man in the street – to emphasize the point, he affectionately nicknamed his airline 'Fredair'. In business, the public saw him as the gallant little underdog who, in his battle to lower air fares, took on the greedy big boys and won. His rivals saw him as a pain in the backside and a threat to their livelihoods. His ongoing fight against companies and governments appealed to the British sense of fair play and he typified the nation's bulldog spirit. Nothing would sway him from his goal. He seemed so invincible that when Laker Airways suddenly crashed to earth in

1982 the news came as a bolt from the blue. The British people had lost a friend.

Freddie Laker was born in the cathedral city of Canterbury, Kent, in 1922. 'Being broke's nothing,' he said later, once again underlining his ordinariness, his working-class roots. 'I was broke when I was born. My father left us when I was five and my mother did everything for me. We knew all about the two-up and two-down, and the loo and the copper in the backyard, and bed bugs and no lino, let alone carpets. And we knew all about hard work.' As a teenager, he would gaze in awe at the sight of the Hindenburg airship and the Handley Page biplane flying over Kent and resolved to pursue a career in aviation. During the war he served with the Air Transport Auxiliary and afterwards, armed with his RAF payoff of £40 and with capital of just £240, he set up his own company to deal in aircraft spares. His big break came in 1948 when BOAC (British Overseas Airways Corporation) offered him 12 Halton aircraft – civilian versions of the Halifax bomber. In June of that year, the Russians imposed a blockade on Berlin in an attempt to force the Allies to withdraw from the city and surrender it to the eastern bloc. The Allies responded by organizing a massive airlift to drop food and other supplies to the beleaguered troops in Berlin. The airlifts went on for several months and, with planes at a premium, Laker's company, Aviation Traders, made a fortune by supplying his BOAC planes to the Air Ministry. In total, Laker's planes flew 2,577 round trips to Berlin.

The money he made from the Berlin airlift set Laker up nicely and enabled him to buy his first Rolls-Royce before he was thirty. He sold his business in 1958 and played a key role in a new company, British United Airways, becoming managing director. He turned BUA into Britain's largest independent carrier but in 1965 he fell out with chairman Miles Wyatt and left to embark on another solo venture. The following year, he launched Laker Airways with share capital of £211,500 held by himself and his then wife Joan, plus £4 million in loans. He unveiled Laker Airways as 'contract carrier to the package-holiday trade' and 'a personalized airline. I will make possible cheaper and longer holidays by efficiency and speedier travel.' It was very much a shoestring operation, starting out with second-hand furniture, a rented hangar and three second-hand BAC One-Eleven aircraft, each capable of carrying 75 passengers. 'This is Fredair,' he used to tell people. 'If we get any bigger than six planes, you can kick my arse!'

By now, Laker was a rich man: he owned a 1000-acre farm, a yacht and a stud with a string of racehorses. The Laker aircraft flew in his racing colours of red and black with the name Laker in surprisingly small letters on the tailplane. It was an era when the British holidaymaker was starting to become more adventurous. Gone were the days of the fifties when the average British family went no further than a holiday camp or a seaside resort and the thought of going abroad was only marginally more likely than flying to the moon. By the mid-sixties, new horizons were opening up of sun, sea and sangria which sounded more appealing than the traditional British fare of rain, wind and Watneys. Foreign travel was still relatively expensive but package holidays helped reduce the cost and make a fortnight in Majorca more affordable. Laker aimed to cash in on this growing market.

Although he concentrated on charter holiday flights at first, Laker saw the opportunity to expand the cheap flights policy to broader markets. As the world continued to shrink, transatlantic air routes caught his eye, not only for Britons wanting to visit the fashionable Florida resorts but also for businessmen with work commitments in the United States. 'We want to open up the market for the forgotten man,' he said.

Laker thought that air travel was too expensive and too

inflexible for the modern traveller. He aimed to cut fares and red tape in unison. He envisaged a transatlantic air service that operated like a train – low fares and no advance bookings. Passengers would simply walk on. By offering a basic, no-frills service and by keeping his overheads to a minimum, he reckoned he could cut fares to the United States from over £300 to less than £100. It was a revolutionary idea but one that Laker was convinced would work. There was a gap in the market, he insisted, that other airlines had failed to spot, adding: 'There is an appalling lack of top-class management in British aviation.' Such comments were not guaranteed to win him any friends among his competitors. But Laker didn't care – the only friend he wanted was Joe Public. Laker decided to call his new venture 'Skytrain' and in 1971 applied to the Air Transport Licensing Board for permission to operate. He was turned down.

Laker appealed and, although the appeal was upheld, it was rejected by John Davies, the Conservative government's Minister of Aviation. And when the Civil Aviation Authority finally agreed to the licence, the Americans turned him down. There was widespread mistrust of the Skytrain proposal in the US. There was a feeling that the scheduled airlines had to take the rough with the smooth – operating profitable routes alongside those that were less economically viable – but now companies like Laker were threatening to move in and skim the cream off the major routes such as the North Atlantic. But Laker was nothing if not a fighter and eventually the American authorities backed down, only for the White House to fail to act on the recommendation. Laker suspected a conspiracy.

Things were becoming increasingly heated. His next move, amidst a blaze of publicity (Laker was always a source of good copy), was to file anti-trust suits against the six principal transatlantic carriers. However, Peter Shore, Trade Secretary with the new Labour government, ruled against Laker who reacted by taking Shore to court. In 1974, angered at what he saw as attempts to block his progress, he labelled civil servants at the Department of Trade 'bums and gangsters', adding: 'If any of them want to victimize me, I will die for England with the Union Jack in my hand.'

He wasn't finished yet. He described the IATA (International Air Transport Association), the body that regulated air fares, as 'that mausoleum of lost causes' and, in another attack, roared: 'I don't want any hammer and sickle in my back'. This was what the British public loved – Laker the patriot standing up to spineless overseas competitors – although the fiercest opposition to Laker's proposals actually came from much closer to home in the shape of British Airways. A number of Conservative MPs championed Laker's cause in the House of Commons. The outspoken Norman Tebbitt, himself a former BOAC pilot, launched a withering assault on Peter Shore in 1975. He demanded to know whether Shore thought that 'Freddie Laker, with three DC-10s and his handful of employees, is such a menace to British Airways with its scores of aircraft and its 60,000 employees that he must be put down in this ruthless manner in order to protect British Airways?' Margaret Thatcher, then the leader of the opposition, joined in: 'Is it not the nub of what the Secretary of State is saying that the private carrier is so efficient and so good for the consumer that the nationalized industry cannot compete?' These were the ideals dearest to her heart, the very root of Thatcherism. She was in full cry and underlined her commitment by choosing Laker Airways to fly her on her first official visit to North America in 1975. Even by Laker's standards, it was a remarkable publicity *coup*. Shore was on the run.

The courts found in favour of Laker. Shore had to back down. On 15 June 1977, US President Jimmy Carter signed the permit to allow Laker to fly the lucrative North Atlantic route and just over three months later, on 26 September, the first Skytrain left Gatwick for New York, carrying 272 passengers at £59 a head. Other operators' standard single fare to New York was £186. Most of the passengers queued for over 24 hours to take advantage of the first walk-on airline and inside they found the cabin of the DC-10 decked out with Union Jacks. Although the service was billed as fairly basic, for an extra £1.75 passengers were offered a meal of pâté, beef in red wine, apple pie, cheese and biscuits and a small bottle of wine. Laker was in buoyant mood and made a point of walking up and down the cabin and thanking each passenger personally for travelling with him and for helping to prove him right. Naturally he didn't let the moment pass without launching another blistering attack on the larger airlines that had fought so hard to thwart him. He accused the half-dozen major operators on the transatlantic route of trying to make Skytrain fail, claiming, in his usual colourful rhetoric, that they 'dared to go for me with a knife and tried to slit my throat. All they have managed to do is to improve our licence and open the floodgates for lower-price air travel all over the world.' Laker had a way with words. His rivals thought he had got away with murder.

Laker made £2,176 clear profit on that trail-blazing first flight. After the six-year struggle to get Skytrain off the ground, it all seemed worthwhile. 'If I may say so,' he said, with his usual lack of modesty, 'I think it is the best idea I have ever dreamed up – certainly the most profitable. So far I have never seen anything quite so profitable.' The figures backed him up. In its first year, Skytrain carried a total of 250,000 passengers between London and New York and returned a profit of £2 million. The success of Skytrain provided overwhelming proof that cheap, readily available air tickets would attract a whole new market of travellers. More passengers meant fuller planes and fuller planes lowered the cost of seats that had previously been kept artificially high through lack of competition. The big airlines were terrified of competition but Laker knew that it was in the public interest – as well as his own. Reflecting on his triumph, he told his supporters: 'I think I am in the heavy sugar. I think I am home and dry.'

Skytrain was no flash in the pan. In 1978, the queues were so long that there was chaos at Heathrow. It seemed that everyone wanted to travel on it – Laker Airways was Britain's favourite airline. Prince Philip was even inspired to compose a short poem:

> Freddie Laker
> May be at peace with his Maker
> But he is persona non grata
> With IATA.

Perhaps he had other things on his mind . . .

In June 1978, Freddie Laker was knighted, amidst mutterings of discontent from some quarters of the aircraft industry still seething about the award of the transatlantic licence. 'A few hundred years ago he would have had brass earrings, a beard and a cutlass', snapped one British Airways executive. For his many fans, Laker still had plenty of enemies all waiting to see him fall flat on his face. It may have been beyond their wildest dreams at the time but Laker was about to sow the first seed that would lead to his ultimate demise.

On a high from the profits on the New York run, in September 1978 Laker decided to extend the Skytrain service to Los Angeles. For the first time, Laker and Skytrain appeared fallible. The Los Angeles extension was a disaster and over the next 12 months came close to wiping out the profits that Skytrain had earned by crossing the Atlantic. So with profits falling, the last thing Laker needed was a stroke of bad luck, a tragedy over which he had absolutely no control.

On 25 May 1979, a DC-10 belonging to American Airlines crashed on take-off at Chicago's O'Hare airport, killing 273 passengers and crew. It was the second major disaster involving a DC-10 and all airlines that operated DC-10s – including Laker – were suitably horrified. The plane that crashed was identical to the six DC-10s that made up Laker's long-haul fleet and was of similar age. Accident investigators looking into the Chicago crash found that the pylon holding the left engine to the wing had failed. This was particularly alarming since it was generally assumed that either the design of the pylon should have prevented an accident or at the very least that the plane should have been able to continue take-off safely on only two engines. As further inquiries were carried out, the likely cause of the pylon's failure was thought to be American Airlines' practice of removing the engine and the pylon from the wing with a forklift truck during overhaul. The rumour sent shock waves through Laker Airways as Laker's own DC-10s – his main financial asset – were overhauled in the United States by American Airlines. The American authorities reacted by grounding all DC-10s for six weeks to undergo safety checks, leaving the British Civil Aviation Authority with no choice but to follow suit. So Laker's entire long-haul fleet was grounded for six weeks. It was a devastating blow, one that cost him an estimated £13 million in lost revenues and threatened to wipe him out altogether.

Yet the initial signs were that Laker could ride the storm. When the grounding was lifted, business picked up steadily – even to Los Angeles. Maybe this lulled him into a false sense of security as he embarked on a further period of rapid expansion. At a cost of £130 million, he ordered ten Airbus A-300s and five more DC-10s. He took delivery of the first of the Airbuses in 1981, but by then both plans to run a European Skytrain and be granted a licence for the route to Hong Kong had been blocked. In February 1981, he applied to the Civil

Aviation Authority for permission to operate Skytrain to Australia. Two months later, the application was turned down. Laker stormed: 'This is a black day for people with relatives in Australia – and just about everybody in this country has relatives in Australia.' From having few planes and a wealth of potential, Laker suddenly found himself with a stack of aircraft but nowhere to fly them.

Meanwhile, the transatlantic big three – Pan Am, TWA (Trans World Airlines) and British Airways – were not prepared to sit idly by and watch Laker Airways steal their custom. Deciding that the only solution was to fight fire with fire, they began drastically cutting the costs of their flights to match Laker's prices. Passengers who had deserted them to join Laker's cut-price revolution now returned to the fold in their thousands, leaving Laker to ponder the fact that customer loyalty, rather like army intelligence, is something of a contradiction in terms. Of course, cheaper air fares were at the very heart of the Laker manifesto but whereas the public were delighted by the widespread reductions, the decision by Pan Am, TWA and British Airways was making a big hole in Sir Freddie's profits. He was being punished for his own initiative. The big companies had such reserves that they could afford to reduce fares in the short term. They knew that once they had seen off the challenge of Laker for good, they would probably be able to raise their prices again. But Laker did not have that massive financial backing and, at a time when he was borrowing heavily to fund further expansion, this loss of trade and revenue wounded him to the core. Any accusations of dirty practice were firmly denied by Pan Am who remarked acidly: 'The only person who will kill Freddie Laker is Freddie Laker.'

Laker had badly overstretched himself and his troubles were compounded by the falling pound. The purchase of the Airbuses and the additional DC-10s was crippling him. His interest payments to banks on the loans were running at over £14 million a year in 1981 – an enormous burden for a comparatively small company to bear. He had to rely too heavily on borrowed money. He chose to borrow virtually all of his money in dollars but most of the company's revenue – out of which the loans had to be repaid – was in pounds sterling. So if the pound fell sharply after Laker had taken out his loans, he would need many more pounds to meet his dollar commitments than expected and would therefore stand to lose a great deal of money. Conversely, if the dollar fell, he could have made a fortune. Gambling with the exchange rates had worked in Laker's favour in 1980 and early 1981 but then the pound started to tumble against the dollar, making Laker's dollar debts more expensive by the minute. The banks started to twitch.

Laker's overheads were now colossal. The expense of operating huge jets such as the DC-10s was frightening. Taking into account parking, landing fees, fuel and wages, the cost of flying a DC-10 from Gatwick to New York and back in 1982 amounted to over £36,000. At Skytrain's cheap return fares which then stood at around £200, Laker needed at least 180 passengers on every flight to and from New York just to break even. And to pay any reasonable share of the airline's horrendous overheads, he needed to fill virtually all 345 seats on every plane. Trade was quite brisk throughout the summer of 1981 but in the winter business slumped alarmingly – a combination of the stiff competition from companies determined to undercut his prices, the traditional winter loss of holiday passengers and a recession. For Britain was a nation in crisis that year. With the number of jobless rising to 3 million and Mrs Thatcher's Conservative government implementing widespread cuts, the youth of the country saw it as an excuse to take to the streets in a succession of summer riots. Throughout July, inner-city areas – London, Liverpool, Birmingham, to name but a few – were turned into battlegrounds as youths lobbed petrol bombs and other assorted missiles at the police. The riots even spread to normally sedate provincial towns, knocking the annual meeting of the townswomen's guild off the front pages of the local papers. On 23 September, the FT index suffered its second worst fall ever. The economy was equally rocky in the US. Inflation was running high, interest rates hit 20 per cent and many companies reported terrible losses. Ford alone lost $1.5 billion over the 12-month period. In the face of such uncertainty, tourism was one of the first industries to suffer. People were not prepared to part with money on non-essential items when they might need it to cover the essentials like food, fuel bills and mortgages. The crisis in confidence hit Laker Airways hard. In the last two weeks of January 1982, the number of passengers on each Skytrain flight between Gatwick and New York averaged only 125 – way below the break-even figure. And on the Manchester–New York run, the average passenger list per flight was just 107.

With revenues falling and debts mounting, Laker was in a desperate position. He tried cancelling some Skytrains in a bid to cut costs but the passenger numbers on those planes that did fly dropped still further.

Nevertheless, Laker remained in bullish mood. 'I said to myself, Laker, you are an innovator. You have innovated the airline business. Now you must innovate the banking business.' He negotiated a six-month rescue package with the Bank of England, which made available sufficient cash to enable him to keep trading through the difficult winter months. For its part, the Civil Aviation Authority was happy to allow Laker to continue operating as long as the banks believed the airline could survive through the next few months. Laker was certain that he had pulled it off and, on 3 February, he was telling the world that he was flying high and that his financial problems were over. 'The future of the company is now very good,' he said. 'In fact we are in a better position than we have ever been.'

Two days later, Midland Bank brought the receivers in and Laker Airways collapsed with estimated debts of £270 million. The bank acted after new figures showed worse than expected ticket sales, combined with disappointing forecasts for cash flow in the months ahead. The gloomy news on Laker's trading position meant that nobody could be confident that he would be able to carry on paying the bills. After the government decided there could be no state rescue (although in the House of Commons Mrs Thatcher declared herself to be 'a Freddie Laker fan'), Laker made a last-ditch attempt to pull off a deal, but to no avail. The 6000 stranded Laker passengers had the return halves of their scheduled tickets honoured by other airlines and Sir Freddie was said to be 'in a state of misery' as he watched potential Skytrain passengers being turned away at Gatwick. The Clydesdale Bank, owned by the Midland, faced losses of between £6 million and £9 million since, in addition to the £9 million overdraft granted to Laker, it had guaranteed a £5 million bond to the Civil Aviation Authority to safeguard Laker holidaymakers.

The outrage that greeted the collapse was remarkable. The British public could not have been more angry if the Queen Mother had been thrown in jail on trumped-up charges. In their eyes, a national folk hero had been betrayed and destroyed by the big banks and airlines. The 385 members of the Laker pilots and crew association said they would continue working for dole money in order to save the company. A petition bearing 50,000 signatures was taken to Downing Street by a posse of Laker hostesses singing:

Land of Hope and Laker
Father of low fares
Skytrain flies the Atlantic –
Freddie always cares.

Prince Michael of Kent sent a telegram offering his backing
and an anonymous businessman, who claimed that Laker had
done more for enterprise in Britain than anyone in the past 25
years, offered £1 million. Terry and Kay Hardy, who ran a
small guest-house in Sussex, announced the setting up of
'Freddie's Friendly Fund' to raise money and a ten-year-
old boy offered 16p in the hope that every little helped. Laker
was visibly moved by the gestures. 'I am overwhelmed by the
public reaction,' he said, 'and the public support. The telephone lines are blocked by people ringing up to ask, "Where
can we send money to and what can we do to help?" '

Even Laker's bitter rivals shed a few crocodile tears so that
they weren't seen to be gloating. Roy Watts, chief executive of
British Airways, insisted: 'It gives us no pleasure.' And British
Caledonian weighed in with 'very sad'. Labour MP Norman
Atkinson was more forthright, declaring Laker Airways to
have been 'the biggest airborne bucket-shop in history'.

Businessman 'Tiny' Rowland told Laker he had been 'selling ten-dollar bills for nine dollars and sooner or later that
catches up with you'. Even so, Rowland tried to join forces
with Laker to start a 'People's Airline', but the idea never took
off.

Freddie Laker was a victim of his own success, his own
publicity. He wasn't satisfied with the transatlantic routes – he
wanted to change the world. He took on too much, too
quickly and made the cardinal sin of spending money that
he simply didn't have. With such heavy loan repayments, any
economic setback – be it the falling pound or the loss of trade –
proved fatal.

For the time being at least, the people's champion was beaten. But he remained proud of his achievements. 'I often look out and think, all the nice people in the world are the ordinary people out there. And if they ever want a final judgement on Freddie Laker, ask those people.'

The 1631 Bible: A Missing Word

In the seventeenth century, London printers Robert Barker and Martin Lucas were commissioned by God-fearing King Charles I to produce a new version of the Bible. Alas, the finished article contained a number of errors, the most outstanding being the omission of the word 'not' from the Seventh Commandment. Thus all readers of the good book were encouraged by the Lord to commit adultery. The king was furious and immediately had all 1000 copies recalled and fined the incompetent printers the princely sum of £3000.

The Hoover Flights Fiasco: Journey into the Unknown

There is nothing like an imaginative, well-organized promotion to boost a company's trade. Unfortunately, to adapt the old music-hall joke, the Hoover initiative of 1992 was nothing like an imaginative, well-organized promotion. Far from boosting Hoover's image, it caused irreparable damage and merely succeeded in alienating customers and parent company alike.

By 1992, Hoover was a British subsidiary of the Maytag Corporation of the United States. In August of that year, Hoover launched an exciting travel promotion, promising that anyone in the UK who bought over £100 worth of Hoover products before the end of January 1993 would receive two free return tickets to the European destination of their choice and that anybody buying more than £250 worth of Hoover products in the same period would win two free return tickets to either New York or Orlando, Florida. Although there is always stiff competition with such promotional schemes, Hoover was quietly confident that the offer would prove attractive to British customers and would help sales of vacuum cleaners and washing machines in the run-up to Christmas.

The British public are bombarded with special 'too good to be true' offers which, to the cynically minded, come under the heading 'junk mail'. Hardly a week seems to go by without the promise of riches to be won in the latest Reader's Digest Prize Draw. But since there is nearly always a catch, most of this literature ends up in the waste-paper bin. However, the Hoover flights promotion was something else. It didn't take long to work out that it was an unbelievably good deal with no strings attached. The free flights to the US were worth as much as £500, yet entrants only had to spend £250 to win them. And the only time limit on the flights was that they had to be taken before the end of 1994. If there was a hidden trap, it was extremely well hidden.

The response exceeded Hoover's wildest dreams but caused such chaos that it turned into the company's worst nightmare. Hoover had expected no more than 50,000 people to participate but the British public rushed *en masse* to the shops to buy just enough Hoover products to qualify for the free flights. The result was that some 200,000 people – four times the anticipated number – took up the offer and went through all the attendant red tape to earn the free travel. Hoover was completely overwhelmed. Believing in the traditional British apathy, the company had calculated that, even if the offer appeared worth pursuing, people would not be bothered to complete all the steps necessary for qualification. It would be too much trouble, too time-consuming. And even if they did, they would surely not all go as far as actually taking the flights. There was bound to be a degree of natural wastage. Once again, Hoover had seriously miscalculated. The lure of a trip to Disneyland for the purchase price of a new automatic washing machine or a trip to Rome for the cost of a new vacuum cleaner was simply too good to resist.

Within days of Hoover advertising its generous offer, stores throughout the land had sold out of vacuum cleaners. This might have been wonderful news for sales, but it spelt financial disaster for the company as it soon became apparent that Hoover was losing money with each flight claimed. Hoover worked with two travel agencies to obtain cheap tickets. The idea was that the travel agencies would earn commissions by selling the flights as part of a holiday package to include hotel, insurance and car rental. Whenever a consumer bought the package, Hoover would receive a proportion of the commission. It was fine in principle but in practice the vast majority of applicants preferred to book their hotel separately. They weren't interested in the package. So Hoover missed out on the commission payments. Furthermore, the demand for Hoover products was so great that the factory in Cambuslang, Scotland, which had been making vacuum cleaners three days a week, had to be placed on a seven-days-a-week, 24-hours-a-day production schedule. The result was that Hoover had to pay overtime to its workers, another unforeseen expense. By March 1994, rumours were circulating that tour operators were actively trying to dissuade customers from taking up the free travel offer because each flight was costing Hoover money. The ploy of offering a prize that was worth twice as much as the amount needed on product expenditure was proving decidedly ill-advised.

Almost as damaging as the financial losses was the mass of adverse publicity that the enterprise attracted. The good name of Hoover was dragged through the mud as irate customers, unable to obtain the promised holidays, besieged the company, demanding compensation or threatening legal action. Hoover and its travel agencies simply couldn't meet the surge of claims for free flights while the volume of paperwork jammed the system to such an extent that by the middle of April only 6000 applicants had actually taken the flights to which they were entitled. Thousands of others never received their tickets, could not get the dates they wanted or had to wait for months. Hoover's original intention had been to rely solely on charter flights but the deluge of applications meant that more costly, scheduled airlines also had to be used. With complaints running at 2000 a day, Hoover was obliged to set up special hotlines to deal with the crisis and instigated a 'task force' to tackle the huge backlog of customers who had yet to receive their free flights. Maytag conceded that the promotion had caused 'tremendous difficulties in administration and implementation'.

As feelings ran high, David Dixon of Workington in Cumbria held a Hoover van to ransom because he claimed the company had failed to honour its promise of two free tickets to the United States after he had bought a £500 washing machine. When a Hoover engineer called to repair the machine, Mr Dixon blocked in the van with his lorry and announced that he would not be moving it until Hoover met its obligations.

Trading standards officers subsequently investigated 2000 complaints relating to the promotion but found that while Hoover was naïve and gullible, the company had not broken the law. In a bid to alleviate the pressure and ensure that customers finally got their holidays, Maytag ploughed another £20 million into the free flights fund. In total, the fiasco cost Maytag an estimated £48 million. It also cost the jobs of William Foust, president of Hoover (Europe), and two Hoover marketing executives. Maytag added solemnly: 'Our production losses forecast for the coming years run into millions of US dollars with 80 per cent of the total attributable to Hoover (Europe).' Little surprise therefore that in 1995 Maytag off-loaded Hoover for a knockdown £106 million. It was the price of incompetence.

The South Sea Bubble: Victims of Greed

In the early part of the eighteenth century, there were three great financial institutions in the City of London: the Bank of England, the East India Company and, the youngest of the trio, the South Sea Company, which had only received its charter in 1711. It was this last-named whose promise of wealth was to bring ruin to thousands in a calamitous episode that became known as the South Sea Bubble.

For 200 years or more, England had been thoroughly envious of Spain, the nation that appeared to have infinite access to the riches of the world via its connections with the gold and silver mines of Mexico and Peru. In times of war and peace, the English had striven to find a niche in the South American market, but to no avail. With the War of the Spanish Succession at its height and, thanks to the efforts of the Duke of Marlborough, the prospect of very real gains to come Britain's way at its conclusion, the House of Commons passed, on 3 May 1711, a resolution establishing the 'Governor and Company of the merchants of Great Britain, trading to the South Seas and other parts of America and for the encouragement of the fishing'. This organization, to be known as the South Sea Company, would be granted exclusive rights to trade with the eastern edge of South America, from the Orinoco River in Venezuela to Tierra del Fuego at the southern tip of Argentina, and along the whole of the west coast.

The purpose of the company was two-fold. Besides allowing

British merchants to explore new avenues of trade in a far-flung land, it was also hoped that it would bail the government out of a deepening financial crisis. Quite simply, whenever there was a war, England found a way of becoming involved. But wars cost money and now – with yet another one to fund – the expense was beginning to take its toll. The national debt was running at a dangerously high level.

In 1713, the War of the Spanish Succession ended with the Treaty of Utrecht. Considering Marlborough's glorious victories at Blenheim, Oudenaarde and Malplaquet, Britain got a pretty raw deal out of the treaty. It picked up Minorca, Gibraltar and Nova Scotia, along with the Asiento contract, the terms of which allowed just one British ship a year to trade with Mexico, Peru or Chile. It hardly represented the most generous of concessions from the Spanish, particularly as the ship's owners had to hand over a quarter of any profits to the King of Spain. Of course, the Spanish hadn't got where they were by handing over all the best trade routes to the British and they made sure they kept the best for themselves. But although the Asiento contract actually yielded precious little, it did not prevent the South Sea Company from claiming that it was on the verge of a major economic breakthrough. As PR exponents, the directors of the company deserve the utmost praise; as purveyors of the truth, less so. But their words were sufficient to convince the British public that wealth for everyone was just around the corner . . . or at least just across the Atlantic.

By 1719, Britain's national debt stood at £31 million so a few nuggets of gold and trinkets of silver would not have gone amiss. George I had been King of Britain and Ireland for five years and, after a slow start, was beginning to get his feet under the throne. With typical Hanoverian efficiency, he recommended to Parliament (in German, because he didn't speak a word of English) that it might be a good idea for the country to start paying off the national debt and invited the Bank of England and the South Sea Company to come up with suggestions as to how it might be done. London merchant Sir John Blunt, one of the leading directors of the South Sea Company, came up with an ingenious plan whereby it offered to take over the debt in return for certain commercial privileges.

Blunt's scheme was for the South Sea Company to sell shares in itself to the public and to use the money received from the sales to fund the national debt. Since the company had gone to such lengths to paint itself as an exciting, go-ahead concern on the brink of greatness, the idea seemed a sure-fire winner. Obviously the government and the company would benefit but so would the lucky public, given the opportunity to buy shares in such a profitable institution. The British people swallowed the propaganda with relish and were soon convinced that they were about to be made the offer of a lifetime and certainly one that was too good to refuse. The only organization to pour scorn on the proposition was the Bank of England who, having been established longer than the South Sea Company, thought that the onus of sorting out the national debt should rest on its shoulders. In other words, it didn't trust young upstarts.

Blunt and his cohorts proposed to the Chancellor of the Exchequer John Aislabie and Joint Postmaster-General James Craggs that the South Sea Company would make a down payment of £3 million towards taking on the national debt. Suddenly the Bank of England took an interest and put in a counter-bid of £5 million but Blunt was not to be outdone and raised the figure to £7.7 million. On 2 February 1720, Parliament formally accepted the South Sea Company's plan.

The effect on the company's stock was immediate and dramatic. In the course of February, it rose from £129 to £184 and in March it rocketed up to £380. Soon it seemed that the entire population of London was buying South Sea stock in the very real hope of making a fortune. They were encouraged in their actions by the sight of everyone from the Prince of Wales down – including MPs, nobles, even French nobles – rushing to buy South Sea stock and by the generous conditions of payment. The purchaser only had to pay 20 per cent upfront with the balance following in two-monthly instalments. So it was seen as an ideal investment for the small businessman or for the householder with not too much capital to spare.

But the biggest attraction by far was the continuing promise of riches from the other side of the world. Despite the fact that Spain had yet to show any inclination even to give Britain the time of day let alone access to its valuables, false rumours were spread by the South Sea Company directors of imminent treaties between the two countries, as the result of which good old Spain had agreed to hand over the Potosi silver mine in Peru for Britain's exclusive use. The public were led to believe that silver would soon be as easily obtainable as iron. And that was not all. Apparently, the Spaniards in Mexico had taken such a shine to cotton and woollen goods from Britain that they were prepared to swap vast quantities of gold for the prospect of a consignment of colourful ponchos. Each story was more outlandish than the last but the gullible public continued to believe every word and continued to buy South Sea stock. One of the few to urge caution was politician Robert Walpole who warned against the dangers of such manic speculation. But his was almost a lone voice of sanity and nobody paid any attention to what he said. Instead people were willing to risk their homes and their livelihoods in pursuit of a romantic image of untold riches from distant shores. Even MPs who had hitherto hung on Walpole's every word fled the chamber of the House of Commons the moment that they knew he was going to debate the South Sea Company. They did not want to hear. If they were afraid of the truth, they had good reason.

As the stock soared and soared, the streets around Exchange Alley in the City of London were thronging with eager speculators. So deep were the crowds that carriages were unable to find a way through, with the result that even the landed gentry had to proceed on foot – surely an unnerving experience. Meanwhile the rumour factory maintained its production rate. Stories circulated about the Spaniards being willing to swap whole regions of South America in exchange for Gibraltar and that the meagre Asiento contract was to be revoked, enabling the South Sea Company to send as many ships as they wished to the lands of gold and silver. Speculation had reached fever pitch.

But behind the scenes, skulduggery was afoot. Blunt formed a special committee comprising the 33 directors of the South Sea Company, including the accountant Robert Knight, to facilitate the smooth passage through Parliament of certain measures that would prove financially advantageous to the company. The chosen means of facilitation was the simple but invariably effective one of bribery. By inventing fictitious purchases and sales of stock, the company was able to distribute £1.75 million to deserving causes – namely MPs and influential peers. And since both Chancellor Aislabie and Postmaster-General Craggs were the proud owners of South Sea stock, it may be assumed that they always had the company's best interests at heart. The whiff of corruption was growing by the day but was smothered by the stench of greed emanating from the populace.

By May, the price of South Sea stock had risen to £500, shooting up to £800 in the first week of June. To keep the money rolling in, the directors decided to make loans to the public secured on the actual shares. These loans could – and were – used to buy more stock. With the shares showing no signs of slowing down, speculators ploughed their life savings into buying as much South Sea stock as they could lay their hands on. The initial 10 per cent deposit on each transaction brought in another £5 million in cash which was immediately used for loans to new investors. The result was that the share prices continued to rise until, on 24 June, they peaked at an astonishing £1050.

The success of the South Sea Company inspired others with entrepreneurial leanings to jump on the bandwagon. Some were legitimate businessmen, eager to duplicate the South Sea money-making machine, but others were nothing more than artful conmen, seeking to capitalize on the public's gullibility. Suddenly all manner of new weird and wonderful joint-stock companies were quoted on the exchange. These new companies were known as 'bubbles'. That they should be called bubbles was rather appropriate since they had a nasty habit of floating off into the distance with your money. And yet closer examination allied to a little rational thinking would have exposed their transparency. Many of these bubbles lasted less than a week, others were slightly more durable but, at the height of the craze in June, there seemed to be a bubble to suit the taste of every potential speculator.

There were at least 100 bubbles afloat at any given time. That normally sane people should have been in such a hurry to pour their hard-earned cash – or, in the case of nobility, their inheritance – into such ventures defies belief. There was a company formed for the 'discovery of perpetual motion', another for the cure of lunatics and yet another for the curing of broken-winded horses. Companies were launched to maintain bastard children or to start a coral fishery or even for the fanciful purpose of extracting silver from lead. Then there was Pollington's Plan to make deal boards from sawdust, Briscoe's Transmutation of Animals, not to mention Mother Wyebourne's Machine Conundrums or Puckle's Machine Company for 'discharging round and square cannon balls and bullets and making a total revolution in the art of war'. The most bizarre of all was 'a company for carrying on an undertaking of great advantage, but nobody to know what it is'. Every subscriber who deposited £2 per share in this particular bubble was promised a dividend of £100 per year. That was all people seemed to need to know. The governor opened an office in Cornhill in the morning, was overwhelmed by hungry investors, raised £2000 in five hours and fled the country that evening with the takings. It was money for old rope – and there was probably a bubble for that too.

Another trickster issued 'sailcloth permits' at 60 guineas a head. In reality these were nothing more than sections of playing card bearing a picture of the Globe Tavern, but would-be investors were told that the card entitled the holder to subscribe to a yet-to-be-formed sailcloth company. Once again, these were snapped up in their thousands before people realized they had been duped.

Many of the bubbles had prominent figureheads to attract investors, none more so than the Welsh Copper Company which boasted the Prince of Wales as its governor. He made a quick £40,000 before withdrawing his name and leaving the investors to rot as the shares plummeted. Satirist Dean Swift lampooned the bubble folly in verse:

> Subscribers here by thousands float
> And jostle one another down
> Each paddling in his leaky boat,
> And here they fish for gold and drown.

Sooner or later a bubble has to burst and these were no exception. Many of the smaller ones were operating illegally, the companies having set up in business without first obtaining the requisite royal charter. In an attempt to put a stop to this abuse of the system, the king issued a royal proclamation on 11 June 1720 whereby the bubbles were declared to be public nuisances and, furthermore, illegal for share transactions. Company directors were threatened with prosecution and hefty fines. Those in the know had seen this coming and had taken the money and run, leaving the more gullible amongst them to foot the bill.

Just as the bubbles were beginning to wobble, so there were the first signs that the South Sea Company itself was reaching the end of the road. On 3 June there had been a frenzy of selling as canny investors reckoned the price could not go on rising much longer. To prevent wholesale collapse, the directors were forced to step in and buy up much of the stock on offer themselves. Although confidence was temporarily restored, the danger signals were there and many more leading investors began to bail out. After the peak of 24 June, prices began to slide although even by August they were still at a level that represented a healthy profit for those who cashed in at that time.

Blunt and his fellow directors had become increasingly worried about the proliferation of bubbles, fearing that the competition would prove fatal. Even in investment-mad London, there was only so much cash to go round and many of the bubbles promised even greater riches than the South Sea Company itself. Seeing investors deserting South Sea in favour of some other equally far-fetched scheme drove Blunt to distraction. He had been hoisted by his own petard. In a desperate attempt to destroy the bubbles, the South Sea Company tried to take legal action against them. A writ was served in mid-August but as well as lowering the prices of stock in the smaller companies, it also had an adverse effect on South Sea stock. Before the serving of the writ the price stood at £900 but within a week it had fallen to £810.

Despite frantic promises from the directors of a 30 per cent dividend at Christmas, the prices continued to plunge as word spread that Blunt and his colleagues had sold up. Confidence in the company slumped, particularly as none of the claims about lucrative deals with Spain showed any signs of materializing. By 9 September, South Sea shares had dropped to £575; by the 21st, they were at £350; and by the 28th, they had sunk to just £190. Thousands of ordinary people lost everything in a day. The bubble had well and truly burst.

The losses were by no means confined to the man in the street. Poet and satirist Alexander Pope lost around half of his investment while royal physician Sir David Hamilton finished up £80,000 worse off. In contrast, Chancellor Aislabie managed to make an obscene £794,000 by selling at the right time. MPs as a whole came out of the episode rather well, hardly surprising since no fewer than 462 of them (plus 122 members of the House of Lords) held South Sea stock. It is estimated that between them they walked off with profits of around £4.5 million. Four of the directors of the South Sea Company were MPs and, smelling a rather large rat, the fleeced investors vented their anger on directors and MPs alike. With South Sea directors being attacked in the streets, the government feared that civil unrest might spread throughout the capital. The king hurried back from Hanover and recalled Parliament. At public meetings, the South Sea Company was denounced from all quarters as investors faced ruin. Five of the directors were arrested but the accountant Knight managed to escape to France. The king demanded his return. The disgraced Aislabie was forced to resign on suspicion of financial irregularity and, just in case he should try and join Knight in fleeing from justice, he was imprisoned in the Tower of London. On his way to the Tower, he was jeered by an angry mob who underlined their feelings by lighting a bonfire and burning an effigy of the fallen Chancellor. All things considered, the Tower was probably the safest place for him.

Walpole, the only politician to emerge from the shambles with his reputation intact, told Parliament that the restoration of public confidence was of paramount importance. Those whose finances lay in shreds should at least receive some measure of compensation, he maintained. To this end, the estates of 35 individuals were confiscated and Blunt, the orchestrator, was permitted to keep just £1000 of his estate. As a result, the majority of creditors got back around a third of their losses. It was better than nothing but not exactly the riches from the gold and silver mines of South America as promised in the brochure.

For its part, the South Sea Company was taken over jointly by the Bank of England and the East India Company. The big breakthrough never did come, the Spaniards never did give an inch and, after years of poor results, the company finally ceased trading in 1748. The South Sea Company had long since had its day before foolhardy, short-sighted investors discovered that when a bubble bursts, all that is left is thin air.

Computer Error: The Holiday of a Lifetime

A computer error gave British sun-seekers the bargain of the year in 1998 – a return flight to Portugal for just £16. Keen-eyed agents at Global Travel in Hull spotted on their booking computer that Thomson Holidays had advertised a two-week flight-only deal from Manchester to Faro as £16, instead of the usual £260. In the time it took Thomson to correct their mistake, Global Travel alone sold 19 of the cut-price flights with many more believed to have been snapped up nationwide. Global Travel boss Andy Kay described it as 'the bargain of the century'. Thomson were understandably less enthusiastic.

The Montreal Olympics: A Fast Track to Financial Ruin

For sporting *aficionados*, the 1976 Montreal Olympics are remembered for the three gold medals won by fourteen-year-old Romanian gymnast Nadia Comaneci, the 5000/10,000 metres double of Finnish distance runner Lasse Viren and the emergence of a new star, long-legged Cuban Alberto Juantorena, who strode to victory in both the 400 metres and the 800 metres. But for the people living in the host city, the Games evoke memories of extravagance and incompetence for which they were still footing the bill years after the last of the competitors had gone home.

It was in the spring of 1970 that the International Olympic Committee announced that Montreal would be the venue for the next Games. Mayor Jean Drapeau was the driving force behind the city's application and was understandably elated when it headed off the competition and was chosen to bring the world's premier sporting event to Canada for the first time. It was a tremendous honour for Montreal and for the whole of Canada and would surely create an upsurge of interest in the country. Tens of thousands of visitors – participants, team officials, IOC organizers, media representatives and spectators – would descend on the city for the duration of the Games. Although the competitors would be housed in the special Olympic village, others would need hotels in which to stay, restaurants in which to dine. It was all fuel for the local economy. Tourism would undoubtedly flourish, not only while the Games were on, but also as a result of the enormous publicity that Montreal and its environs would receive. Thanks to the wonders of television, pictures of the Olympics would be seen everywhere from Ankara to Adelaide, from Tokyo to Trinidad. How many viewers would be captivated by the images of the great outdoors flashing on to their TV screens and would see it as the ideal holiday destination? Nobody could hazard a realistic guess of course but with a worldwide audience running into hundreds of millions, all concerned were confident of a veritable tourism bonanza – another major boost to the Canadian economy.

The award of the Games should have been a time of rejoicing for the citizens of Montreal but, as is always the case, there were a few killjoys around asking awkward questions such as: who is going to pay for the Olympics? Not to worry, insisted Mayor Drapeau, the Games would be self-financing. In a phrase that would return to haunt him, he boldly declared that the Montreal Games had no more chance of running a deficit than a man had of producing a baby. By the end of the Games, Canadian economists were consulting medical books.

Cojo, the organizing committee for the Montreal Olympics, came up with two central schemes for raising sufficient money to finance the Games: a lottery and the issue of commemorative gold coins. However the government said there was not enough time to vote through the necessary law before the summer recess and so the coin idea had to be scrapped. This left Cojo and its president, Roger Rousseau, with something of a problem. Forced to act swiftly to keep on schedule, Cojo entered into a deal whereby it reportedly paid a colossal $68 million for the use of the Olympic village for around two months. Amid allegations that he had been ripped off by promoters who, it is said, made a profit of 250 per cent in two years, Rousseau cited the delays in getting federal government permission for the issue of the coins and the lottery tickets. Those delays, he said, meant that Cojo had to get the project moving in a hurry without too much regard for the small print. Media commentators described it as a costly oversight for a graduate of New York University in business administration.

Soon the build-up to the Olympics was attracting more than

its fair share of controversy around Montreal. Allegations were flying everywhere. There were accusations of favouritism in the tendering of contracts and of general mismanagement. The equestrian centre situated in the resort of Bromont came under particularly close scrutiny. The facilities at Montreal had been considered inadequate and so new ones were to be built at Bromont. Originally it was envisaged that temporary grandstands should be erected for the equestrian events but somehow Bromont ended up with its own special Olympic village. The result was that the initial estimate of $875,000 rose to a staggering $26 million.

The cost of staging the Games was rising faster than the pole vault champion. Mayor Drapeau's vision of the self-financing Olympics was beginning to look about as realistic as a Mountie in drag. But Montreal had gone too far down the line to back out now and so the City Council kept on voting for credit. In March 1975, the City Council authorized an extra $250 million for site construction. It was now blindingly obvious that, despite all the claims to the contrary, the Games would produce a deficit. The income from the Games was expected to total around $600 million but expenditure had risen to $840 million, leaving an anticipated deficit of $240 million. Whilst this was hardly an ideal situation, it was not thought to be too disastrous. Indeed, some considered it a small price to pay for the opportunity of hosting such a fabulous spectacle.

Alas, the escalating costs did not stop there. Nor was the situation helped by widespread industrial unrest. Sensing that they could hold the Quebec government to ransom, construction workers on the $320 million Olympic stadium – the showpiece of the site – downed tools in a demand for more pay. They knew that the government would have to give in sooner rather than later or run the risk of not having the stadium ready in time for the opening ceremony. After two months of inactivity which threatened to jeopardize the entire Games, the government could afford to hold out no longer and ordered contractors across the province to pay their employees an extra 85 cents an hour. Interpreting the concession as a sign of weakness, the construction workers promptly went on strike again in October 1975, this time for four days. Plumbers and electricians working on the stadium were even accused of sabotage. Things were turning ugly.

The strikes, coupled with a run of inclement weather, meant that there was now a real danger that the Olympic stadium would not be ready for the following July when the Games were due to open. In the event of Montreal failing to meet its deadlines, Mexico City, which had staged the Games in 1968, was placed on standby.

The much-delayed Olympic lottery finally got under way and not a moment too soon. By May 1976 – two months before the opening ceremony – the deficit had risen more than three-fold to an estimated $900 million. To help cover the increased costs, it was announced that the lottery was to be extended for another three years.

Despite their noble concept, the Olympic Games tended to attract controversy. And Montreal was no exception. Most of the African athletes were set to boycott the Games because the IOC refused to discipline New Zealand over its continued links on the rugby field with apartheid-ridden South Africa. It seemed that everything that could go wrong, did.

There was a precedent for an Olympics starting with incomplete facilities. Preparations were so poor for the 1900 Games in Paris that the competitors in the long jump, triple jump and other field events had to dig their own pits! Naturally, Montreal had no wish to join the list of shame and made every attempt to ensure that the international swimmers didn't have to compete in the shallow end at the public baths or that the gymnasts didn't have to hire out the local church hall . . . provided, of course, that they didn't clash with the flower-arranging class. But the cracks were there for all to see – sometimes literally. On 11 July, just seven days before the start of the Games, the roof of the brand-new Olympic swimming pool was found to leak in the rain. The cracks in the roof were hastily repaired but come the big day, Montreal's Olympic site was still not the finished article. Two Olympics hotels were still not completed while the Olympic stadium itself was in a far from satisfactory state. The problem lay with the flooring, much of which was still raw concrete and emitted clouds of dust at the slightest hint of disturbance. Vast areas still bore an uncanny resemblance to a building site. Another bad omen concerned the Olympic flame which traditionally burns for the duration of the Games in a huge urn at the main stadium – a symbol of the Olympic movement. Here at Montreal a sudden cloudburst doused the eternal flame for several minutes. Anxious glances were exchanged.

Nevertheless the Games went ahead as planned and passed off largely without incident, although the closing ceremony was interrupted by the appearance of a streaker. Some spectators thought he was the last relay runner still brandishing his baton. The organization did not meet with wholesale approval and brought this rebuke from IOC executive director Monique Berlioux: 'The athletes are penned up in an iron collar,' she complained, 'and one doesn't feel the kind of holiday spirit that should prevail. These Games have no soul.' The Seoul Olympics were, of course, yet to come.

But the most damning criticism came from the Montreal press, furious at the $1 billion deficit left to the city after staging the Games. The *Gazette* referred to 'the crippling expense' and went on: 'While Montreal revelled in the exuberance of the Games, one quarter of the city's population struggle to maintain, at best, a standard of living that is little more than survival.' *Le Devoir* added: 'It remains for us to pay, perhaps for many years, the price of this beautiful folly.'

As Canadian police launched an inquiry into allegations of corruption and fraud, it emerged that the cost of the Games had almost doubled in the past year to a figure of around $1.5 billion, leaving Montreal with the biggest debt of any host city. The price of security alone had risen to $100 million, of which $1.5 million went on walkie-talkie sets. Another £1 million was spent on renting 33 cranes for the construction work when it would have been considerably cheaper to have bought them outright, but the biggest waste of money was surely the £500,000 paid to the Montreal Symphony Orchestra and Chorus for miming to pre-recorded tapes played over the stadium loudspeakers!

When he had been lobbying for the Olympics to come to Montreal, Mayor Drapeau claimed that a by-product of the Games was that they would help rejuvenate Canadian sport. Unfortunately Canada became the first host country in the history of the modern Olympics to fail to win a gold medal. One sport in need of much encouragement was cycling. There were only 50 registered track cyclists in Canada at the time but surely they would be galvanized into heroic feats by the new $50 million Velodrome, the cost of which thus worked out at £1 million per cyclist. But, contrary to the claim that the facilities would pay for their own upkeep after the Games had ended, the 10,000-seater Velodrome attracted just 300 paying customers to its first national championships. Montreal had been saddled with a white elephant of mammoth proportions.

Montreal had got its sums hopelessly wrong. Any similarity between the original estimates and the final figures was purely coincidental. And now that the circus had left town, somebody had to pay for it. Montreal property owners were faced with a special Olympic Tax – a memento of the occasion – while the Province of Quebec raised the tax on tobacco in a bid to erase the debt. And there was always the lottery. With the Games over, there was a mass clearance sale of more than 3700 tons of second-hand Olympic goods, but the money raised barely scratched the surface. After all, there were only so many things you could do with a pair of boxers' bootlaces.

Day by day, the debt continued to rise. Quebec Sports Minister Claude Charron calculated the cost of running the Olympic complex to be around $5.5 million a year, but with a likely income of just $2 million. So unless the stadium and other venues could be made to pay their way, Montreal would be losing another $3.5 million annually. Strenuous efforts were made to attract big names to the stadium. Pink Floyd and ELP played concerts there and the Montreal Alouettes football team took up residence. But major money-spinning exhibitions could not be lured to the site until improvements had been made. So, at great expense, smart floors were laid complete with a new wiring system. Then in 1987, a roof was added to the Olympic Stadium. And roofs don't come cheap. Nowadays the stadium plays host to sports events, trade fairs and concerts. Over 20 years on and it is finally paying its way. But it has been a long struggle. As Claude Charron said of the Olympic site back in 1977: 'It is a monstrous heritage, born out of outrageous expense, socially unjustified and economically unrealistic.' The people of Montreal continue to hope that there is more chance of a man producing a baby than of their city making the same mistakes again.

Raise the Titanic: The Ultimate Disaster Movie

From the moment on that chilly April night in 1912 when the *Titanic*, on its maiden voyage from Southampton to New York, collided with a massive iceberg in the North Atlantic and plunged to the depths of the ocean with the loss of 1513 lives, a legend was born. The story of the demise of the supposedly unsinkable liner – the biggest ship in the world – and its passenger list that spanned every stratum of society has been passed down through the generations. The tales of heroism and cowardice, folly and greed, mystery and controversy have inspired hundreds of books and no fewer than 17 films. Quite simply, no Hollywood screenwriter could have dreamed up a more gripping yarn. The first movie, the silent *Saved From the Titanic*, hit the big screens in May 1912 – just a month after the tragedy – and was co-written by and starred actress Dorothy Gibson, one of the survivors; the most recent was James Cameron's epic *Titanic*, in 1998, which broke all box-office records. In between were the good and the not so good, along with one that was almost as big a disaster as the ship itself. Enter *Raise the Titanic*.

In many ways *Raise the Titanic* was a meeting of two legends: the immortal vessel and the world's most celebrated showbusiness entrepreneur, Lord Lew Grade. With his trademark cigars and one-liners (of his production *Moses the Lawgiver*, he told journalists, 'It looks good in the rushes') and his love of the charleston (he was the world charleston champion of 1926), Grade had long been the consummate showman. His company, Associated Television (ATV), produced some of the most popular – and bestselling – British television shows of the fifties, sixties and seventies: *The Adventures of William Tell, Sunday Night at the London Palladium, The Saint, The Prisoner, Thunderbirds, The Persuaders, The Muppet Show, Jesus of Nazareth, Space 1999* to name but a few. 'I did space before Spielberg did space,' he once said. He could have added that he did Robin Hood before Costner. Lew Grade was used to being ahead of the game.

He was never able to resist a good story, whether in the form of script or anecdote. Whilst denying that he ever considered cutting the number of apostles to six to reduce the costs on

Jesus of Nazareth, he liked to recount how noted screenwriter Lord Ted Willis bet him that he couldn't name all 12 apostles. 'I said, "Of course I can! Matthew, Paul, Luke, Peter . . ." and then I stopped. He said: "I knew you couldn't name them all!" And I said, "I haven't finished reading the script yet . . ." '

Lord Grade's speciality was always the transatlantic market, dealing with the big American players. Besides the cigars, the jokes and the charleston, he was famous for his quick decisions – many a major deal was struck in no more than a minute – and for arriving at his London office at seven o'clock in the morning. For years, the story was that he used to get into work at 5.30 a.m., but that was just one of the many legends associated with this larger-than-life character. One of his most-quoted lines was: 'All my shows are great. Some of them are bad. But they're all great.' *Raise the Titanic* was certainly great in the Grade sense.

By the second half of the 1970s, Grade was into his seventies himself but had lost none of his golden touch. *The Muppet Show* was doing great business and Robert Powell was earning accolades for his portrayal of Jesus in the multi-million pound *Jesus of Nazareth.* Sure, there was *Crossroads* but nobody's perfect. Grade was beginning to think on an even bigger scale than usual and was particularly keen to expand his empire to encompass the world of feature films – an obvious move insomuch as that if anyone was cut out to be a movie mogul, it was Lew Grade.

In 1977 Clive Cussler's thriller *Raise the Titanic* was published. Telling the story of a race between the Americans and the Soviets to recover a mysterious element, byzantium, hidden somewhere in the vaults of the sunken liner, it went on to become a bestseller. Cussler's agent from the William Morris Agency approached Grade and asked him whether he would be interested in the film rights to the novel. By a

strange coincidence, Grade – or six-year-old Louis Winogradsky as he then was – had first arrived in England by ship
from Hamburg in 1912, just a few months after the sinking of
the *Titanic*. He had come with his mother Olga and brother
Boris (later Lord Delfont) to join father Isaac Winogradsky, a
Russian Jew from the Crimea. But in spite of this loose
historical connection, Grade was not exactly thrilled by the
prospect of making a film about the *Titanic* because he
thought the subject had been, in his own words, 'done to
death'. And he naturally assumed that Cussler's book was yet
another narrative about the ship's sinking in an already
crowded market. So he politely declined the offer to read
the manuscript.

Shortly afterwards, Associated Communications Corporation, the vast entertainments conglomerate of which Grade
was the head (ATV was a subsidiary), went into partnership
with Dick Smith, the chairman and chief executive of General
Cinemas, the biggest circuit of cinemas in the United States.
On a business trip to London early in 1978, Smith handed
Grade a box and, telling him that it contained a manuscript,
asked him to read it when he had a moment. Grade put it to
one side until two nights later, by which time Smith had left
London – thinking he had better read the manuscript as
promised. He opened the box to find that it contained an
800-page manuscript entitled *Raise the Titanic*. Grade's heart
sank. He began reading it at ten o'clock that night but found
that he couldn't put it down. Four hours later, he reached the
final page and knew instinctively that he wanted to make the
movie.

Once Grade's mind was made up, he didn't believe in hanging around. In the movie business, he who hesitates finds
someone else has beaten him to it. So, sensing that the film
might inspire a series along the lines of James Bond, he called
Clive Cussler's agent the very next morning. Grade later

recounted the conversation to the *New York Times*. 'I said, "I've read the *Titanic*; I want it." He said, "I've got several offers." I said, "I'm coming to New York Monday – you be at my hotel." He came in the afternoon about four o'clock. I said, "I want to do a deal, you won't leave this room until we do a deal. I don't want bidding. You are either in a position to do a deal, or else I forget it." He said, "I'll have to go back to Clive Cussler." I said, "Do it now, or I withdraw my offer. Here's the telephone." And he telephoned Clive and Clive said, "OK, provided I have a walk-on part and one sentence." '

In fact, Grade discovered that the manuscript had already been submitted to Oscar-winning producer/director Stanley Kramer (*High Noon, The Wild One, The Caine Mutiny, Guess Who's Coming to Dinner* etc.) but Grade used his powers of persuasion to talk Kramer out of bidding against him. Grade ended up paying $400,000 for the rights to *Raise the Titanic*, part of the deal being that Kramer would come on board as producer/director, with Martin Starger, Grade's number one man in the US, as executive producer. Everything was finalized and Kramer set to work on the construction of a $6 million model of the *Titanic*, built in the course of a year by a team of 30 highly paid, highly skilled craftsmen.

The plan was to use a vast water tank at CBS Studios to simulate the Atlantic and to film the model in the tank. But at 55 ft long, 12 ft high and weighing 12 tons – two or three times larger than Grade had envisaged – Kramer's model was far too big for any tank. Indeed, it was intended that the tank should be able to accommodate models of eight ships at the same time. In addition to the *Titanic*, there had to be room for four US warships, two tugs and a New York Harbour fireship. Furthermore, the tank needed to be deep enough so that, when photographed, it would convince an audience that the action on screen was really taking place 6000 ft beneath the surface of the Atlantic. When it became apparent that there wasn't a tank in the world large enough to take the model and photograph it from underwater, the plan to film at the studios was scrapped and the search began to find an alternative site.

Meanwhile, there were 'artistic differences' with Kramer, as a result of which he was taken off the picture and replaced as director by Jerry Jameson. The script was also causing considerable headaches. In total, there were over ten drafts before the screenwriters hired to adapt Cussler's book got it anywhere near right. With millions of dollars having being spent already and fresh problems arising daily, Grade's deputy, Bernard Kingham, suggested that it might be an idea to cancel the entire project before it got out of hand. But Lew Grade would not be swayed. Kingham remembered: 'I was told to mind my own business and go away!'

The worldwide quest for a suitable water tank took the production team to the Mediterranean. On the island of Malta, they found a large tank, but it still wasn't big enough to take the various vessels. However, it had the advantage of being surrounded by a plot of land on which it was possible to build an extension. Work on the tank began in November 1978. 'I asked when it would be ready,' said Grade, 'and they said January. But they didn't say which January!'

To fulfil the filming requirements, the tank had to be 35 ft deep, 300 ft long and 250 ft wide and be capable of holding 9 million gallons of water. But even with Europe's biggest bulldozers at work, the tank took ten long months to build and construction costs soared to $3 million. Some $200,000 was frittered away on a giant metal gantry which was supposed to haul the model *Titanic* in and out of the tank while the tank itself was being emptied. The first gantry was built in Los Angeles but, on arrival in Malta, was found to be too short for filming purposes. So it was decided to extend it by 40 ft. However, when it was subjected to stress tests, the gantry proved hopelessly incapable of picking anything up and appeared in constant danger of collapsing under its own weight. It was not a success. Another useless innovation was a turntable brought in to revolve the model *Titanic* while it rested at the base of the tank. First, it failed to turn – a fairly basic necessity for a turntable – and then its wheels collapsed under the sheer weight of water. In any case, a turntable was superfluous to requirements because a cameraman filming under water is weightless and would therefore simply be able to turn himself around. So there was no need to rotate the ship. The water pressure inside the tank was also a constant problem. It was so great that pipes kept bursting and had to be replaced, all of which cost money and time. It had also been hoped to construct an underwater camerahouse in the tank to photograph the action through glass. This too was an unnecessary extravagance but fortunately the idea was scrapped when it became obvious that no glass would be tough enough to withstand the pressure from so much water.

One of Grade's former associates admitted: '*Raise the Titanic* lurched from one disaster to the next. There was a lot of local corruption in Malta that held up filming, and then they found that the glue which held together the model of the *Titanic* wouldn't stick in salt water. Ironically, I think part of the problem was the success of *Jesus of Nazareth*. Lew had got into hock on that but threw money at it, and it came out right. He thought he could do the same again.'

Grade himself outlined his frustrations in his autobiography: 'We had been promised a completion date,' he wrote, 'which came and went without the tank having been finished. Meanwhile the crew and cast were all standing by on full salary. When work on the tank was finally completed we discovered that the pressure of the water crushed the submersibles. So we had to keep on making more submersibles with the result that the film overran its shooting schedule by a disastrous four months.'

The last straw was when Maltese Prime Minister Dom Mintoff decreed the tank to be a tourist attraction because it was situated on the approach to the airport. So he ordered the production team to landscape it with trees – yet another drain on the budget.

'They kept on telling me the budget would be $18 million,' groaned Grade. 'In the end it cost $35 million, and they didn't finish the film until the day I had scheduled it for release, so there wasn't even a chance to do any proper editing. We had committed ourselves to dates throughout the United States, and therefore had no alternative but to show the film without the luxury of "sneak previews" prior to doing a final edit on it.'

Raise the Titanic opened in the United States in the summer of 1980, grossly over budget. It had no star names, apart from cameo performances from Jason Robards and Alec Guinness. Steve McQueen, Paul Newman and Robert Redford had apparently all turned down the lead role of marine biologist Dirk Pitt, a part that subsequently went to the relatively unknown Richard Jordan. So it needed all the help it could get. Yet unwittingly the film was dealt a fatal blow by Lord Grade's own brother, Lord Delfont. At the time Delfont was Managing Director of EMI's Entertainment Division and had a production company based in the United States that was making TV movies and mini-series. Among the latter was a four-hour mini-series entitled *SOS Titanic*, based on the sinking. A turkey by any standards (despite the presence in the cast of Helen Mirren), it bombed spectacularly on American television when it was shown in 1979. In an attempt to recoup some of its losses, Delfont's company decided to edit the TV version for theatre release. According to Grade, his brother did try to halt the making of *SOS Titanic* but since his head of production had already committed himself, Delfont didn't want to override him. EMI's powerful foreign distribution meant that *SOS Titanic* was seen all over the world except in Japan where executives left it to gather dust on a shelf because they had already paid out for *Raise the Titanic*. It seems no coincidence that the much-maligned *Raise the Titanic* was the top-grossing film of the year in Japan. Grade certainly thought so. 'I really believe that the failure of the film was inadvertently, and ironically, due to my brother Bernie . . . I believe that the final outcome of *Raise the Titanic* would have had an altogether different complexion had the film been completed three or four months earlier, and had *SOS Titanic* not been made.'

But to heap the blame on a rival production is to ignore the critical mauling that *Raise the Titanic* received. *Variety* wrote: 'It hits new depths hitherto unexplored by the worst of Lew Grade's overloaded ark melodramas. This one wastes a potentially intriguing premise with dull scripting, a lacklustre cast, laughably phoney trick work and clunky direction that makes *Voyage of the Damned* [a 1976 Grade film starring Faye Dunaway] seem inspired by comparison.' *Screen International* described *Raise the Titanic* as 'a waterlogged mass of unresolved subplots, insufficiently identified characters and a complexity of technical jargon'. The *Guardian*'s reviewer was equally unimpressed. 'The longer it all goes on, the more one hopes that, if they ever do raise the *Titanic*, they'll heave the film overboard to replace it!' These reviews scarcely amounted to a vote of confidence.

The critics' views were by no means in the minority. Clive Cussler says he actually retched when he saw the film. 'The screenwriting was pathetic, even the editing was terrible,' he says. 'I really don't know where the money went. It looked, from start to finish, like a cheap production.'

To recoup the enormous expenditure on production, *Raise the Titanic* had to do outstanding business in the United States. But American cinema audiences were getting younger

– at the time 75 per cent of US cinema-goers were under the age of twenty-four. And there wasn't really anything in this version of the *Titanic* story to appeal to younger audiences. So they gave it the thumbs-down with the result that it took just $8 million at the box office. Of that, ACC's American film division share was 45 per cent – $3.6 million. But well over $8 million had been spent on printing and advertising, leaving the division facing a hefty loss.

The failure of *Raise the Titanic* was to prove more far-reaching than Grade or anyone else could have anticipated. The original plan had been to use the expensive models again in a series of three epic sea films which would justify the cost of their manufacture. But that scheme depended on the success of *Raise the Titanic*. The sequels went down with the *Titanic*. ACC's film division ended up losing $26.4 million in 1981, Grade revealing that the 'major loss-maker' was *Raise the Titanic*. The blow effectively killed the company as a major force in film production in its own right and from then on ACC only embarked on feature films in association with strong financial partners. The *Titanic* disaster also weakened Grade's grip on ACC and helped make it vulnerable to a takeover bid in 1982 by the Australian corporate raider, Robert Holmes à Court. Grade's empire – the foundations of which had been so carefully laid over the years – was sold.

Raise the Titanic was therefore more than just another loss-making movie. It was a blunder of epic proportions. As Lord Grade himself so sagely remarked in its aftermath: 'It would have been cheaper to lower the Atlantic.'

DeLorean: The $250 Million Gamble

The charismatic American John Zachary DeLorean was seen as the saviour of Northern Ireland. Along with his plans for a radical new, top-of-the-range sports car, he brought the promise of hundreds of jobs at a time when it was as difficult to attract outside investors to the strife-torn province as it would be to lure igloo manufacturers to the Sahara. Biting his hand off before he changed his mind, the British government gleefully poured millions of pounds of taxpayers' money into the project, only to discover, when it was too late, that DeLorean could not deliver. Government, investors and suppliers ended up losing over $250 million on the deal. The car of the future simply didn't have one.

John DeLorean was born in Detroit on 6 January 1925. His father Zachary, a Romanian immigrant, worked in the foundries of the Ford Motor Company. His mother was Austrian. Unlike many American children raised in the 1930s, DeLorean did not experience genuine poverty and was talented enough to qualify for a musical scholarship (he played the clarinet) to the Lawrence Institute of Technology. From there he graduated to the automobile industry and worked his way to the top of Chevrolet, one of the most prestigious management jobs in the American motor industry. He enjoyed the trappings of wealth and decided to opt for a more glamorous, movie-star lifestyle. He split up from his wife of 17 years, went on a crash diet, dyed his silver hair jet black and had a major facelift which included the insertion of a foam-like material in his chin to give him a 'more manly' jutting jaw.

The transformation certainly appeared to do the trick because before long the 6 ft 4 in DeLorean was one of the most eligible bachelors (or divorcés) around town. Beautiful women who usually had Rolexes on their arm now had DeLorean. The media celebrity circus snapped his every move, photographing him with a string of lovelies, including Hollywood star Ursula Andress, before he married twenty-year-old Kelly Harmon, daughter of the CBS broadcaster and former all-American half-back, Tom Harmon. Kelly was 24 years

DeLorean's junior and the age difference quickly told, the marriage lasting less than two years.

It was not only DeLorean's appearance and wives that changed around this time. Publicly, at least, he was adopting the fashionable viewpoints that would endear himself to the American public. He declared that he was pro-civil rights, pro-consumer, pro-safety and pro-fuel efficiency. Presidents have been elected with fewer attributes. With his flashy clothes, sideburns, dyed hair and trendy political stance, DeLorean was seen as a refreshing alternative to the faceless big businessmen for whom the bottom line is always money. America loved him.

None of his bosses at General Motors cared how he dressed or whom he was dating as long as he continued 'making his numbers', i.e. delivering the goods. This he continued to do and by the start of the 1970s he was president of GM's North American car and truck operation, just one step away from becoming president of GM, the world's largest car manufacturer. But his sudden concern for the environment – a somewhat ironic position in view of the number of gas-guzzling cars he had introduced over the years – began to manifest itself in a succession of speeches attacking the American motor industry. He started to make enemies within GM and when some internal documents were leaked and traced back to DeLorean, he was asked to resign. The bush telegraph hinted at darker reasons behind DeLorean's departure while the man himself perpetuated the story that he left of his own accord because he refused to toe the party line. In May 1973, a month after his resignation, he married his third wife, the glamorous model Cristina Ferrare, and told journalists: 'I want to do something in the social area.' But what he really wanted was to make more and more money to support his lavish lifestyle. To do that, he needed somebody to believe in him. And that was where the British government came in.

Image was all-important to DeLorean and the right image needed the right car. Somehow a Reliant Robin did not fit the bill. DeLorean was a sports car man and now, freed from the constraints of General Motors, he dreamed of setting up his own company to manufacture a revolutionary sports car in his own image. It would be sleek, stylish, safe, economical and fast. He visualized a car made from an alternative material to fibreglass – perhaps a new plastic that was stronger than steel and almost half the weight. It would be produced by a process called elastic reservoir moulding, or ERM. The only drawback to ERM was that it couldn't be painted so DeLorean decided to cover the plastic with the most durable material available – stainless steel. Although the car would therefore only come in one colour, that colour would be silver. Again it fitted DeLorean's image – at least until he started reaching for the bottle of hair colourant. The silver machine would give the car the futuristic, space-age look that DeLorean craved and because it only came in one colour, repair shops would find it easier to stock DeLorean panels. The stainless-steel finish would also prevent the great bodywork curse of rust, ensuring that the vehicle itself enjoyed a longer life. People would know that when they bought a DeLorean, it would last them many times longer than any comparable car on the market, somewhere between 20 and 25 years. It might not be cheap, but it would be durable.

DeLorean liked to be perceived as the consumer's friend and so he placed the emphasis on safety features. He wanted to make airbags standard equipment, along with bumpers that could withstand impact at 10 mph without any damage (the industry standard was only 3 mph). When he awoke from his dream, he had created the great 'ethical' car – the one that, he claimed, Detroit had not allowed him to build, the one that they dared not build.

To realize his dream, he established the John Z DeLorean

Corporation and hired the services of experienced Italian car designer Giorgetto Giugiaro. By July 1975, the design was all but completed. Apart from the stainless-steel finish, its most startling concept was its remarkable gull-wing doors. The DeLorean would look like no other car on the road. Like DeLorean himself, it would stand out above the crowd and would be aimed at the very top of the US automobile market. At the start of 1976, DeLorean was talking excitedly about production being 'less than two years away'. All he had to find was somewhere to build his factory – preferably a land of large grants and cheap loans.

He began by searching for possible locations in the United States but the likes of Maine, Rhode Island and Ohio would not come up with sufficient cash towards funding the project. Puerto Rico expressed an interest but they wanted DeLorean to put up considerably more money than he was prepared to. So he cast his net further afield and alighted on the Republic of Ireland. Irish government officials were keen to do business but began to get cold feet when they realized the extent of DeLorean's ambitions. He started talking in meetings about building a giant company that would eventually be in a position to make an offer for shares in General Motors. They came to the conclusion that he was probably just a shade too ambitious for them. For the Irish government, it was a lucky escape.

DeLorean then turned his attentions to Northern Ireland, knowing that the British Labour government was desperate to attract any form of industry to the province. Since 1969, Northern Ireland had been plunged into a state of civil unrest. With no end to the 'troubles' in sight, despondency and unemployment were high and new companies were reluctant to move there lest their workforce should come under attack from the various sectarian paramilitary forces. Quite rightly, the government thought that a major new employer would provide a much-needed boost to the people of Northern Ireland, reducing the jobless total and thereby going some way towards easing the social tension. Quite wrongly, it thought that John DeLorean was the man for the job.

DeLorean reckoned that the government would welcome him to Northern Ireland with open arms and fistfuls of dollars in handouts, but even he couldn't have believed how easy it would be. Taking candy from a baby would have proved a tougher challenge than relieving the British government of vast sums of money. Before they entered into negotiations, DeLorean executives estimated that they needed $90 million from investors in order to start production. Just 45 days after the first meeting between DeLorean and officials of the Northern Ireland Development Agency in New York, an agreement was signed whereby the British government offered DeLorean a total of $97 million to build his factory in Belfast, of which almost a third was an outright grant. When DeLorean first heard about the offer, he could hardly believe his luck. 'It was too good to be true,' he told an associate.

Ever the master salesman, DeLorean had succeeded in selling both himself and the car to the government even though both had considerable flaws. Stories about DeLorean's flamboyant lifestyle were dismissed out of hand although the government did claim to have looked into the reasons why he left Detroit. His somewhat chequered past was brushed aside with equal haste, the government believing that it was entirely natural for an entrepreneur to have a few companies go bankrupt in his early years. As for the car, the government was convinced that it knew a good thing when it saw one. For a start, there were those amazing gull-wing doors. Nobody had ever seen anything like them. That was because they couldn't remember the Mercedes 300 SL of the 1950s which featured almost identical doors. In fact, far from being an exciting innovation, the doors turned out to be a major headache, particularly in bad weather. On snowy nights, moisture would gather in the door seals and when the temperature dropped further, the water would turn to ice and succeed in freezing the perimeter of the gull-wing shut. If the driver happened to be inside at the time, that was where he stayed. But there was always the hi-tech stainless-steel finish. The difference between that and the doors was that the bodywork was a nuisance all the year round. It was supposed to look shiny and spotless but in winter, when icy roads were salted, showers of salt left tell-tale white spots all over the stainless steel. And in summer, fingerprints and handprints showed up on the bodywork. Small wonder that many owners chose to paint over the stainless steel. In truth, both the stainless steel and the gull-wing doors were gimmicks, calculated to make the car look different from its better-designed, better-engineered and invariably cheaper rivals. They hid the fact that the DeLorean was basically a very ordinary car, with standard components and engine. It was mutton dressed as lamb. But it looked good enough on paper to secure the participation of the gullible British government.

DeLorean had little trouble in worrying Britain into signing the deal. He showed officials the written offers from Puerto Rico and the Republic and said that unless the government could promise a deal within the next few weeks, he would accept one of his rival suitors. What the government apparently failed to realize was that the Republic had already withdrawn its offer of a free factory and cash grants, while the Puerto Rico deal, although technically still alive, had long since run into seemingly impenetrable difficulties. The government took the view that if the basic concept had been good enough for those two countries, it was good enough for Britain. Terrified of losing their man, they gave DeLorean everything he wanted . . . and more.

On 3 August 1978, the short stocky figure of former miner

Roy Mason, the Secretary of State for Northern Ireland, and the tall suave John DeLorean stood head to shoulder and announced that DeLorean's company was setting up a 550,000 sq. ft factory in Dunmurry, just outside Belfast, an area with the highest unemployment rate in western Europe, to build a new sports car aimed at the American market. The project would create an initial 800 jobs just for building the factory with the promise of 600 permanent jobs after 1979 and another 1500 as the factory hit its full production target of 30,000 cars a year. 'We aim to move from cow pasture to production within 18 months,' said DeLorean. It was a proud day for the people of Northern Ireland.

Precise details of the financial package were not disclosed although the look of contentment on the faces of the DeLorean executives should have been an indication that it was an extremely favourable deal from their point of view. What particularly appealed to them was the leeway they were given – enough rope to hang the population of China. Not only hadn't the government asked too many questions but it was happy to give DeLorean all the freedom in the world. Although the government was putting up the money, it was perfectly willing to allow DeLorean himself to retain control and to let his team hire whoever they wanted and use whichever suppliers they wanted. All that mattered was that the local economy was receiving invaluable aid and that jobs were being created. And if DeLorean made a nice, fat profit out of government investment, that suited everybody just fine. That way, the Northern Ireland Development Agency would be able to attract other manufacturers to Belfast and surrounding districts.

Three and a half years later, when the DeLorean exercise had backfired disastrously, Roy Mason tried to defend the government's part in proceedings. He wrote in *The Times*: 'DeLorean happened at a time when no private enterprise would have entered West Belfast without government intervention, government cash, and had bold decisions not been taken by ministers.' Answering criticisms that the DeLorean project had been hurried through without a proper feasibility study, Mason stated that at least 15 government departments had been involved in the decision (a case of too many cooks if ever there was one) and that there had only been a few dissenting voices in the House of Commons expressing concern about the cost of the plan and about the economic wisdom of government involvement with a private business. So that was all right then.

DeLorean's ability to charm the birds from the trees earned him other investors, although on a slightly smaller scale. American chat-show host Johnny Carson agreed to put in around $500,000, some 345 American car dealers joined forces and contributed $8.6 million to the cause and a consortium assembled by Wall Street promised to add a further $18 million. Thus without putting up much money himself and without relinquishing power, DeLorean had acquired a great deal of working capital. One businessman who ultimately decided not to invest in DeLorean was Saudi magnate Ojjeh Akram. Before committing any portion of his accumulated wealth, he commissioned an independent report to examine the potential of DeLorean's new operation. The report was less than favourable. It found that the sports car market was not a growth area and that DeLorean would face ferocious competition at the upper end of the range from both Porsche and Jaguar. It also cast grave aspersions on the gull-wing doors and even predicted that serious financial difficulties lay ahead. Not surprisingly, Akram decided to invest his money elsewhere. The British government should have heeded the warning.

DeLorean had recruited Colin Chapman, founder of Lotus, a name synonymous with sports cars and Formula One cars for some 20 years, to help turn his prototype into a production model. At the highest level, the two men got along famously but the respective company subordinates enjoyed a less than harmonious relationship. And the resultant friction brought the first signs that all was not well at Dunmurry. The root of the problem was that Lotus did not rate the DeLorean car's three basic design concepts: the gull-wing doors, the stainless-steel bodywork and the rear engine. The DeLorean team wanted to hurry things along – they had an exacting schedule to meet – but the Lotus engineers insisted on solving problems when they arose. The constant disagreements and alterations conspired to delay production. Lotus were startled to discover that, with the production date only a few months away, the car's electrical components had not been chosen nor the windows designed. Not all of the parts had specifications and some parts didn't even have drawings until the very last minute. One Lotus engineer remarked: 'The first thing you usually design for a car is the wiring. But with DeLorean, we put it in last and had to move around everything that was already in place.' The feeling from within Lotus was that the DeLorean people were trying to run before they could walk and that more time needed to be spent on the car before the first vehicles rolled off the production line.

The delay to production meant that DeLorean needed more money and so he went back, cap in hand, to the government, now a Conservative administration under the leadership of Margaret Thatcher. Although the new government had declared its intention to slash public spending, Northern Ireland Secretary Humphrey Atkins agreed to hand over another $25 million with the promise of an additional $16 million at a later date. Fortunately the DeLoreans were able to maintain their opulent lifestyle and John arranged for a $53,000 Mercedes, wrapped in a huge ribbon, to be delivered to Cristina at her favourite San Diego health farm.

The advertising campaign was starting to get into gear. 'Live the dream,' pleaded the commercials. 'Your eyes skim the sleek, sensuous stainless steel body and all your nerves tell you, "I've got to have it." The DeLorean – surely one of the most wanted automobiles in automotive history.' Even by advertising standards, this proved to be an extreme case of hyperbole.

The DeLorean DMC 12 was finally ready for the road early in 1981. In February, the first pilot car was air-freighted from Belfast to the States for the Los Angeles National Auto Dealers Convention. However, there was a portent of things to come when the DeLorean company's mid-west technical manager was summoned to the airport to release the doors of the vehicle which had jammed shut. Everyone shrugged it off as just a minor hitch.

Two months later, the first batch of 400 cars was shipped across the Atlantic for distribution in Delaware and California. But, because of the poor preparation and insufficient time allowed for ironing out faults, those first models left a great deal to be desired. Complaints included headlights that wouldn't switch off, indicators that didn't work, fuel gauges that didn't operate properly, engines that refused to start (this became a frequent bone of contention) and, if that wasn't enough, occasionally the glass in the driver's window fell out when it was lowered. The much-vaunted doors fell off on a regular basis and the hood could be downright dangerous to open, prompting one executive to describe the vehicle as 'a British car with body by Wilkinson Sword'. As for the stainless steel, it was stained before the cars even made it on to the road. Another DeLorean chief confessed: 'You get warranty claims on all cars. Car companies average three or four claims for each car produced in the course of a year. But the DeLorean was pulling three or four claims per car per month.'

The dream car's most public humiliation took place when

its highest-profile owner and champion, Johnny Carson, drove his new DeLorean on its maiden journey to a nearby drugstore. In front of a large crowd of onlookers, journalists and photographers, the battery failed. The publicity stunt had backfired spectacularly and word began to get around that the DeLorean was unreliable.

Fearing that future sales would be jeopardized if the car acquired a poor reputation from the outset, DeLorean demanded instant improvements, particularly to the door seals, the door lock (drivers had problems getting the key to fit) and the radio which suffered dreadful interference. On a bad day, it sounded as if Sinatra was tramping through a field of corn flakes. At one point, DeLorean went so far as to suggest buying back the first 5000 cars off the assembly line and giving customers the option of purchasing the next DeLorean model instead. Whilst such a gesture would have restored his position as the consumer's friend, it would have cost in the region of $115 million. Therefore it was quietly forgotten.

Even leaving aside its collection of faults, the DeLorean fell way short of the claims made by its founder. DeLorean had never been one to undersell either himself or his product, but the car that first stuttered off the production line did not live up to expectations. In 1979, DeLorean had told *Newsweek* that the new car would be priced at around $15,000 and could accelerate from 0 to 60 mph in less than eight seconds. But when it finally appeared, it cost $26,000 – $7000 more than its chief rival in the US market, the Chevrolet Corvette – and it took 10.5 seconds to get from 0 to 60, considerably slower than most other sports cars. Neither the promised airbags nor strong bumpers ever materialized while claims of a lightweight vehicle were dashed when it weighed 900 lb more than the original estimate. DeLorean had also predicted a ten-year, 100,000-mile guarantee on the car, but in the event the company offered nothing more than the standard one-year,

12,000-mile protection. And even when adjustments were made, the outcome was not always an improvement. The car was redesigned in such a way that it was lowered but this left the driver with a poor view through the rear window, rendering parking a hazardous assignment.

Despite the sticky start, things soon picked up and by the early autumn of 1981 some cars were selling for $35,000 – $8000 above the suggested retail price – and in October monthly sales rose to 710, more than the previous two months combined. DeLorean celebrated by treating himself to a $3.5 million, 430-acre estate in New Jersey. He reckoned he deserved it.

The trouble was that although sales were picking up, they were still nowhere near the rate of production. Back in August 1978 at the press conference with Roy Mason, DeLorean had stated categorically: 'We have orders as of now for 30,000 cars.' And, despite opposition from his executives, he was determined to push towards production of a minimum of 30,000 cars a year. In July 1981 when the car was undergoing all manner of teething troubles, DeLorean stunned his colleagues by insisting that production at Dunmurry should be upped to 1600 a month, making a target of 20,000 a year by the autumn. So even the increase in sales accounted for less than half of the cars being produced. Thus half of the cars being made each month remained unsold despite DeLorean's bold claim that he could sell every car the factory could make.

It was a disastrous decision but DeLorean's ego and ambition knew no bounds. He was convinced that people would buy the cars just for the privilege of owning a DeLorean. And he was not one for hanging about – caution was not a word in his vocabulary. Everything had to be done in a hurry. His insistence on increasing production flew in the face of all of the company's market research. His marketing experts had predicted a maximum sale of 20,000 cars a year . . . if the price had remained below $18,000. At $24,000 per vehicle, they estimated that annual sales would dip to just 10,000 and at $28,000 (which, with taxes and delivery charges, was pretty much the price of a DeLorean), the company could expect to sell fewer than 4000 cars a year. If DeLorean had settled for making 6000 or even 8000 cars a year, he might well have broken even, but a figure of 20,000 rising to 30,000 was beyond comprehension. Then again, John DeLorean didn't believe in doing things by halves. He was certain that people would pay for the right product, particularly if it bore what he saw as the ultimate status symbol – his name. Accordingly, at a business lunch at the end of October 1981, he declared: 'We have 3000 highly motivated employees who are producing 80 cars per day. The consumer and dealer reception has been spectacular. In fact, on the basis of public reaction, we have raised our production targets up to 30,000 for 1982. In 30 years in the business, it's the first time people have told me our price is too low – and we're sold out through the end of 1982.'

DeLorean's rousing rhetoric may have sounded good to the British government and his employees but it cut no ice where it mattered – in the market-place. DeLorean may have been talking optimistically about a new four-door model, but declining sales figures spelt out the harsh reality of the situation. Figures for November fell to 578 cars sold with the prospect of winter – traditionally the worst time for sports car sales – to come. That winter saw the worst weather in the United States for a century and, with echoes of the hapless Sinclair C5, orders for sports cars ground to a standstill. As early as the start of December, there was a sudden, unexpected rush of cancellations from dealers, requesting shipments of DeLorean cars to be put on hold until further notice. With DeLorean unwilling to cut production for fear of damaging an impending share flotation which he hoped would raise $20 million, the unsold cars began to pile up. Soon there were 1000 sitting at Belfast docks, desperately in need of US customers. As the situation worsened – only 25 cars were sold in the final week of the year – a desperate DeLorean tried to negotiate cut-price sales in a bid to raise some much-needed cash. At one point Budget Rent-A-Car was reportedly interested in taking 2000 of the cars that had accumulated in DeLorean's American warehouses.

The proposed share flotation on Wall Street was called off. Rumours began circulating about DeLorean's business activities and sales failed to pick up. By January, there were over 1800 unsold cars at Belfast. It seemed that DeLorean, the master salesman, couldn't give them away.

Before Christmas, DeLorean had assured James Prior, the latest Northern Ireland Secretary, that production would rise, the share issue would go ahead and that sales would increase steadily, so four weeks later when he returned from the festive break, Prior was somewhat disturbed to find the Dunmurry plant on a three-day week, the share issue dead and sales in a precarious position – just 259 cars were sold in January. DeLorean wanted a reported $65 million in credit from the government to tide him over but this time Prior refused. There was to be no more money.

Meanwhile, the banks began taking a closer interest in the company and insolvency specialist Sir Kenneth Cork was appointed to report on its financial state. He found losses of around $40 million. In early February the Dunmurry plant had been put on a one-day week and then on the 19th, the British government placed the factory in receivership. Prior told journalists: 'I had to reiterate to Mr DeLorean that there was no question of further public money.'

DeLorean was unaccustomed to admitting defeat and immediately looked for someone to blame. The city of Belfast seemed a convenient scapegoat and DeLorean was quoted as claiming that the factory had suffered repeated firebomb attacks and that his executives had been targeted by snipers. Later he accused the British government of reneging on its agreement. Prior concluded sombrely that there had been 'very considerable management and marketing mistakes' in the running of the company.

The government set a deadline of 18 October by which DeLorean could regain control of the plant if he came up with the sum of $10 million. He failed to do so.

The car that everyone was supposed to have wanted had sold barely 4000 by the summer of 1982. DeLorean's claim of firm orders for 30,000 had been nothing more than sales talk – the figment of a vivid imagination. If DeLorean had thought smaller and set more modest targets, he might have realized his dream, but that simply wasn't his nature. Everything had to be big. As for the government, it should have investigated DeLorean's background and track record much more closely and conducted adequate feasibility studies before throwing so much money at the company. The motives may have been honourable but the thinking was flawed. But then Roy Mason had bought the dream. He had fallen for the charms of both manufacturer and machine. Alas, in the end, where the De-Lorean was concerned, virtually the only people taken for a ride were the British government.

Bramber Council: A False Economy

In 1974, cash-strapped Bramber Parish Council of West Sussex passed a resolution to save money by switching off all street lighting in the village for three days. At the next meeting, the parish treasurer was happy to announce that, following the economy measures, electricity to the value of £11.59 had been saved. Before his colleagues could burst into an appreciative round of applause, he felt he ought to add that the bill for switching off the electricity was £18.48 and the bill for switching it on again was £12. Thus it had cost the council £18.89 to spend three days in the dark.

Bibliography

Blundell, Nigel, *The World's Greatest Crooks and Conmen* (Octopus, 1982)

Blundell, Nigel, *The World's Greatest Mistakes* (Octopus, 1982)

Brough, James, *The Ford Dynasty* (W. H. Allen, 1978

Carroll, Paul, *Big Blues: The Unmaking of IBM* (Weidenfeld & Nicolson, 1994)

Eglin, Roger and Ritchie, Berry, *Fly Me, I'm Freddie* (Weidenfeld & Nicolson, 1980)

Fay, Stephen, *The Collapse of Barings* (Richard Cohen, 1996)

Franklin, Charles, *The World's Greatest Mistakes* (Odhams, 1969)

Gordon, Stuart, *The Book of Hoaxes* (Headline, 1995)

Grade, Lord, *Still Dancing* (Collins, 1987)

Gunston, Bill, *Giants of the Sky* (Patrick Stephens, 1991)

Harris, Robert, *Selling Hitler* (Faber and Faber, 1986)

Harry, Bill, *The Ultimate Beatles Encyclopedia* (Virgin, 1992)

Hartley, Robert F., *Management Mistakes and Successes* (John Wiley & Sons, 1994)

Hughes, Murray, *Rail 300* (David & Charles, 1988)

Leeson, Nick, *Rogue Trader* (Little, Brown, 1996)

Levin, Hillel, *John De Lorean: The Maverick Mogul* (Orbis, 1983)

Lewisohn, Mark, *The Complete Beatles Chronicle* (Hamlyn, 1992)

Marshall, Dorothy, *Eighteenth-Century England* (Longmans, 1962)

Masefield, Sir Peter G., *To Ride the Storm: The Story of the Airship R101* (William Kimber, 1982)

Newham, Richard, *The Guinness Book of Fakes, Frauds and Forgeries* (Guinness, 1991)

Pendergast, Mark, *For God, Country and Coca-Cola* (Weidenfeld & Nicolson, 1993)

Pile, Stephen, *The Book of Heroic Failures* (Futura, 1979)

Regan, Geoffrey, *Historical Blunders* (Guinness, 1994)

Bibliography

Schama, Simon, *The Embarrassment of Riches: Dutch Culture in the Golden Age* (Collins, 1987)
Yapp, Nick, *Hoaxes and Their Victims* (Robson Books, 1992)
Yenne, Bill, *The World's Worst Aircraft* (Bison Books, 1990)

Index

Index

Index

Index